PATTERNS OF COMMUNICATION
Literary and Non-literary

PATTERNS OF COMMUNICATION
Literary and Non-literary

Vinod S Dubey

GYAN

Published by

GYAN

Gyan Publishing House
5, Ansari Road
Daryaganj, New Delhi-110002
Phone: 011-47034999, 9811692060
E-mail: books@gyanbooks.com

Distribution Network
gyanbooks.com
India, USA, Canada, UK, Australia, France

ISBN: 978-81-212-9081-4 (HB)

First Published, 2023

Printed at: Gyan Press, Delhi.

PATTERNS OF COMMUNICATION: LITERARY AND NON-LITERARY
Author: VINOD S DUBEY

Dedicated to the sweet and ever-lasting memory of
My dearly beloved wife
SUMITA DUBEY
The inspiring spirit behind my efforts to write this book,
Indeed my guiding angel all my life,
Who passionately anchored and emboldened my efforts to write this book
Till the last breath of her life as it was nearing completion.

Acknowledgements

I would first offer my prayerful tributes to the memory of late Professor S K Verma, an internationally renowned linguist and leading authority on Indian English and ex-Vice-Chancellor, Central University of English & Foreign Languages, Hyderabad, as well as my guru-supervisor of the PhD research, for constantly inspiring me to access higher peaks of academic excellence, always and ever.

I also offer my reverential tributes to late Professor Damodar Thakur, an internationally-acclaimed scholar of English language and literature, as well as of the Gita, Upanishads and a number other Hindu scriptures, and, above all, a generous soul for his unwavering support and precious comments all through the period of writing of this book. I owe him my abiding gratitude, specially for his great words of appreciation of the title of the book.

My warm blessings to my sons, Vivek and Vinayak, for tremendous help with their software expertise in multiple ways at various stages of production of the book, to my daughters-in-law, Smriti and Archana, and my daughter, Tanushri, for their standby support in more ways than one in completion of the book. I warmly wish my dear grand-daughters, Bhargavi and Sambhavi, for taking good care of me in several ways as I was at work on the book. I must add my loving blessings to my other little cute grand-daughters, Aadriti and Atula, and my darling grandson Vipul Anugrah, whose beaming smiles and sweet words over video chats from the USA always infused me with renewed vigour to finish my work well in time. I am grateful to my elder brother, Ashutosh Dubey, for his moral support, as well as to my younger brother, Sanjiva Shankar Dubey, for his assistance and suggestions in bringing out this book.

I am really thankful to Munindra Misra, himself an author-translator of several Hindu religious texts, for his personal suggestions and help when the book was at publication stage.

I am much thankful to Madan Manjunath Naik for helping me with his computer skills in publication of this book.

To all my friends and well-wishers, not named here, I owe more than a word of formal gratitude for their support and best wishes in writing this book.

I am also grateful to the Gyan Publishing House, New Delhi for doing an excellent job.

Bengaluru
26 January 2023

Vinod S Dubey

Preface

We exist as humans if singularly because we are born with infinite and inherent ability to communicate with others in one form or the other, which is crucial not only for our very survival as humans but also for our cultural growth and advancement in every facet of life. Noticeably, all other living things of the world such as animals, birds, fish, insects, plants and trees are also endowed with a measure of communicative ability, yet their potential for this ability is abysmally limited in range and distinctly variant according to their kind of species. Scientists cite, among other things, even the example of forest trees how they communicate their signals of vital importance through their 'wood-wide web' of underground networks. Tacit and tactile communication are some other examples of how humans as well as other living beings are genetically programmed to communicate between themselves.

What seems though unique about human communication is its limitless room of expanse of creativity and infinite ambit of communication. Even as language remains their crucial communicative medium, humans have innate ability to communicate in a variety of other subtle ways besides language, such as by gesture, posture, signs, and even by telepathy, and so on. Also, recourse to nonverbal ways of silent communication such as *sparsh* (touch), *maun* (silence), *aanshu* (tears) and *muskan* (smile) are considered primordial forms of human communication. Researchers say that the Hindu Vedas, Puranas, smritis as also Buddhist and Jain scriptures are replete with numerous references to *sparsh* (touch) as a form of human communication.

Lately, display of images/signages in public places, in place of language, as caution advisories and access guide to restrooms, elevators, escalators, restaurants, etc. is an accepted norm of communication globally. So is the global pattern of option for signs/signages, instead of language, as user-friendly guide to everyday consumer goods, electrical and electronic items, etc. More recently, emojis are fast displacing texting in cell phones, twitters and in other forms of digital communication.

Despite multiple and emerging avenues of human communication, language remains, and will ever remain, pivotal and most comprehensive form of human communication. This is not just because language is a species-specific trait of humans, but crucially because the core structure of language follows a self-creative system and pattern. From the initial level of speech sounds and phonemes, morphs and morphemes upwards that of lexis, syntax, semantics, text and discourse, language is intricately structured as a system, layered within layers with inbuilt ancillary systems, despite arbitrary features of divergence that distinguish one language from the other.

Even as the structure of language follows a comprehensive system and pattern, these have little communicative value per se. Language gains its communicative viability only in a speech society, envisaging speaker/writer--listener/reader participatory tie, without which it cannot function. The functional expanse of language thus covers the entire spectrum of communication of a speech society, from everyday parlance through an extensive canvas of more patterned forms of language use, literary as well as non-literary.

Notably, what seems to be language is in fact only its 'observable product', text—spoken/written—created by a speaker/writer, through a dynamic process of communication, called discourse. The complex process of how language functions as discourse is crucially conditioned by a number of overlapping factors, such as profile of its user participants, functional purpose/register of its use, context of the text/situation of its use, choice of type of the text—literary or non-literary, and its sub-varieties. Concomitantly, the dynamics of linguistic discourse is impacted by a range of other critical dimensions of language use as well, such as those of stylistics, pragmatics and socio-semiotics of the speech society.

A note on the dynamics of linguistic discourse above, though brief, would seem relevant in that it prefaces the central concern of all the studies in this volume that explore the discourse dynamics of a variety of texts, literary and non-literary. Since the core concern area of all of its chapters is independent of each other, an ingenious approach and topic-tailored format has been devised to study each of them in-depth individually. Interestingly, such a study framework of the volume has helped offer a rainbow view of variegated patterns of the dynamics of linguistic discourse, literary as well as non-literary, and, what is more, that of native, non-native and nativised varieties of English.

This book broadly caters to widening interest areas of a growing cross-section of general readership, gifted with an overriding passion to explore new avenues of reading pleasure, irrespective of their professional leanings. However, academics, research scholars/ students in the area of English language and literature, stylistics, Indian English, communication studies, as well as media and advertising professionals, language planners, etc may find the book worth their special interest and in-depth attention.

Vinod S Dubey

Contents

1
GM Hopkins' Pied Beauty : A Semantic-stylistic Interpretation

Pied Beauty

Glory be to God for dappled things;
For skies of couple-colour as a brinded cow;
For rose-moles all in stipple upon trout that swim;
Fresh-fire coal chest nut-falls; finches' wings;
Landscape plotted and pieced –fold, fallow and plough;
And all trades, their gear and tackle and trim.

All things counter, original, spare, strange;
Whatever is fickle, freckled (who knows how?)
With swift, slow; sweet, sour; a dazzle, dim;
He fathers-forth whose beauty is past change:
Praise Him.

Gerard Manley Hopkins (1844-1889) was a unique English poet in more senses than one.[1] He was born in the Victorian period, yet was deeply imbued with the religious fervour of a George Herbert and the over-arching sense of the senses of a John Keats. Nevertheless, his poetic fame in the twentieth century, indeed ever after, belated and posthumous, is essentially anchored in his matchless poetic craftsmanship and stylistic innovations.

Noticeably, the entire body of Hopkins' prolific poetic output offers abundant room for in-depth research. However, it is his oft-read and most-anthologised sonnets that hold our immediate attention *per se*, if only for their outstanding stylistic reasons. Hopkins' **Pied Beauty** happens to fall into this select class of his outstanding sonnets.

The poem is called a 'curtal' sonnet—a class distinctly apart from the conventional types of sonnets—only because its structural limit spans ten lines and a half. The curtal sonnet is therefore largely noted for being a structural innovation, and aptly so. However, the underlying functional value of this curtal sonnet goes far beyond its face value. Indeed, it seems crucially derived from, as well as foreshadows, the sonnet's core pattern of message organisation. This is quite evident from the critical significance the tail-piece sentence has in the concluding half-line of the curtal sonnet. The tail-piece sentence has pivotal value in the entire text in that it encapsulates its focused message, lucidly and conclusively. Its peak prominence is well marked in that the half-line sentence is the *solitary* sentence to occur in the concluding line of the text.

The stylistic dimensions of **Pied Beauty** are multi-layered, structurally as well as semantically. Therefore, each of them in their multiple ways deserves focused attention singularly. For this overriding pragmatic concern as well as limitation, attention is restricted here to its semantic-stylistic dimension, which indeed seems to be the bedrock of the poem.

Pied Beauty features expression of what Steiner calls 'total significance' of the message through employment of 'language in a condition of special use', through the poet's 'special level of deliberation' and 'special intensity of conscious focus' (Steiner 1971:114-115). This 'special level of deliberation' and 'special intensity of conscious focus' give rise together to what may be termed the *semantics of form* and the *form of semantics* which, despite being largely complementary to each other, are marked by subtle distinction in terms of their orientation and focus.

Whereas the *semantics of form* stipulates absorption of the content in the form, the *form of semantics* focuses on the form structured to match the semantic content of the text. The two notions are of course too intricately coalesced with each other to distinguish, and more so, spell out as to which overrides the other in the given context of a text. However, an imperative and pragmatic need often arises in a stylistic study as the present one for such a subtle distinction between the two notions.

Elaborating the significance of the *form of semantics* in poetry—the relation between poetic form and its meaning— Roger Fowler observes :

> "We must believe that the formal description not only leads to, but is, a statement of meaning ..... significant, valuable statements when we describe the form of poetry." (Fowler 1971 :234)

Pied Beauty draws our attention mainly on account of the form it has, the *form of semantics*. This *form of semantics* has 'value' in Richard Gunter's sense of the term (cited in Fowler 1972 : 02), for it has both 'a grammatical identity' and 'a content' (Nixon 1972).

The *form of semantics* the poem features is of, to employ Stankiewicz's phraseology (cited in Fowler 1966: 75), 'autonomous value' as it is 'more highly organised or more deviant than ordinary language' (*op. cit.*: 12). To deal with its autonomous *form of semantics*, I have approached the poem under two sub-heads as below :

(a) Semantic Structure, and

(b) Semantic Components

Semantic Structure

It seems viable to take an organic view of a poem in that the totality of meaning of a poem is more than the sum total of its parts even as the parts always remain critical components in its ultimate making. The basic presumption here is that "the primary unit of stylistic description is a whole text seen as a unit, not as a string of sentences. " (Fowler 1966 : 20) A poem thus, in the first place, ought to be considered as a whole before it is dissected into parts. Obviously, this would guard us against the error of mistaking the woods for the trees even as the trees, in their variegated individual beauty, make up a beautiful forest in no insignificant ways.

Apparently, **Pied Beauty** offers a happy example of Hockett's well-known classic notion of a poem being a long idiom (Hockett 1958). The entire poem seems to be in the nature of a *raison d'etre,* with a forthright command tagged to it at the end. Right from line 1 to line 10, the poem abounds in phrases/clauses/sentences which have, *in the overall semantic structure of the poem*, the functional value of adverb phrases/clauses (Adv Phrs/Cls) of reason, overtly or covertly. The following clippings from the text seem much like a string of wide range of formidable reasons offered to highlight why one ought to pray for 'Glory be to God' (1.1) :

for dappled things—(1.1);
For skies of couple-colour (1.2);
For rose-moles all in stipple— (1.3);
(for) Fresh-fire coal—(1.4);
(for) finches' wings—(1.4);
(for) Landscape plotted and pieced—(1.5);
And (for) all trades, their gear—(1.6);
(for) All things counter, original— (1.7);
(for) Whatever is fickle, feckled—a dazzle, dim—(II.8 -9);
(and for) He fathers-forth whose beauty is past change:—(1.10).

Plainly, minus the phrases/clauses/sentences mentioned above, all of which have functional value of an AdvPhr/Cl of reason in *the overall semantic structure of the poem*, the poem would be ultimately reduced to the following two sentences of an 'obligatory' sentence type[2] :the first half of the first line —'**Glory be to God**'— and the last half-line tail-piece of the poem—'**Praise Him**'. The functional value of these two sentences is thus critically significant as they together help cohere the core semantic structure of the entire poem.

DSS1, begins results in augmented focused value of DSS1+2+3 many times over.

Interestingly, the sudden shift of focus from the earlier expansive discourse on *pied beauty* to a simultaneous shift of focus back to the underlying message of the text is conveyed in the dovetailed lines, 10 and 11, with which the text concludes:

> '**He fathers-forth whose beauty is past change :** (l.10)
> **Praise Him.**' (l.11)

The process of *arrest* and *release*, effected by means of deflective discourse on *pied beauty*, has thus critical discourse value in the entire text. By delaying progression of DSS1, '***Glory be to God***' (l.1), till as far as the penultimate sentence of the text (l.10), the intervening section on *pied beauty* functions as a discourse catalyst in thematic evolution of the text.

The functional value of arrest and release may well be guessed if DSS 1, 2 and 3 were to occur together in that sequence at the beginning of the text, followed by discourse on *pied beauty* till end of the text, or, in the reverse sequence order, for that matter. Obviously, such a hypothetical variation would render the text utterly pointless, insipid and uninspiring.

The discourse on *pied beauty* in the intervening section of the text may well be viewed from a somewhat different angle as well. After experiencing a vision of the world of *pied beauty*, described earlier in the text, one would perceive later in the text (l.10), perhaps more sharply, the stark contrast between the supremacy of God and His creation of the world of *pied beauty*. The cardinal reason for acceptance of ultimate command, '**Praise Him**', (l.11) further lies in that the world of *pied beauty* remains ***evanescent*** whereas, by contrast, that of its fountainhead progenitor-creator, God, is '***past change*** (eternal)' (l.10). One would not have ever, even naively, accepted the *command,* '**Praise Him**' (l.11), even if it were to occur earlier on in the ***thematised***[6] initial sentence of the text.

The deflective discourse on *pied beauty* in between DSS1 and DSS 2+3 assumes indispensable functional value in the evolution of discourse structure of the poem. Indeed, *Pied Beauty*, right from the title of the poem through its entire text to the end, follows a neat five-stage pattern of semantic progression, beginning with its surface semantic structure (SSS) and closing finally with its deep semantic structure (DSS) :

- Stage I: (SSS1) : **Pied Beauty** (Title of the poem)
- Stage II : (DSS1) : '**Glory be to God**' (l.1): *Invocation*
- Stage III : (SSS2) : Discourse on *Pied* beauty : *Deflection* (from the latter half of line 1 until line 9)
- Stage IV: (DSS2) : '**He fathers-forth whose beauty is past change**' (l.10) : *Enunciation and Pronouncement*
- Stage V: (DSS3) : '***Praise Him***' (l.11) : *Command*

Deflective discourse on *pied beauty* is thus not only neatly designed and coherently structured but also given expansive space in the text to underscore its critical value. What is worth noting is that it gets one's riveting attention as well solely because of its hallmark feature of stylistic singularities and innovations. (More discussion on this point follows in the section on Semantic Components).

Embedding (s) and Conjoining (s)

Deflective discourse on *pied beauty* gains its functional viability in the text solely because it is structured at two-fold levels of **embeddings** and **conjoinings**. Each of these linguistic devices functions independently as well as concomitantly to help cohere the semantic structure of the text. This implies that they have each their own independent functional value in the text even as they work in tandem with each other in building up its semantic structure.

Broadly, the notion of **embedding** in linguistics/stylistics is a *vertical* syntactic notion in that it implies inclusion of same or different element (s) of grammar, such as a sentence, clause, phrase or word, one within the other, which is a common occurrence in language. For instance, in the sentence, '*Mary, who I have known since her childhood, is now a lecturer at the university.*'

the underlined clause is embedded within the main clause, not underlined. Embedding assumes stylistic significance though when its recurrence follows a pattern in a text such as the present one.

The notion of **conjoining** in linguistics/stylistics, by contrast, is one of *linear* syntactic relation, precisely, one of concatenation or chaining together of same or different element (s) of grammar at the levels of both syntax and discourse. Though a common feature of language, conjoining acquires stylistic significance through their patterned recurrence in a text such as the present one. In the sentence, '*John met Mary and Susan, and they together met Mike and Lara, and they all planned to visit…….*' the **conjoins/ conjuncts** that help effect conjoining are underlined.

Embeddings and *conjoinings* are extensively employed in the entire text of **Pied Beauty**, except its last line. Yet, what marks them off as a hallmark feature of the text is their high density of occurrence in the elaborate discourse on *pied beauty*. The description of the world of *pied* beauty is a *deflective piece of discourse*, plainly because it digresses one's attention from the core underlying theme of the text (discussed earlier).

Embeddings and conjoinings, intricately employed in the text, have a discourse value for two-fold reasons. First, they help sustain prolonged focus on deflective discourse on *pied beauty*. Secondly, all at once, they hold back one's attention from the underlying theme of the text far too long, until line 9 of the text of 11 lines. They have thus a pivotal value in the text. The elaborate pattern of embeddings and conjoinings in the text critically serves as a catalyst of **arrest** and **release** of one's attention (discussed earlier), in that they help evolve ultimate and augmented focus on the core theme of the text.

Embeddings

The sonnet has layers of embeddings/sub-embeddings whose functional value is to help elaborate, in micro- as well as macro-details, the semantic spectrum of its *base semantic phrase/base semantic clause/sentence*. The *base semantic phrase*, '**dappled things**' (l.1) is a key phrase of the text, until line 9, because it functions as an umbrella term of reference to the world of *pied*[7]/ variegated beauty described in the text. Thus, what follows in the text until line 9 is an elaborate and exclusive discourse on the world of *pied beauty*. The *base semantic sentence* of the text consists of a single full-sentence (finite) clause in line 10, which has a crucial discourse value of in the entire text : '**He fathers-forth whose beauty is past change**' (l.10).

Even as base semantic phrase, '**dappled things**' has reference to manifold dimensions of the world of *pied beauty*, a discreet difference in their embedding pattern of reference is distinctly noticeable between its octave and sestet sections. While the embedded items in octave are largely focused on micro-details of the world of *pied beauty*, those in the sestet are, on the whole, focused on its panoramic facets.

Obviously, the elaborate matrix of embeddings/sub-embeddings, reinforced by their lexical and syntactic components, holds thematic significance in the text. This aspect of embeddings is given in-depth attention later in the section on Semantic Components.

Whereas base semantic sentence of the text (except its last line), is derived from its initial '*core-sentence clause*'[8]

Quirk and Greenbaum mean that "given the use of a particular verb in a particular sense, the sentence is SVA (in bold font), its base semantic phrase is derived from its '*optional sentence element*' (in italics) : '**Glory be to God** *for dappled things*' (l.1).

The initial core-sentence clause functions as the superordinate core-sentence clause[9] of the entire text because of its broad reference to the entire text, except its last line. This is well marked overtly by occurrence of the conjunct **for**, together with a *dash* **(—)**, with which the first line/sentence of the text concludes.

The superordinate core-sentence clause of the text (in bold font), '**Glory be to God** for *dappled things*— ' (l.1), has a phrase (in italics) which is a constituent of its clause structure. Though an optional element of its clause structure it has a critical discourse value as a *semantic phrase*, as well as the *base semantic phrase* of the entire text until line 9.

The embedded items, occurring from line 2 until line 9, amplify a range of ramifications of base semantic phrase of the text, '**dappled things**' (l.1), in very many innovative ways. All the words/ phrases/ clauses, from line 2 until line 9, thus function as variant forms of **embeddings/sub-embeddings** that connote a wide range of implications of the base semantic phrase. This results in elaborate structure of deflective discourse on *pied beauty*.

Like base semantic phrase, *base semantic sentence* (underlined), having an embedded clause (in italics), is also derived from the superordinate clause of the text (in bold font) :

'**Glory be to God**' (l.1) — ' (and for) He fathers-forth *whose beauty is past change*'. (l.10).

The embedded clause in the base semantic sentence has a crucial importance in the entire text. The embedded clause, '**whose beauty is past change**' (l.10), is well positioned in the penultimate line/sentence of the text (l.10), so as to sharply contrast the beauty of God, which is 'past change'/*immutable* (l.10), with the world of *Pied* beauty of '**dappled things**' (l.1), which is *evanescent.* This pattern of discourse evolution progressively helps narrow down augmented and ultimate focus on *immutable* beauty of God Himself vis-à-vis *evanescent* world of *Pied* beauty of 'dappled things', created by Him, its fountain-head progenitor-creator.

The entire sentence in line 10, '**He fathers-forth whose beauty is past change**', thus holds crucial significance in the text. Not only does it help make an ***enunciation*** of the immutable beauty of God vis-à-vis the world of *Pied* beauty of '**dappled things**', but, more importantly, a categorical ***pronouncement*** as to why, in the first place, one should crave for '**Glory be to God**' (l.1) Himself, rather than, by implicature[10.] the world of *pied beauty* created by God, howsoever fascinating *per se.*

Detailed below is a break-up pattern of embeddings/sub-embeddings in the text under the heads : Base Semantic Phrase and Base Semantic Clause:

***Base Semantic Phrase*: '*dappled things*' (l.1)**
Embedding (EMBDG)s/Sub-embeddings (SEMBDG)s: OCTAVE

Note : EMBDGs and SEMBDGs are indicated below by an arrow sign (→).

EMBDGs of '*dappled things*'→

Line 2:	EMBDG1:	'skies of couple colour as a brinded cow'→
	SEMBDG1	: 'skies' —'of couple colour as a brinded cow'→
	SEMBDG 2 :	'of couple colour' →'as a brinded cow'
	SEMBDG 3 :	'of couple colour' →'colour' → 'of couple'
	SEMBDG 4 :	'brinded cow' →'cow' →'as a brinded'
Line 3	EMBDG 2	: 'rose-moles all in stipple upon trout that swim'→
	SEMBDG 1:	'rose-moles' →'all in stipple upon trout that swim'
	SEMBDG 2:	'rose-moles'[11]→'moles' → 'rose'
	SEMBDG 3:	'all in stipple upon trout that swim'→
	SEMBDG 4:	'all in stipple upon trout'→' (trout) that swim'
	SEMBDG 4:	'trout' → 'all in stipple upon'
Line 4	EMBDG 3:	'Fresh-fire coal chestnut-falls' —
	SEMBDG 1:	'chestnut-falls'→'Fresh-fire coal'
	SEMBDG 2 :	'chestnut'→'falls'
	SEMBDG 3:	'fire coal' →'Fresh'

	SEMBDG 4:	'fire' — 'coal'
Line 4	EMBDG 4:	'finches' wings'→
		'finches' →'wings'
Line 5	EMBDG 5:	'Landscape plotted and pieced→fold, fallow and plough'
	SEMBDG 1:	→'Landscape'→'plotted and pieced'
	SEMBDG 2:	→'fold, fallow and plough'
Line 6	EMBDG 6:	'all trades, their gear and tackle and trim' →
	SEMBDG 1	:→'all trades'→'their gear and tackle and trim'

EMBDGs/ SEMBDGs : SESTET

Base Semantic Phrase : '*dappled things*' (l.1)

EMBDGs/ SEMBDGs of '*dappled things*'→

Line 7	EMBDG 7:	'All things counter, original, spare, strange'→
	SEMBDG 1	: 'All things' →'counter, original, spare, strange'
	SEMBDG 2:	→'Whatever is fickle, freckled (who knows how?) →
Line 8	SEMBDG 3:	'Whatever is fickle, freckled'→ (who know how?) →
Line 9	SEMBDG 4:	(who knows how?)→'With swift, slow; sweet, sour; a dazzle, dim'

Base Semantic Clause/Sentence :'He fathers-forth whose beauty is past change' →

Line 10	EMBDG 1:	'He fathers-forth' →'whose beauty is past change'

The detailed break-up of embeddings/ sub-embeddings above would show how intricately woven and densely distributed they are in the text. More than that, their ingeniously crafted pattern of embeddings/sub-embeddings, often first-time coinages ever, **arrests** one's immediate attention, quite often a long while, to peel off innovative shades of their meaning. Notably, such an elaborate matrix of EMBDGs/SEMBDGs helps ensure prolonged focus on discourse on *pied beauty*. As a result, it appears sharply distinctive and deflective piece of discourse in the text.

Conjoinings

Conjoinings play a key function by conjoining and cohering the widely distributed embedded items across the text in a logical sequence. The conjuncts, **for** and **and**, help secure compactness of discourse by chaining together the embedded items of the text at various levels of grammatical structure, word/ phrase/ clause/ sentence.

Despite their key functional value, the occurrence of these conjuncts in the text is mostly covert/implicit, yet markedly perceptible. The total number of the conjuncts, **for** and **and,** occurring in the text overtly, is only four whereas their number, occurring implicitly, is sizeable. Such a choice pattern of their occurrence seems a text/discourse necessity. Obviously, once these conjuncts have marked their pan-reference pattern by their overt occurrence a few times early on in the text (II.1-3 and 6), there seems to be little reason why they should recur in the text later obtrusively many more times over.

First and foremost, it needs a special mention that the well-wrought matrix of embeddings, so well employed in the text extensively to build up its semantic structure, would not have passed off as a coherent piece of discourse without conjoinings being there as its cohesive component. This can be well imagined if one were to decipher the central message of the text in its existing format, i.e. without a reference to implicit occurrence of these conjuncts, indicated within brackets below.

Detailed below is the occurrence break-up of the conjuncts, **for** and **and**, occurring overtly/covertly. The break-up would show how these conjuncts help chain together *coherently* and *sequentially* the widely distributed embedded items across the text into a cohesive piece of discourse, until line 10. The conjuncts that occur in the text overtly appear in bold font below whereas those occurring covertly/ implicitly appear within round brackets:

Base Semantic Phrase : '*dappled things*' (l.1)

Line 1 : Glory be to God **for** dappled things ——

Line 2: (and) **For** skies of couple colour ......brinded cow;

Line 3: (and) **For** rose-moles .... swim;

Line 4: (and for) Fresh-fire coal chestnut falls;

Line 4: (and for) finches' wings;

Line 5: (and For) Landscape................ plough;

Line 6: **And** (for) all trades...................... trim;

Line 7: (and for) All things .... strange;

Line 8: (and for) Whatever is fickle, freckled ....

Line 8: (and for) ...... (who knows how?)

Line 9: (and for) (whatever is) With, swift, slow; sweet, sour; a dazzle, dim

Base Semantic Clause/Sentence : 'He fathers-forth whose beauty is past change' (l.10)

Line 10: (And for) He fathers-forth whose beauty is past change

The overt occurrence of the conjuncts, **for** (II.1-3) and **and** (l.6), and their covert/implicit occurrence in the rest of the text, point to a neat pattern in which they help conjoin and cohere the entire text until line 10. So much so that the text until that line seems essentially derived from its superordinate core-sentence clause, '**Glory be to God**' (l.1).

The functional value of **for** and **And** (for) that occur in the text overtly is too explicit to need elaboration. Nevertheless, the clipped citations from the text below are given by way of illustration:

'Glory be to God...'. (1.1)

→'***for*** dappled things......' (Base Semantic Phrase) (1.1)

→'***For*** skies...'(1.2)

→'***For*** rose-moles...'(1.3)

→ '***And*** *(for)* all trades...'(1.6)

In the rest of the text, the conjuncts, **for/ and/ And for,** occurring implicitly, have also the same indispensable discourse value at the levels of both base semantic phrase and base semantic clause. At the level of base semantic phrase, '**dappled things**', they help conjoin and cohere a range of reasons, elaborately spelt out in its embedded items, behind the invocation, '**Glory be to God**'. In the process, these conjuncts help amplify exponentially the reasons behind the invocation. The discourse value of these conjuncts could be well guessed if one tried to decode the message of the text without a reference to their implicit occurrence in the text.

Similarly, the conjuncts, **and for**, occurring implicitly before base semantic clause/sentence, '**He fathers-forth whose beauty is past change**', help explicate lucidly the reason for the invocation, '**Glory be to God**'. This can be guessed if one were to decode the discourse value of the base semantic sentence in the given format of the text, i.e. without a reference to their implicit occurrence.

Significantly, despite their critical discourse value, the occurrence of '**And** (for)' before base semantic clause/sentence seems too implicit/oblique in the text to be perceived at a first glance. Plainly, this seems thoughtfully designed to elicit one's priority attention to the base semantic clause/sentence because it has a key discourse value in the entire text.

Apparently, these conjuncts have a two-fold crucial discourse value in the text. Not only do they conjoin and cohere implicitly the base semantic clause/sentence with the invocation, '**Glory be to**

God', but, more notably, conjoin and cohere it with the preceding deflective discourse on *Pied* beauty as well, anaphorically, sequentially and logically.

Consider the discourse value of the conjuncts, **for** (l.1) and **and for** (l.10), occurring respectively, overtly and covertly, in base semantic phrase and base semantic clause of the text:

(a) **Glory be to God→for** *dappled things*: Base Semantic Phrase (including its embedded items) (II.1-9)

(b) **Glory be to God→**He fathers-forth whose beauty is past change**:** Base Semantic Clause/Sentence (l.10)

(b^1) **Glory be to God→(And for)** He fathers-forth whose beauty is past change (l.10)

In (a), the conjunct **for,** occurring overtly, helps conjoin and cohere the superordinate core-sentence clause (in bold font) with its base semantic phrase (in italics), thus effecting a meaningful discourse. By parallel contrast, coherence between superordinate core-sentence clause and its base semantic clause/sentence in (b), as in the text, is difficult to figure out for want of a conjunct to conjoin them. However, coherence between superordinate core-sentence clause, '**Glory be to God**' and its base semantic clause/sentence, as in (b^1), which is a varied version of (b), would emerge if one conceives, as here, implicit occurrence of the conjuncts, (And for), before its base semantic clause/sentence (l.10).

I have mentioned earlier that, like base semantic phrase of the text, '**dappled things**' (l.1), its base semantic clause/sentence, '**He fathers-forth whose beauty is past change**' (l.10), is also derived from the superordinate core-sentence clause, '**Glory be to God**' (l.1). However, being the penultimate clause/sentence of the text, its discourse range is obviously much wider and crucially significant than that of its base semantic phrase. Noticeably, its discourse range has implicit anaphoric reference to, and impact of, the preceding deflective discourse on *pied beauty*, as well as implicit cataphoric reference to the last half-line sentence of the text, '**Praise Him.**' (l.11), that follows it.

The functional value of **for** (l.1) and **And for** (l.10) lies in not only conjoining the twin parts of the single-piece discourse, one centred around its *base semantic phrase, together with its embeddings*, and the other its *base semantic clause and its embedding*, into a compact piece of discourse (until line 10), but, in the process, in spelling out a parallel and pointed rationale behind why one must crave for glory to God:

Glory be to God→*for* dappled things—— (l.1)

——————————→ ***(And for)*** He fathers-forth whose beauty is past change (l.10)

Notably, a couple of reasons behind the invocation, '**Glory be to God**' (l.1), both coherent, are somewhat dissimilar from each other. The first reason for the craving for glory to God stems from His munificent creation/gift of the world of *Pied* beauty/'**dappled things**', extensively elaborated in the following lines (II.1 -9), whereas the second one is rooted in the premise that God Himself '**fathers-forth whose beauty is past change**' (l.10).

The conjuncts, **for** (l.1), and **And for** (l.10), occurring overtly and implicitly, respectively, have thus a two-fold function in the text. First, they help project binary focus on somewhat dissimilar reasons for selfsame invocation, '**Glory be to God**'. Secondly, notwithstanding contrary reasons for the invocation, these conjuncts help cohere them together all at once into a cohesive piece of discourse (until line 10). Significantly, this happens as the conjuncts, **and for**, though occurring implicitly before the penultimate sentence of the text (l.10), help cohere it with the earlier discourse on *pied beauty* anaphorically.

The parallel contrasting reasons for the invocation, '**Glory be to God**', expounded in the text in a sequential order—first, at the level of semantic phrase, together with its embeddings, followed next by semantic clause/sentence, together with its embedding—indicate a holistic discourse implicature. The occurrence of semantic clause/ sentence (l.10) towards the end of the text, much later than semantic phrase (l.1), comes with a transparent implicature that the semantic clause/sentence has a priority discourse value in the text.

Considered as a single-piece discourse until line 10, the invocation thus seems inspired, primarily and essentially, by God, '**whose beauty is past change**'/*immutable* (l.10), rather than, as the earlier section of the text initially seems to suggest, by the world of *pied beauty* of '**dappled things**' (l.1). This is so because the world of *pied beauty*, despite being wondrously charming, remains, after all, only a creation which God '**fathers-forth**'. Further, its *evanescent* beauty sharply contrasts with *immutable beauty* of God Himself/ '**whose beauty is past change**'. This brings out the pivotal value of semantic clause/sentence (l.10) in the text vis-à-vis its semantic phrase (l.1).

The penultimate clause/sentence (l.10) has a critical discourse value in that it helps effect sudden shift of attention away from deflective discourse on *pied beauty* while restoring it back to the invocation, '**Glory be to God**', with which the text begins. Further, it helps explicate the rationale behind the ultimate command at the end of the text, '**Praise Him**' (l.11) to which it has cataphoric reference. Indeed, it functions as a discourse bridge in between what precedes it earlier—the initial **invocation** of the text, followed by deflective discourse on *pied beauty*—and what follows it next, the pithy **command**, '**Praise Him**'/**God** (l.11). The **command** acquires peak prominence in the text if only because **enunciation** of core message of the text, coupled with a **pronouncement**, in the penultimate sentence of the text helps reinforce its ultimate discourse value.

Kernel word

A refreshing angle of viewing the semantic structure of the poem would be to consider it with reference to its **kernel word**, or base word. Apparently, **beauty** is the kernel word of the poem, just because it broadly covers its entire gamut of manifestations, the *evanescent* world of *pied beauty*, created by God, as well as the *immutable* beauty of God Himself, its fountain head progenitor-creator. Notably, the text spells out the message that the evanescent world of *Pied* beauty/ '**dappled things**' (l.1) owes its origin to its creator, God, '**whose beauty is past change**' (l.10).

In a way, the kernel word, *beauty*, is the **topic** of the poem whereas the rest of it is a **comment** on it. Nonetheless, the poem is titled **Pied Beauty,** and aptly so. This is plainly because the poem is overwhelmingly focused on *pied beauty* in a major section of the text. More so, this is because the title is discourse-wise ingeniously designed to hold back climactic focus on its core message, DSS, until the concluding section of the text. Noticeably, this is done while, at the same time, according prime and elaborate focus on SSS, its deflective discourse on *pied beauty*.

The poem is thus distinctly marked by a progressive shift of attention, from SSS2 —the *evanescent world of pied beauty*— to DSS2— the *immutable beauty of God Himself*:'**He fathers-forth *whose beauty is past change***' (l.10). This evolutionary discourse pattern of *enunciation and pronouncement* (l.10), is well firmed up next by DSS3, the ultimate command in the last sentence of the text, '**Praise Him**'/*God* (l.11). Considered in this perspective, the title of the poem, **Pied Beauty**, crucially functions as a catalyst to the discourse structure of the entire text.

Semantic Components

This section on semantic components carries forward the earlier discussion on semantic structure of the text, though in a more focused way. The specific quest is here to explore in-depth how semantic structure of the text is built up, so to say, brick by brick, by its semantic components, intricately and in innovative ways. Going by their distinctive discourse value, the semantic components of the text will be considered in a focused way under the following sub-heads:

(a) Lexical Components, and

(b) Lexico-grammatical Components.

(a) Lexical Components

Lexical components of **Pied Beauty** are discussed here from a dual and overlapping perspective, namely, thematic and descriptive,

- 'swift, slow; sweet, sour; adazzle, dim' (l.9).

Apparently, the specific discourse value of the adjectives in the sestet lies in mapping a broad contour of thematic structure of the sonnet. Their sole function is thus to give a synoptic overview of the multi-faceted world of *pied beauty* in the concluding section of the text. The adjectives, '*counter, original, spare, strange*' (l.7) function as a cover-term of reference to the **pervasive** dimension of the world of *pied beauty; 'fickle, freckled*' (l.8) denote its **evanescent** aspect; '*swift, slow*' (l.9) reflect its **dynamic** dimension; and, its **sensual** range, both oral and ocular, is denoted, respectively, by the antonym pairs of adjectives, '*sweet, sour*' (l.9) and '*adazzle, dim*' (l.9). It needs to be mentioned that these aspects of the world of *pied beauty* were not encompassed earlier in the octave. (see Fig. 1)

A noticeable variation is marked between the adjectival pattern in the earlier section of the text (ll.1-9), featuring AdjNPhrCl/AdvPhrCl clusters and adjectives of general attributes, and the one followed in the penultimate sentence of the text, '**He fathers-forth *whose beauty is past change***' (l.10). Though the restrictive relative/adjective clause, '***whose beauty is past change***', plainly refers to the *immutable beauty of God*, the choice of a clause to amplify this point comes with a marked discourse value. The implicature of the choice of a predicative/adjective full (finite) clause, '***whose beauty is past change***', in preference to a short synonymous phrase, '*immutable beauty*', is to lucidly explicate its core thematic value in the text.

By contrast, the expansive discourse on *pied beauty*, despite being elaborately structured by a string of AdjNPhrCl/AdvPhrCl clusters, as also adjectives of general attributes, does not get core discourse value in the text. This is plainly because the discourse on *pied beauty,* despite being expansive, singularly lacks even a solitary reference that explicates its overriding discourse value in the entire text.

Interestingly, the penultimate clause/sentence of the text, '**He fathers-forth whose beauty is past change**' (l.10) (DSS2) has a critical thematic function. As mentioned earlier, the clause/sentence not only helps shift attention away from deflective discourse on the world of pied beauty (II.1- 9), (SSS2), but simultaneously helps restore central thematic focus back on the invocation, '**Glory be to God**' (l.1) (DSS1), with which the text begins. Significantly, being positioned as a discourse bridge in between what precedes it in the text and what follows it next, it helps explicate the rationale for why one ought to '**Praise Him**'/God (l.11), (DSS3), rather than His creation of the world of *pied* beauty *per se*).

Descriptive perspective

Lexical items

The lexical density of the poem that reinforces its thematic design, also needs to be considered with reference to their elaborate structural constituents, AdjNPhrCl clusters. The functional value of these clusters, or encapsulated lexical items, lies in giving in-depth description of various facets of the world of *pied beauty* in amazingly novel ways. Therefore, these clusters are discreetly designed to augment maximal focus on the multi-faceted dimensions of the world of *pied beauty.* Most of them thus stand out as a hallmark feature of the text.

Out of ten lines and a half that structure the entire poem, lines 2 to 9 are packed full of AdjNPhrCl clusters. The *italicised portions* below would show how these clusters, containing graphic details of various facets of *pied beauty*, help conjure up their *virtual image* to one's mind :

(1) '(skies of) *couple-colour as a brinded cow*' (l.2)

(2) '(rose-moles) *all in stipple upon trout that swim*' (l.3)

(3) '*Fresh-fire coal chestnut-falls*' (l.4)

(4) '(Landscape) *plotted and pieced – fold, fallow and plough*' (l.5)

(5) '(all trades,) *their gear and tackle and trim*' (l.6)

(6) '(All things) *counter, original, spare, strange* (l.7)

(7) '(All things)*Whatever is fickle, freckled (who knows how?*) (l.8)

With focus on archetypal patterns of the world of *pied beauty*, the lexical sets, employed in the text, not only span its diverse dimensions but also mirror it through iconic images. The images have thus a wide range of reference to a cross-section of orientations, namely, **elemental, occupational, dynamic, sensuous, cyclic** and **volatile**. (see Fig. 3).

The lexical set having **elemental** orientation has reference to all the five core elements that are believed to be quintessential constituents of the cosmos, as also of the human body: the *earth*, *water*, *air*, *fire* and *sky*.[12] The elemental lexical set in the text makes reference, directly or indirectly, to each one of these core constituent elements of the cosmos.

The reference to the element **earth** occurs in '*Landscape* ...' (l.5); the reference to the element **water**, though oblique, occurs in 'trout that *swim*' (l.3); the reference to the element **air**, again oblique, occurs in 'finches' *wings*' (l.4); the remote reference to the element **fire** occurs in 'Fresh-*fire* coal' (l.4); and, the reference to the element **sky** occurs in '*skies* of couple-colour' (l.2). Note, all these references, transparent or oblique, are chosen most discretely and thoughtfully to unfold, in one way or the other, the elemental sweep of the world of *pied beauty*. One of course needs to sift through these descriptive details judiciously to be able to perceive the elemental and cosmic range/pattern of *pied beauty*.

The lexical set, having **occupational** orientation, has reference to primordial occupation of agriculture and farming as indicated by '*Landscape plotted and pieced—fold, fallow and plough*' (l.5). This lexical set also includes reference to all primordial trades, their vocations and tools, as revealed by '*all trades, their gear and tackle and trim*' (l.6). Observe that a reference to all trades is followed up with a sample list of their professional tools, '*gear*', '*tackle*' and '*trim*' (l.6), which, in turn, has implicit correspondence with their primordial vocations, namely, *fishing*, *hunting* and *boating*. Thus, '*gear*' has reference to fishing and hunting whereas '*tackle*' and '*trim*' have reference to fishing and boating, respectively.

The lexical set having **dynamic** orientation of *pied beauty* comprises lexical items, '*swift, slow*' (l.9), whereas the one focused on its **sensuous** dimension, precisely, its oral and ocular aspects, is referred to by the lexical items, '*sweet, sour*', '*adazzle, dim*', respectively.

The lexical set, focused on **cyclic** dimension of *pied beauty*, precisely, its cyclic change from one season to another—here, implicitly, from winter to autumn—is discreetly marked by corresponding lexical items, 'Fresh-*fire* coal' and 'chestnut-*falls*' (l.4), respectively. The image of 'fresh-***fire*** coal' reminds one of reddish brown freshly-burning coal in the fire place during winter, whereas the sight of fallen chestnuts conjures up the image of autumn, the time when chestnuts fall off the tree.

The lexical set, '*fickle, freckled* (who knows how ?)' (l.8) that highlights **volatile** aspect of *pied beauty* unfolds yet another dimension of its archetypal pattern.

Lexico-Grammatical Components

Lexico-grammatical components of the text have a vital discourse function in building up its thematic structure, though they are not so perceptibly marked overtly because of their nuanced discourse value. For this reason, this aspect of the text needs to be given adequate attention separately.

Noticeably, there are five hyphenated compound words in the entire text, each of which helps describe a variant pattern of thematic structure of the text in deviant ways. The compound words, '***couple-colour***' (l.2) and '***rose-moles***' (l.3), are each a nonce formation because of a hyphen occurring in between them. As a result, these words acquire item-specific adjectival value in relation to their referent. Thus, '**couple-colour**', a constituent of the lexical item, '**skies of couple-colour as a brinded cow**', has reference to the changing colour patterns of 'skies' (l.2)—**not** 'sky'— akin to varieties of colour pattern of '*a brinded cow*' (l.2).

Likewise, ***rose-moles***, as contrasted with "dark-brown" regular colour pattern of moles (LDCE 2004 : 1060), typify an ingenious colour configuration, restrictive to '*all in stipple upon trout*', which again is further delimited to '(trout) *that swim*' (l.3). Obviously, because of this nonce-formation, the lexical item, '*rose-moles all in stipple upon trout that swim*', envisions a unique spectacle of the world of *pied beauty*.

The compound words, '***Fresh-firecoal***' and '***chestnut-falls***' (l.4) that together make up one lexical item has reference to the colour of the chestnut, fallen off the tree, that looks glowingly reddish-brown, much like the freshly-lit firecoal. This nonce formation, however, needs to be further looked into in detail.

'*Fresh-firecoal*' and '*chestnut-falls*' that structure one lexical item are hyphenated compound words, each having *inter se* similar grammatical structure, Adjective + Noun. These compound words do not though function discourse-wise precisely the way they appear overtly marked lexico-grammatically. Apparently, '*Fresh-firecoal*' is a semantic compression of the clause, 'Firecoal is freshly lit', having implicit reference, in the given context, to the *colour* of the firecoal when it is freshly lit, rather than that of firecoal which is fresh. Similarly, '*chestnut-falls*' is a semantic compression of the clause, 'Chestnut has fallen off the tree', having implicit reference to the *colour* of the 'chestnut that has fallen off the tree', as contrasted with the *colour* of the 'chestnut on the tree'. In this sense, 'Fresh-firecoal' and 'chestnut-falls' function together as instances of '*dynamic adjective*' and '*dynamic noun*',[13] respectively.

Interestingly, both the compound words, a semantic compression of the corresponding clauses from which they are derived, entail some *activity/transition*:'Firecoal is freshly lit' and 'Chestnut has fallen off the tree'. This explains their deviant structure: '*fresh*' being hyphenated with '*firecoal*', and '*chestnut*' being hyphenated with '*falls*'. The configuration of '*Fresh-firecoal*' with '*chestnut-falls*', having semantic value of a *dynamic adjective* and a *dynamic noun,* respectively, as a single nonce lexical item thus helps project **dynamic** dimension of the world of *pied beauty*.

In the fifth and last hyphenated compound word of the text, '***fathers-forth***' (l.10), the focus sharply shifts to core theme of the poem, the beauty of God Himself, the fountain head progenitor-creator of the world of *pied beauty*, as well as His eternal act of creation. Such a diametrical shift of focus remains opaque, though initially, obviously because of sharply deviant lexico-grammatical structure of this lexical item. Consider the incongruence, both structural and semantic, of the nonce lexical item, '**fathers-forth**', that occurs in the penultimate sentence of the text :

'*He fathers-forth......* **(what ?)** ...... **whose beauty is past change* (?).'

Apparently, the lexico-grammatical deviance of '*fathers-forth*' stems from its dual overlapping discourse function in the text.

Looked at from one of these orientations of discourse functions, the deviance of '***fathers-forth***', a transitive verb, lies in being complemented by a Cs, '*whose beauty is past change*', instead of an Od which is its *obligatory* sentence element. Considered thus, '***He fathers-forth***' functions discourse-wise as an NP, '**He +fathers-forth**', which seems somewhat a stylistic variant of NP structure, '**He, the father**'.

Viewed thus, the adjective clause (in italics) that follows it next as Cs, as in 'He **fathers-forth**/the father, *whose beauty is past change*', helps amplify eternal beauty of God.

Apart from its specific discourse orientation, discussed above, ***fathers-forth***, concurrently functions as a VP as well. Notably, both of its dual functions have a parallel and paramount discourse value in the text. This is apparent from '***fathers-forth***', functioning as a VP in its simple present tense form that entails unrestrictive reference to infinite span of time, ranging from past to future (cf. Leech 1971: 7). Thus, '***fathers-forth***', functioning as a VP, helps here amplify focus on God's *eternal act of creation* —ranging from past to future —which is distinct from God's *eternal beauty,* discussed above. The deviant lexico-grammatical structure of 'fathers-forth, has thus critical discourse value in the text.'

Consider ***fathers-forth***, occurring as an NP in (a) and as a VP in (b) below, with reference to their *stative/dynamic* discourse value in the text :

(a) 'He **fathers-forth** — He, the father/*creator – whose beauty is past change*.' : NP (stative)

(b) 'He **fathers-forth** — He fathers/*creates* (simple present) → eternally *whose beauty is past change*' : VP (dynamic)

The discourse value of '**fathers-forth**'in the penultimate sentence of the text thus lies in projecting core focus on eternal beauty of God, as well as on God's eternal act of creation, detailed in (a) and (b), respectively. Notwithstanding its pivotal functional value, '**fathers-forth**' seems, paradoxically though, obtrusively incongruent and incomprehensible, necessitating a careful re-think. This is plainly because the lexico-grammatical structure of this nonce lexical item is ingeniously crafted to highlight at once its dual and overlapping discourse value in the text.

G M Hopkins' **Pied Beauty** appears much like a hymn in quite a few distinctive ways. The poem begins on a note of glorification of God (l.1), elaborates abiding sense of gratitude to God for His munificent creation/gift of the world of *pied beauty* (II.1-9), extols God for being eternal beauty Himself, as well as for His eternal act of creation (l.10), and, finally, concludes on a note of forthright command to the target readership to '**Praise Him**'/God (l.11). Even so, **Pied Beauty** stands out, above all, as a poem *par excellence*.

Despite its underlying religious thrust, the poem is titled **Pied Beauty**, and for a valid reason. Among the notable ways the poem appears outstanding is how imperceptibly it evokes and sustains, initially and largely, one's overwhelming aesthetic response to the world of *pied beauty*, elaborated in a major section of the text. The poem also stands out as a class apart if only because of its multiple stylistic innovations, those of semantic structure and semantic components, which are its hallmark feature.

Pied Beauty displays a matchless feat of poetic craftsmanship as it strikes a delicate balance between what it highlights extensively in the text—God's creation/gift of the wondrous world of *pied beauty*— and what it centrally focuses on so transparently — God's eternal beauty Himself and His eternal act of creation, followed finally by a laconic clear-worded edict to the target readership to '**Praise Him** (God)'. Such an excellent feat is accomplished solely because the poem displays, from beginning to end, thematic singularity of discourse structure, as well as its organic unity. [14]

Notes

1 This chapter is a revised version of my paper published in the *Indian Journal of Applied Linguistics*, Vol. II, No. 1, Bahri Publications, New Delhi. 1976.

2 Quirk and Greenbaum (1973 :7. 2) identify these 'Obligatory or Core' Sentence/ Clause types as (1) SVA, (2) SVC, (3) SVO, (4) SVOA, (5) SVOC, (6) SVOO, and (7) SV.

3 The labels 'surface' and 'deep' are not used here in Noam Chomsky (1957) 's sense of the term.

4 Note, '**perennial**' implies "continuing for a very long time; happening again and again" (OALD 2015 : 1141).

5 In linguistics/stylistics, 'arrest' and 'release', are commonly used terms, especially in discourse analysis.

6 Thematisation and topicalisation are commonly used interchangeable terms in linguistics/stylistics to assign focused value to an element of clause/sentence structure/discourse structure of the text.

7 The word *pied* has a restrictive denotation, having reference to "(especially of birds) of two or more different colours, especially black and white." OALD (2004 : 1159). But, in the context of the poem, the word seems marked by semantic extension to mean 'variegated'.

8 Quirk and Greenbaum (1973 : 7.2) identify seven 'core' sentence type clauses, having obligatory elements to each, namely SVA, SVC, SVO, SVOA, SVOC, SVOO and SV. By 'core'/'obligatory' elements of clause structure, Quirk and Greenbaum mean that "given the use of a particular verb in a particular sense, the sentence is incomplete if one of these elements is omitted." They go on to

explain that the sentence, 'I put the book' (core/obligatory sentence Type Clause (SVOA) is unacceptable as it omits the obligatory element A (adverbial), for instance, 'on the table'.

9 For a brief note on superordinate clause/sentence, cf. Greenbaum and Quirk (2008 : 289-90).

10 In pragmatics, 'implicature' contrasts with 'explicature'. Implicature has reference to 'what a speaker intends to communicate' which is 'characteristically richer than what she directly expresses : linguistic meaning radically undermines the message conveyed and understood'. (cf. Horn in Horn and Ward 2005)

11 Note, 'rose-moles' is a coinage attributed to G M Hopkins.

12 Apparently, the **elemental** dimension of *pied beauty* seems drawn from the primordial notion of microcosm/macrocosm that has existed long since in various spiritual/religious traditions of the world. According to this notion, man is viewed as a miniature version of the larger whole of the cosmos, and vice versa. In the Hindu religious tradition, the core constituent elements of the cosmos, just as of man, called the *panchabhuta* (the five elements) and numbered five, are identified as *chhiti* (Earth), *jal* (Water), *pawak* (Fire), *gagan* (Ether/Sky) and *samira* (Air). This notion finds a specific reference in a most celebrated Hindu religious classic of the 16th century, **Shri Ramcharitmanasa** by Goswami Tulasidas. Consoling the grieving Tara over the death of her husband, Bali, Lord Rama thus dispels her shroud of *maya*/ illusion of earthly life: "This despicable trash of the human body is composed of *chhiti* (earth), *jal* (water), *pawak* (fire), *gagan* (ether/sky) and *samira* (air), the five core constituents the human body, which is only a microcosm of the larger macrocosm of the cosmos." *(Kishkindhakand* of **Shri Ramcharitmanas**, *doha* 10, *pada* 2 (English translation of the Hindi text).

13 For more on the notion of 'stative' and 'dynamic', see Leech (1971); Quirk and Greenbaum (1973).

14 This discussion was focused on Hopkins' **Pied Beauty** *per se.* No reference was therefore made to either the poet's other poems, or a poem by any other poet, so as to retain central and solitary focus of the discussion to the poem itself. Naturally, a poem ought to be understood and appreciated, in the first place, by itself independently before it is critically evaluated, if at all, in relation to any other poem(s).

References

Chomsky, Noam (1957): *Syntactic Structures.*

Fowler, Roger (1966) : *Essays on Style and Language*, Routledge & Kegan Paul, London.

________(1971) : '*Some Linguistic Contributions to criticism*'. *The Language of Literature*. Eds. Chatman S & Levin S R. Routledge & Kegan Paul, Boston.

________(1972) : *The Language of Poetry*. Vol. I, No. 1. University of South Carolina, Columbia.

Greenbaum and Quirk (2008) : *A Student's Grammar of the English Language*. Pearson Education, Delhi.

Hockett, C.F.A. (1958) : *A Course in Modern Linguistics.* New York : Macmillan.

Horn, Lawrence R., & Ward, Gregory (eds.) (2005) : *Handbook of Pragmatics.*

LDCE (2004) : *Longman Dictionary of Contemporary English.* International edition, 2004.

Leech, Geoffrey N. (1971) : *Meaning and the English Verb*. Longman.

Mc Namee, M.B., Cronin J.A. & Rogers, J.A. (1971) (eds.) : *Literary Types and Themes*. Holt, Rinehart & Winston.

Minis, Noel (1971): *Linguistics at Large*. (self-edit) Holt, Rinehart and Winston Inc. 2nd edition.

Nixon, Nell (1972): '*Pied Beauty*'. *The Language of Poetry*. Vol. I, No. 3 : 1972. University of South Carolina, Columbia.

OALD (2015): *Oxford Advanced Learner's Dictionary.* OUP. 2015.

Quirk, R and Greenbaum, S. (1973): *A University Grammar of English.* Longman.

Steiner, George (1971): 'Linguistics and literature'. In Minis, Noel edit. (1971), *Linguistics at Large.* Holt, Rinehart and Winston Inc. 2nd edition.

Tulasidas, Goswami : *Shri Ramcharitmanas,* Geeta Press, Gorakhpur, India. 2016.

2
Some Aspects of Foregrounding in GM Hopkins' The Starlight Night

The Starlight Night

Look at the stars! look, look up at the skies!
O look at all the fire-folk sitting in the air!
The bright boroughs, the circle -citadels there!
Down in dim woods the diamond delves! The elves'-eyes!
The grey lawns cold where gold, where quickgold lies!
Wind-beat white beam! airy abeles set on a flair!
Flake-doves sent floating forth at a farmyard scare!
Ah well! it is all a purchase, all is a prize.

Buy then! bid then! –What?—Prayer, patience, alms, vows.
Look, look : a May-mess, like on orchard boughs!
Look! March-bloom, like on mealed-with-yellow sallows!
These are indeed the barn; withindoors house
The shocks. This piece-bright paling shuts the spouse
Christ home, Christ and his mother and all his hallows.

It seems relevant to begin with the following statement by Dylan Thomas (1914-1953), a reputable poet-critic of the 20th century, inasmuch as it offers an insider's view of the poet's process of poetic composition: "The best craftsmanship always leaves holes and gaps in the work of the poem so that something that is *not* in the poem can creep, crawl, flash, or thunder in." (Dylan Thomas. In MacNamee, *et al.* 1970 : 482)

Apparently, there is an element of substantial commonality between what Dylan Thomas metaphorically calls the 'holes and gaps in the work of the poem' and the stylistician's notion of *foregrounding*. Both saliently feature the obtrusive character of poetic structure at its best, both tax and rivet the reader's mind in the first instance, both indeed are "sufficient incentive for him to re-read (the poem, as here), if only formalistically" (Roger 1971 : 220), and, above all, both are a precondition for him to unravel the manifold *unexplored* stylistic ramifications of the poem that generally go unnoticed.

A re-reading of a poem, or apiece of literary text for that matter, of the type mentioned above is quite essential for its full-measure aesthetic appreciation and enjoyment, let alone heightened understanding of its encoded message, or its 'micro-language with a micro-grammar' (Freeman 1970 : 10).

Foregrounding

The notion of style as difference is, by and large, prominently associated with poetic language. A common—though not absolute—assumption prevails that poetic language "deliberately breaks the rules in order that a given passage be noticed *as language*", which derives from the corollary assumption that "the hallmark of literary language is foregrounding" (Freeman 1970 : 06).

Foregrounding has thus reference to norm-breaking features of language. In the process, it has concurrent reference to setting up of new linguistic norms of the language that remain, though largely restrictive, to the context of the text itself. This happens because the new linguistic norms are structured by a pattern of 'consistency and systematic character' (Mukarovsky 1970 : 44). Foregrounding is therefore norm-breaking as well as norm-setting feature of language.

Foregrounding thus helps build up 'micro-language' of the poem as it 'exploits linguistic unorthodoxy' for the purpose (Leech 1970 : 121). It is indeed the very warp and weft of the 'highly structured' language of the poem since, as Mukarovsky points out, the 'function of poetic language consists in the maximum of foregrounding of the utterance' (Mukarovsky 1970 : 43).

Foregrounding is, by its very nature, set against the process of automatisation: 'automatisation schematises the event; foregrounding means the violation of the scheme' (*ibid*). It would thus seem that a poem quite often, though not always, stylistically 'ticks' because of its foregrounded features.

How crucial the functional value of foregrounding is in poetic composition is brought out in the following remark by Leech : "whether or not the concept (of foregrounding) is applicable to any great extent to other art forms, it is certainly valuable, if not essential, for the study of poetic language" (Leech 1970 : 121).

However, foregrounding gains its functional value depending a great deal on how suitably its contrastive function is set against a certain norm that prevails over the entire text. Apparently, just as too much of compliance of the norm in a text results in the standard language, surfeit of foregrounded features nullifies its desired stylistic effects, thus, in turn, rendering the text even obtuse or insipid.

In violating the norm, foregrounding follows a set system and pattern of its own. Elaborating this crucial aspect of foregrounding in poetry, Mukarovsky remarks : "The *violation of the norm of the standard, its systematic violation* (the italics are mine), is what makes possible the poetic utilisation of the language; without this possibility there would be no poetry." (Mukarovsky 1970 : 42)

Stylistic Context

The poser now is : Violation of which norm? Whether the norm of the standard language of the period, or the norm of the standard language of the genre? In either case, the norm remains a rather relative concept and hazily defined as it always remains in a flux.

In this scenario, the pragmatic approach seems to look for the norm within the text itself. Michael Riffaterre aptly suggests replacing 'the notion of overall norm with that of stylistic context' of the text as it is 'automatically relevant', 'immediately accessible' and 'variable', thus constituting a 'series of contrasts to the successive stylistic devices' (Riffaterre 1960 : 431).

The text would thus, in itself, be an entirety, providing for both the background of the norm and the foreground of the foregrounded stylistic features, or what Michael Riffaterre terms 'stylistic context' and the 'stylistic device' (*ibid*). Elaborating the point, Michael Riffaterre remarks :

"Style is not a string of stylistic devices, but of binary oppositions whose poles (context/stylistic devices) cannot be separated. Far from concentrating on the stylistic devices just because they are the salient, easily classifiable features, style analysis (and later, esthetic meta-analysis) must devote as much attention to the unmarked elements of the opposition. (Riffaterre 1960 : 432)

Close to Riffaterre's views, cited above, are those of William R Cantrall. Cantrall, affirming the significance of such an artistic use of contradiction, even calls it the 'chief determiner of style' (Cantrall 1972 : 217).

Viewed in this perspective, Gerard Manley Hopkins' sonnet, **The Starlight Night**, is to be reckoned as a stylistically outstanding poem if only for its foregrounded features alone, 'unique, creative innovations of poetry' which are not 'routine deviations' as they follow 'a certain rationale of .. (their).. own' (Leech 1970 : 57).

Foregrounding has *deviation* and *parallelism* as its twin major components. The distinction between the two is neatly explained by Leech in the following way : "Obtrusive irregularity (poetic deviation) and obtrusive regularity (parallelism) account for most of what is characteristic of poetic language" (Leech 1969/74 : 73). The foregrounded features of Hopkins' sonnet are therefore discussed below with reference to these broad parameters of foregrounding.

Deviation

Hopkins' **The Starlight Night** draws the reader's attention, first and foremost, on account of its unique structure, featuring both obtrusive irregularity/deviation as well as obtrusive regularity/ parallelism. The poem's pattern of obtrusive irregularity, or deviation, being focused in this section, appears neatly schematised, perhaps too much so as to give it a semblance of regularity.

Deviation in the poem is set against the backdrop of both 'macro-context' and 'micro-context' (Riffaterre 1960 : 433-37). The macro-context of the poem is the pervasive spell of wonder and rapture that the *starlight night* evokes in the mind of a *perceptive* beholder. The micro-context of the poem, by contrast, is restrictive to intra- context of the nonce lexical items coined to describe, as it were, piecemeal, the pervasive macro-context of the text.

The foregrounded features of deviation in the poem, as the following discussion would show, seem markedly prominent at the levels of lexis and semantics. The poem is therefore discussed below with pointed reference to these aspects of deviation.

Lexical Deviation

The Starlight Night draws one's instant attention to the state of ecstasy that grips the beholder at the sight of *starlight night*. This happens mainly on account of the poem's innovative and rich inventory of lexical items, hyphenated as well as non-hyphenated. Interestingly, most of these items are freshly coined hyphenated lexical items, nearly evenly spread across the entire text, that have central value in the discourse structure of the poem.

Hyphenated lexical items

Notably, the sonnet of fourteen lines contains as many as nine hyphenated lexical items, each of which comprises at least one nonce hyphenated-compound words to structure it. Their functional value lies in giving perhaps a first-ever sharp visual image of kaleidoscopic range of the beholder's ecstasy at the sight of the *starlight night.*

The nonce lexical items, having hyphenated-compound words (in bold fonts), listed below, seem crisp, though unorthodox, so much so that each of them looks much like 'encapsulation of a newly formulated idea' (Leech 1974 : 44); what is more, they underline the 'concept-making power of neologism' (*ibid*) :

'all the **fire-folk** sitting in the air' (l.2), '**circle-citadels**' (l.3), '**elves'-eyes**' (l.4), '**wind-beat** white beam' (l. 6), '**Flake-doves** sent floating forth at a farmyard' (l. 7), '**May-mess**, like on orchard boughs' (l.10), '**March-bloom**, like on **mealed-with-yellow** sallows' (l.11), and '**piece-bright** paling' (l.13).

In line 2, the lexical item, '**all the fire-folk sitting in the air**' is marked by deviation at the levels of both macro-context and micro-context. The deviation at the macro-context level lies in the stars in the *starlight night* being referred to as 'fire-folk', or *fire people,* that are '*sitting* in the air'—not '*up* in the air'. Even as the coinage somewhat taxes the reader's mind it, nevertheless, ingeniously serves to whet and perhaps even widen the range of his visual imagination to appreciate it.

At micro-context level, 'fire-folk' is marked by a collocative clash :'folk' does not go with 'fire'; instead, what it normally goes with are such words as common/ village/farming, as in '*common* folk', '*village* folk', '*farming* folk', etc. Yet, the nonce formation, 'fire-folk', helps conjure up the image of *living folk* image of the stars, as contrasted with their non-living image, 'sitting-in-the- air', that twinkle, indeed, burn much like the flickers of the firelight. The remaining lexical items in the list are likewise a deviation at both macro- and micro-context levels.

The lexical item '**circle-citadels**' (l.3), a reference to the stars, is a deviation as the stars do not normally collocate with citadel/ place of refuge or safety. At micro-context level, the collocation of 'circle' with 'citadels' is also deviant in that it has a specific reference to the *circular* citadel, a neologism[1]. The foregrounded value of this deviance particularly lies in projecting the stars, appear as they do, like dots of light in the starry sky, much like illuminated '*circle-citadels*'/circular fortresses in the sky, distant in seclusion and independent in their distinctive identity.

The reference to the stars as '**elves'-eyes**' (l.4) is again deviant in both the contexts. Obviously, the stars, in the first place, do not collocate with elves, which are 'imaginary creature (s) like a small person with pointed ears and magical powers' (LDCE : 508). The deviation lies further in that, herein, the visible objects —the stars— are described with reference to objects/creatures that are themselves imaginary, unreal and invisible.

The deviance gets sharper at micro-context level on account of two reasons. First, assuming that the stars seem like the eyes of elves who none has ever seen before, how can one possibly go a step further to figure out the visual image of their eyes? Secondly, the lexical item is a revealing neologism as it helps evoke in one's mind an uncanny image of stars as 'elves'-eyes', conjured up in the starlight night. It is worth noting that this neologism is not even remotely connected with the prominent features of elves—their 'pointed ears and magical powers' (*ibid*)—commonly spun in make-believe fairy tales.

The foregrounded value of 'elves'-eyes' thus remains in not only re-inventing a deviant image of the firmament in the *starlight night*, but indeed tickling the reader's bygone memories of the children's world of elves and fairies to savour its spectacle. The common image of 'sparkling'(?) eyes, particularly associated with the supernatural, thus comes in handy for a description of the twinkling stars as 'sparkling' eyes of the 'elves'. The pre-condition that needs to be complied with to appreciate this nonce image of the stars is of course one's flight of fancy to grasp the aesthetic range of this deviant lexical item.

In line 6, '**wind-beat white beam**' is an incredible coinage if only because of its sweeping range of deviance. On the face of it, the coinage does not suggest even remotely its reference to the stars. At micro-context level, the deviance is so marked that the item provides, if at all, only an opaque reference to them.

However, if the reader were to stretch his imagination a little bit too far indeed and make up for what Dylan Thomas metaphorically calls the 'holes and gaps in the work of the poem' to which I referred earlier, its reference to the stars would appear transparent. Obviously, the reference here is not to the 'wind-beat white beam' tree as such, but to the blossoms of the tree. Apparently, the stars that lie scattered all over in the moonless night sky, emitting white/silver beams of light, seem much like the little white blossoms strewn all around as the white beam tree is tossed about by the wind in the springtime.

In line 7, '**Flake-doves sent floating forth at a farmyard**' is a deviant item in both the contexts, and again quite opaque at a first glance like the item discussed above. Apparently, the reference here is not to the stars for the stars do not appear as 'doves' at all —whatever be the kind—that float, or appear 'sent floating forth', because the stars are considered 'stationary' in common perception. Apparently, the item seems to have reference, as its structure suggests, not to the stars themselves but to the floating dove-like white/silver flakes of light in the starlit sky that they transmit from afar, as if at a farmyard.

The intra-context deviation of the item lies in 'doves' being collocated with 'flake'——' a small thin piece that breaks away easily from something else' (LDCE : 606). Nevertheless, such a collocative clash helps build a visual image of swift and smooth dove-like passage of 'flakes' of thinly-spread light from the distant stars.

In line 10, '**May-mess, like on orchard boughs**', a metaphorical reference to the stars, is again a deviant lexical structure because of its intra-collocative incongruence. The collocation of 'May-mess' with 'like on orchard boughs', renders the lexical item quite opaque to the reader. What the common reader, despite his best initial efforts, gets the most out of it is only a somewhat hazy image of the stars in the starry night.

At the intra-context level *per se*, the deviance of the lexical item appears sharper. In the hyphenated-compound word,

'May-mess', the deviance lies in 'mess' being collocated with 'May' : 'May' cannot be 'in a mess'; a room, for instance, can be. However, the occurrence of 'May-mess' along with 'like on orchard boughs' envisions a graphic image of the 'exotic blooms of the orchard' in the month of May.

Indeed, the functional value of the deviant item stands out in projecting a graphic image of the countless, widely scattered, rather disorderly stars— stars that seem to be 'in a mess'— in the cloud-free night-sky, much like the disorderly, cluttered clusters of fruits resting on orchard boughs in the month of May.The appreciation of this image of the starry night, of course, largely rests on whether the reader is able and willing to give, if at all, his probing attention to the item for quite a while.

In line 11, the item, '**March-bloom, like on mealed-with-yellow sallows**' has a structural pattern similar to the one discussed above. The only difference is that the structure here is more condensed and more opaque. It has two hyphenated words, instead of the poem's prevailing norm of one, which results in increasing degree of its deviance and semantic opaqueness.

The item, again a reference to the stars in the starry night, seems deviant to the point of obtuseness as it involves telescoping of several images into one. Thus, at the macro-context level, what the reader tends to guess from the item is only a hazy contour of the starry night.

At the micro-context level, the deviance is structured two-fold. First, 'March-bloom', which has reference to the springtime blooms/catkins hanging on tree branches in the month of March, hardly makes much sense because of its collocative clash with 'like on mealed-with-yellow sallows'. Secondly, one is left wondering about the implication of 'mealed' collocating with 'sallows' — sallow/ willow trees.

Nevertheless, the functional value of deviance of the item reveals itself when looked at closely. Apparently, the stars that cover the entire firmament in the night sky look much like the pervasive '*yellow*'/yellowish pollen, '*mealed*'/floured from the blooms of sallow trees in the month of March/'*March-bloom*' : 'March-bloom, like on mealed-with-yellow sallows'. To appreciate the intricate structure of this deviant item, the reader is of course required to travel an extra mile.

The deviant structure of '**piece-bright paling**' (l.13) is rather complex again. The item involves both lexical and semantic dimensions. Attention for now is focused on its lexical dimension; its semantic dimension, that has much bearing on it, will be discussed later on.

The item is deviant at both macro- and micro-context levels. At macro-context level, its deviance makes it even obtuse because the item offers little clue to help infer its reference to the stars or the starry night, the focal point of the running discourse. The collocation of 'piece-bright' with 'paling' thus sends the reader on a wild goose chase about its possible reference point.

At intra-context level, the deviance in the hyphenated compound word, 'piece-bright', instead of 'bright-piece', is not quite unusual, being an instance of hyperbaton— a regular poetic license—that allows such reversals of normal syntactic/lexical structures in poetry.

However, the functional value of this nonce item lies in presenting a unique image of the stars in the starry sky, with wide semantic implications. Apparently, each of the stars, looking 'piece-bright' or bright piece, seems to piece/string together with other stars to make up the Milky Way of the night sky. In this way, the stars form a kind of 'paling'/fence for the enclosure —conceivably heaven, beyond the stars–that 'shuts the spouse' (l.13)— 'Christ home, Christ and his mother and all his hallows' (l.14).

Non-hyphenated lexical items

The non-hyphenated lexical items also fall in with the deviant lexical pattern of the poem, though they do not seem, by and large, as sharply foregrounded in the text as the hyphenated ones. This is so because their number in the text is much smaller, being restricted to four, as against nine of the hyphenated items. More notably, their structure is fairly less complex and quite less opaque as compared to the hyphenated items.

In line 3, the item, '**bright boroughs**', a reference to the stars, is a slight variant of 'circle-citadels' that immediately follows it in the same line (discussed earlier). Only that this nonce formation has restrictive reference to the stars as being 'bright'/illuminated 'boroughs'/towns, instead of the larger image of 'circle-citadels'/ circular fortresses that immediately follows it.

The functional value of this deviance is specially marked at macro-context level. The reference to the stars as *illuminated towns,* or 'bright boroughs', naturally conjures up the image of a town/ borough with a *population*, making it thus a 'living' image which is not just innovative but indeed incredibly delightful.

In line 4, '**Down in dim woods the diamond delves**' has obvious reference to the stars, like the item that follows it, 'elves'-eyes' (discussed earlier).Despite this, the item remains deviant and opaque at macro-context level because of its structural deviance at intra-context level as well. Apparently, the collocation of 'Down in dim *woods*' with 'the diamond *delves*'[2] seems rather incongruous, even opaque, just because caves normally collocate with mountains, rather than woods.

The functional value of this deviant item comes out though on a closer look. Apparently, 'dim woods' looks akin to the shade of greyish-black night sky, much like the dim/ darkish woods. The image thus provides a contrastive visual back-drop for the stars to twinkle in the night sky, much like 'diamond delves', or caves of diamonds. The choice of *mountains*, in place of *woods*, would not have ever served this purpose at all; hence the collocation of *woods* with *delves* to structure this lexical item.

A similar pattern obtains in the following line (l.5) in the item, '**The grey lawns cold where gold, where quickgold lies**'. Like the item discussed above, it has two components, 'The grey lawns cold' and 'where gold, where quick gold lies', that together make up a reference to the stars in the night sky.

Even as this nonce formation suggests at macro-context level a quick, though hazy, image of the starry sky, it remains deviant because of its opaqueness at intra-context level. The first component of the item, 'The grey lawns cold', has obvious reference to the extensive carpet of the night sky that looks like greyish-black lawns. Conceivably, it is 'cold' as well —'grey lawns cold' —because of its infinite altitude and remoteness in the sky. However, its incompatibility with the remaining component of the item, 'where gold, where quick gold lies', makes it not only deviant but also opaque.

Nevertheless, the functional value of the item lies in picturing the image of the starry sky in a singularly distinctive way. The neologism, '*quickgold*', coined by analogy with '*quicksilver*' and discreetly chronicled step-wise in that order, from being tentative to being definitive — *gold* being followed by *quick gold*, 'where *gold,* where *quick gold* lies'—renders the image of the starry night increasingly more visual and wondrous.

Apparently, the image of the stars, twinkling as *gold,* would seem inappropriate without *gold* being additionally endowed with the *mercurial attribute* of quicksilver so as to liken it with the flickering, unsteady light of the stars. Hence, the thoughtful choice of a blend 'quick gold', instead of just *gold*, to structure this lexical item.

In line 6, the item, '**airy abeles set on a flare**', has again reference to the starlit night, though in a way outright different from the item that precedes it. Despite its deviance and opaqueness at both macro-and micro-context levels, the item occurs with an added functional value.

At macro-context level, even as the item evokes, metaphorically though, a broad hazy image of the stars, likened to something 'set on a flare', it remains elliptical, because of its structural deviance at intra-context level as well. To appreciate this singularly deviant image of the item at intra-context level, one needs to overstretch one's visual imagination. One must therefore conjure up the starlit night sky as a kind of wide sprawling canopy of '*airy* **(not** earthly) *abeles*' — white poplar trees in the sky —whose inverted branches seem to be '*set on a flare*'/ lit up by torch-like beams of light from the stars.

Semantic Deviation

Despite its title having focused reference to **The Starlight Night** the poem is not quite about the wondrous beauty of the starlight night as such. On the contrary, it is essentially marked by religious note that permeates all through the poem, though the reader gets to perceive it clearly only in the latter half of the poem.

The religious note finds an overt mention in the text, only briefly and in passing, as a semantic deviation (II.9 and 12-14).Yet its mention is well sequenced nearly midway in the text, and thereafter, so as to starkly contrast it with elaborate description of beauty of the starlight night, the macro-context of the poem. As a result, the religious note acquires a pronounced foregrounded value in the text.

Foregrounding of religious note is noticeably well-crafted and well-sequenced in the structure of the entire text. This would explain why even as the reader's attention is never allowed to flag or ramble off from the beautiful spectacle of the starlight night– just because of its pervasive and gripping description in the entire text— it is ultimately the religious note that holds supreme sway over the reader's mind.

Line 8, **"Ah well! it is all a purchase, all is a prize"**, the last line of the first stanza, has a pivotal discourse value in the text in that it foreshadows reference to the religious note of the next line, as also the following stanza. This exclamatory statement only sums up the wondrous beauty of the starlight night in its entirety, calling it a 'purchase' or 'prize' that is up for a grab, but does not go any further to elaborate its message.

However, the interjection in the next stanza, line 9, **"Buy then! bid then! –What? –Prayer, patience, alms, vows."** amplifies, loud and clear, the religious overtone of the earlier statement (l.8). A visibly clear semantic deviation is thus marked in the poem in its ongoing discourse on the beauty of the starlight night. The statement here begins on a note of self-query about how one can access this 'purchase' or 'prize' target, "Buy then! bid then! – What?". This is concurrently followed by a range of options, suggested in the same statement later, as possible means to access it : "Prayer, patience, alms, vows".

Line 9 thus clearly spells out the religious import of *prayer, patience, alms* and *vows* as unequivocal conditions of religious piety that must be met with by those coveting this celestial 'purchase' or 'prize'. Obviously, by extension, this also implies that those not fulfilling these basic criteria of piety would just not be able to access this celestial 'purchase' or 'prize'.

Note, the semantic deviation in line 9 is flanked by elaborate description of the starlight night on either side, whereas the concluding lines, 12 to 14, also featuring semantic deviation, are flanked by its description on one side only, i.e. towards the end of the text. What is most significant here is that this occurrence pattern of semantic deviation as a stylistic device in between the macro-context of the starlight night on either of its sides or both, is what ensures it pronounced foregrounded value. The pattern followed here is similar to the one stipulated by Michael Riffaterre (1960):

Context — Stylistic Device (SD)— Context.

Herein, semantic deviation as Stylistic Device (SD) gains its crucial foregrounded value because of the sequence pattern of its occurrence in the Context of the text.

Semantic deviation as SD seems to acquire a special foregrounded value in the concluding lines of the poem (II.12 to 14) in more ways than one. First, these lines are preceded—not followed—by description of the sensual macro-context of the poem. Notwithstanding the preceding extensive focus on the starlight night, the prime focus ultimately narrows down to the religious note of the poem, thus giving it a finale value. Secondly, these concluding lines, culminating on a religious note, present an inverse semantic contrast to – indeed a semantic progression from —the initial lines, highlighting the sensual aspect of the starlight night, with which the poem starts off.

Consider the two sets of lines below (II.1 and 2 vis-à-vis II. 13 and 14) for their underlying semantic contrast, one focused on the sensual aspect of the starlight night and the other highlighting its religious dimension, respectively :

Look at the stars! look, look up at the skies! (1)
O look at all the fire-folk sitting in the air! (2)

This piece-bright paling shuts the spouse (13)
Christ home, Christ and his mother and all his hallows . (14)

Unlike the description of the starlight night in sensual terms in *most part* of the poem, from the beginning till now, the concluding lines of the poem, 12 to 14, are a clear departure from the preceding pattern of discourse. The image of the starlight night is now finally and exclusively conceived in religious terms. As a result, these lines acquire a special foregrounded value. Note, the metaphorical image of the starlight night, as below,

(These are indeed) the barn; within doors house (12)
The shocks. This piece-bright paling shuts the spouse (13)
Christ home, Christ and his mother and all his hallows. (14)

has all reference to the Christian religion and mythology. This unique image of the starlight night can therefore be best explored exclusively in religious terms.

Viewed in this purely religious perspective[3], the starry sky replicates the image of a heavenly barn — the reference being made here is to the old Protestant hymn "*Bringing in the Sheaves*" —- that houses within doors not only the redeemed souls but also, as here, shuts behind its 'piece-bright paling', or fence of bright stars, *Christ* in his *home*, i.e. heaven, *his mother* Mary and *all his hallows*[4], or all saints of Christ. This extended religious image of the starlight night only goes to finally answer the self-query, raised earlier, why the wondrous spectacle of the starlight night is indeed such a coveted 'purchase' or 'prize', suggested earlier (l.8).

Parallelism

Parallelism and deviation are both key stylistic mechanisms to foreground the obtrusive features of language. However, they are sharply opposite from each other in their stylistic function. Stylistic deviation brings out the *irregular features* of language whereas stylistic parallelism focuses on its *features of extra-regularities*.[5] Nevertheless, they are both important, and even complementary tools of foregrounding, with immense stylistic value in their own distinctive ways, as in the present text.

The significance of parallelism in poetry is highlighted in G M Hopkins' notable remark that 'the artifice' of poetry "reduces itself to the principle of parallelism." (cited in Leech 1969/74: 65) This is further underscored by Leech's own comment, "The importance of parallelism as a feature of poetic language almost rivals that of deviation. It is certainly the principle underlying all versification." (*ibid* : 65)

Much like deviation that gains its stylistic value because of its distinctive pattern of contrastive occurrence (discussed above), the structural pattern of parallelism is also marked by a contrastive feature. However, the contrastive pattern of parallelism typically stipulates "an apportionment of invariants and variables" (Roman Jakobson 1966, quoted in Leech 1969 /1974: 65), or what Leech calls the essential occurrence of "an element of identity and an element of contrast""which are 'parallel' with respect to their position in the pattern." (*ibid* : 65 and 66)

Parallelism and deviation, indeed foregrounding in general, are not quite an unusual feature of language in everyday speech situation. But, because of their trivial nature of commonplace occurrence, they do not generally by themselves merit stylistic attention. What makes each of them stylistically significant though is the extent or 'degrees of foregrounded irregularity (deviation) and 'degrees of foregrounded regularity' (parallelism) (*ibid*: 64) to which each is patterned in the relevant text. Further, the stylistic value of both parallelism and deviation also hinges a great deal on their multi-layered 'inter-locking' of a wide range of 'foregrounded patterns' (*ibid*: 66)—phonological, lexical, etc. – that vary from text to text.

Parallelism is, however, a holistic notion, with multi-dimensional functional value and has thus more facets to it than what the discussion above may seem to suggest. Its functional value ranges across diverse art-forms, both "inside and outside poetry" "including the "language of music." (Leech 1969/74 : 67) So far as poetry is concerned, even the "simple principle of equivalence" highlights the significance of parallelism as a crucial means of foregrounding, as we shall see below. (*ibid*: 67)

What has been observed above may serve as a valid reference point for further consideration of **The Starlight Night**, with focused reference to poetic use of parallelism. Deviation apart, Hopkins' poem displays, at a first glance, quite a few distinctive features of extra-regularities of language that seem to converge, leading to its structural cohesion and semantic coherence. The poem will be discussed below with reference to these features of extra-regularities of language at various levels of parallelism, namely, lexical, syntactic and semantic.

Lexical Parallelism

The entire poem is a fervent exhortation to the reader/listener to rush outdoors and watch the wondrous spectacle of the starlight night. No wonder, the key word extensively chosen in the text to make this exhortation is **look**. Notably, the word 'look' occurs seven times in the text overtly, having just about an even distribution across it——four times in the octave and three times in the sestet. In rest of the text, except its lines 8 and 9, the word occurs only implicitly to ensure discourse compactness, as also to avoid its obtrusive recurrence in the text *ad nauseum*. What really gives it stylistic value as an eye-catcher in the entire poem is not its repetition *per se*, [6] but how each time of its occurrence as an '**invariant**' eye-catching word in the text, whether overt or implicit, is followed by a wide range of '**variables**' which are '**parallel**' to each other syntactically, **"with respect to their position in the**

pattern" of the text (*ibid*: 65 and 66).Consider the relevant lines from the text below that substantiate this point :

> **Look at** the stars! **look, look up at** the skies! (1)
> ***O* look at** all the fire-folk sitting in the air! (2)
>
> **Look, look**: a May-mess, like on orchard boughs! (10)
> **Look**! March-bloom, like on mealed-with-yellow sallows! (11)

The overt recurrence of the 'invariant' word, 'look', followed by a range of 'variables', listed below, that occur parallel to each other in the syntactic pattern of the text, serves to augment attention to the starlight night in manifold ways :

'the stars', 'the skies' (l.1), ' all the fire-folk sitting in the air' (l.2), 'a Mess-mess, like on orchard boughs' (l.10), 'March-bloom, like on mealed-with-yellow sallows' (l.11).

The same pattern is followed in rest of the text, except its lines 8 and 9, wherein the 'invariant' word 'look', occurs implicitly, though followed by a range of other 'variables' having parallel position to each other syntactically :

> **Look at** : 'The bright boroughs' (l.3); 'the circle-citadels there' (l.3), 'Down in ....delves' (l.4),
> 'The elves'-eyes' (l.4), 'The grey lawns ....lies' (l.5), 'Wind-beat ....flair' (l.6),
> 'Flake-doves ....scare' (l.7), 'These are indeed .... his hallows' (II.12-14)

Apparently, the 'invariant' word, 'look', like a prime mover of the text, draws persistent attention to the starlight night by constantly shifting its focus from one variable to another. Noticeably, each of these variables has *inter se* parallel syntactic position, and each of them functions as a viable referent of the starlight night : ' the stars'/ 'the skies'/ ' all the fire-folk sitting in the air', and so on.

Interestingly, the instances of parallelism mentioned above are given emotive intensity through successive repetition of 'look' in an identical order in lines 1 and 10. There is, however, a slight and singular variation in this pattern in line 2. Here, contrary to the regular pattern of its occurrence in sentence initial position, 'look' is preceded by the emotive interjection 'O': "O look...". Even as this structural variation results in 'irregular'/'free' parallelism[7]—seemingly a 'disturbance' in the running pattern of discourse –it has the rhetorical effect of raising the addresser's pitch of sustained exhortation to the reader/listener to the level of forthright informality[8].

It may be added that the discourse value of the invariant word, 'look', remains crucially significant in the text, whether it occurs overtly or implicitly. However, its occurrence in the text in one way or the other seems conditioned by exigencies of discourse compactness, as also avoidance of its obtrusive recurrence in the text.

Syntactic Parallelism

The discussion above largely centred around '**look**', the 'invariant' key word in the poem —-its frequency and distribution in the text —with direct and pointed reference to the adjacent variables, each having distinctive discourse value and occurring parallel *inter se* in the syntactic pattern of the text —-'the stars', 'the skies', and so on. However, the functional value of this key word in the text as a stylistic tool of foregrounding extends far beyond these adjacent variables.

Given a closer view, it appears that 'look' is not just an invariant word in relation to its adjacent variables mentioned earlier, with a limited foregrounded value. Indeed, the word functions as '*an element of identity*' for the entire poem (except its lines 8 and 9) to which the rest of it, schematised in its elaborate semantic pattern, parallels *syntactically*— at the levels of sentence, clause or phrase —-as the '*element of contrast*' (*ibid*: 65). Plainly, this implies that the variables, 'the stars', 'the skies', and so on, the *element of contrast*, will have little message value in the text without reference to the invariant key word, 'look', the *element of identity*. This can be easily guessed if one tries figuring out the message value of these variables in the text in isolation, independent of any reference whatsoever to this key word.

Considered thus, the entire poem (except its lines 8 and 9) features the syntactic structure of a 'superordinate sentence', embedded largely with exclamatory sentences/clauses/phrases of the text (marked in italics below), wherein 'look' functions as the verb phrase (VPhr). Interestingly, 'look' functions synchronically as a VPhr in the 'superordinate sentence' of the entire text (except its II. 8 and 9), as well as in all its embedded sentences/clauses/phrases, directly or indirectly. 'Look' occurs in the text explicitly in the embedded sentences/clauses/phrases in lines 1, 2, 10 and 11, and implicitly in lines 3, 4, 5, 6, 7 and 12 to 14. This pattern of foregrounding of VPhr not only helps retain persistent focus on 'look'— the keyword of the text —but also helps circumvent its obtrusive repetition in the text many times over.

Viewed in this perspective, what remains minus 'look', a key constituent (VPhr) of the 'superordinate sentence' of the entire text (except lines 8 and 9), is its direct object (O_d), consisting of embedded sentences, clauses or phrases. Significantly, these varied manifestations of O_d—sentences, clauses, or phrases—essentially function as variables (marked in italics below and numbered) of the 'superordinate sentence', which are all parallel and equivalent *inter se* in the schematic pattern of the poem. The following break-up of this pattern will elucidate this point further :

Look at *the stars*! (1) **look, look up at** *the skies*! (2)
O **look at** *all the fire-folk sitting in the air*! (3)
(Look at) *The bright boroughs*, (4) **(Look at)** *the circle-citadels there*! (5)
(Look at)*Down in dim woods the diamond delves*! (6) **(Look at)** *the elves'-eyes*! (7)
(Look at) *The grey lawns cold where gold, where quick gold lies*! (8)
(Look at) *Wind-beat white beam*! (9) *airy abeles set on a flare*! (10)
(Look at) *Flake-doves sent floating forth at a farmyards scare*! (11)
Look, look (at) : *a May-mess, like on orchard boughs*! (12)

> **Look (at)!** *March-bloom, like on mealed-with-yellow sallows*! (13)
> **(Look at)** *These are indeed the barn ..... his hallows*. (14)
> (II. 12 to 14)

Therefore, the foregoing break-up indicates how, in the entire text (except its lines 8 and 9), 'look'—'the element of identity'—is indispensable to syntactic structure, as also semantic relevance, of all the co-occurrent variables —'the element of contrast', directly or indirectly. 'Look' is overtly an integral part of the syntactic structure of the variables 1, 2, 3, 12 and 13, and implicitly in those numbered 4, 5, 6, 7, 8, 10, 11 and 14. The critical value of 'look' can well be guessed if one tried deciphering their message value, *in isolation*, i.e. minus this key word from the text. Consider the syntactic congruity/message value, or lack of it, of any of these variables listed above, without reference to the key word, 'look':

> 'the stars' (?), ' the skies' (?), ...'The grey lawns....' (?), and so on.

Noticeably, all these variables are critically positioned in the text syntactically. Even as all of them function parallel and equivalent to each other *inter se*, they occur in a certain order of sequence. Such a configuration of parallelism proves to be most efficacious in structuring the core message of the poem. This would explain why the variable 14 (II. 12-14), having outstanding message value in the text, occurs towards the concluding and climactic lines of the text, not at its beginning. (I shall come to this point again in the section on Semantic Parallelism)

In a sharp departure from the earlier pattern of variables, variable 14, spanning over three lines (II.12 to 14), pictures the starlight night from an outright revealing perspective. This results in an amazing metamorphosis of the on-going discourse orientation of the text. The entire spectrum of beauty of the starlight night is conceived afresh in variable 14, now metaphorically in terms of elaborate reference to the Christian religion and mythology — a sharp contrast with earlier variables of the text centrally focused on the wondrous spectacle of the starlight night as such. (cf. the earlier section on Semantic Deviation). The discourse value of 'look'—- the VPhr of the 'superordinate sentence' (except its lines 8 and 9)—-is thus pivotal in that it helps draw the reader's pointed and persistent attention, though implicitly, to the variable 14. This could be figured out easily if one considered the syntactic congruity and message value of the extended variable14, when it is preceded by (implicit) occurrence of 'look', as in (a)/the text vis-à-vis (b), a hypothetical illustration when it is marked by its absence :

(a) **(Look…)**{These are indeed the barn; within doors house
The shocks. This piece-bright paling shuts the spouse
Christ home, Christ and his mother and all his hallows.} (14) (II.12- 14)

(b) **(X)**{These are .... hallows.} (14) (II.12-14).

Apparently, (a) gains its syntactic coherence and semantic relevance just because the extended variable 14 (II.12-14), functioning as Od in the 'superordinate sentence' of the text, derives its discourse value from VPhr, 'look', the element of identity of the entire text.

Lines 8 and 9 need a special mention as their pattern of parallelism sets them apart from rest of the text in a number of prominent ways. First, they do not share the matrix of parallelism of the text built up earlier around the invariant word of 'identity', 'look', and its whole gamut of co-occurrent variables, its 'element of contrast'. Secondly, lines 8 and 9, placed centrally in the text of 14 lines, functions as a catalyst to help unravel the core message of the text. Thirdly, and most significantly, they fore shadow transition of focus from the sensual beauty of the starlight night to its divine perception, precisely the clearly-worded stipulation to access it.

Line 8 occurs at the end of octave of the sonnet whereas line 9 occurs at the beginning of the sestet. In a way, they are both juxtaposed to each other in terms of their varied orientations of focus. Line 8 summarises the sensual beauty of the starlight night —"Ah well! It is all a *purchase*, all is a *prize.*" (italics mine)— while line 9 immediately follows it up with a rhetorical declamation "*Buy* then! *bid* then!—What?—*Prayer, patience, alms, vows*." (italics mine)

Despite their divergent focus, both the lines share features of intrinsic coherence between them, whether of similarity or contrast, which go to highlight their relationship of equivalence, or parallelism.[9] Line 8 sums up the sensual beauty of the starlight night as '*purchase*'/ 'a *prize*' worth coveting whereas the first half of line 9 pronounces its next logical corollary: (If it is so) '*Buy* then! '*bid* then!'. Note, the parallelism of 'purchase' and 'prize' in line 8 with their converse words, 'buy' and 'bid', respectively, in the first half of the next line 9 neatly foregrounds the syntactic and semantic coherence between the two sentences.

What needs special attention here is that the functional value of this pattern of parallelism extends much beyond what has been just pointed out above. Apparently, this pattern, streamlined in two critical stages, foreshadows the core message of the text unequivocally. In the initial stage, line 8 and the first part of line 9 puts ole focus on the sensual beauty of the starlight night —'Ah well! .... bid then!' –whereas, by equivalent and parallel contrast, the latter half of line 9—'Prayer ... vows'— lays bare the salient pre conditions of piety one must comply with for divine perception of sensual beauty of the starlight night :

> *Ah well! it is all a purchase, all is a prize.* (l.8)
> *Buy then! bid then!* —What?— *Prayer, patience, alms, vows.* (l.9)

Significantly, 'What?' functions in the text as a bridge word that helps connect and evolve these two stages of parallelism. In the first stage, the euphoric exclamation at the wondrous beauty of the starlight night, called 'a purchase' and 'a prize' (l.8), is followed next in line 9 by a sense of wonder if the same is accessible, if at all, by 'buying' and 'bidding'. However, in the second stage, the reference to 'bidding' and 'buying' is promptly questioned by the bridge word, 'What?', and revised suitably in the latter half of the same line 9, by *parallel reference*—equivalent and contrastive—to 'Prayer, patience, alms, vows', the crystal clear stipulations for such an access.

The functional value of this pattern of parallelism lies in not just simply foregrounding the core message of the text, but in evolving it credibly and gradually in stages until their climax. The word, 'What', is thus pivotal as it helps shift and prioritise attention in the on-going discourse, from one stage to another, precisely, from the sensual beauty of the starlight night to the clearly-worded specific stipulations of one's piety for its divine experience. The reference to 'Prayer, patience, alms, vows' only betokens these essential stipulations.

Semantic Parallelism

Semantic parallelism in the poem functions synchronically in tandem with its lexical and syntactic parallelism. Consequently, it pervades the thematic structure of the entire poem. While the two levels of parallelism—lexical and syntactic—are restricted to an '*immediate*' interpretation, semantic parallelism, having an all-inclusive sweep in the text, is subject to a '*wider*' and holistic interpretation.[10]

The very title of Hopkins' poem, **The Starlight Night**, entails semantic parallelism in a most outstanding way. Despite extensive description of the starlight night in a major portion of the text, the poem does not glorify its beauty *per se*. Instead, by parallel contrast, it projects, in its concluding lines, an elaborate vision of divine dimension of beauty of the starlight night. This pattern of semantic parallelism—equivalent and contrastive—is reflected in the neatly-worded pattern of contrast, transparently visible in the text, between how it begins and expands through most part of it, with focus on the sensual beauty of the starlight night, on the one hand, and how it finally concludes with peak prominence on its divine dimension :

> Look at the stars! Look, look up at the skies! (l.1)
> ....
> This piece-bright paling shuts the spouse (l.13)

Christ home, Christ and his mother and all his hallows. (l.14)

The same pattern of semantic parallelism is sustained and fortified in the middle of the text as well. As noted in the section on Syntactic Parallelism, lines 8 and 9 are crucially positioned at the centre of the text of 14 lines even as, at a first glance, they do not quite seem to cohere with each other in the discourse pattern of the text. Nevertheless, their discourse value comes out soon enough as they critically help foreshadow—in microcosm, just about midway in the text—the semantic parallelism that features the entire poem. This is reflected in the discourse format of the lines 8 and 9, being juxtaposed with each other.

While line 8 sums up the beauty of the starlight night as 'a purchase'/'a prize', this observation is complemented by its logical corollary in the very first half of the next line 9 : (If it is so) 'buy then!', 'bid then!'. By equivalent and parallel contrast to this, the concluding part of line 9 stipulates the preconditions of piety that must be complied with to access this coveted 'purchase'/'prize'. The reference to 'Prayer, patience, alms, vows' in line 9 only helps amplify these stipulations.

The text also reveals yet another notable pattern of semantic parallelism that operates at yet another crucial level. Viewed in this perspective, the poem appears to comprise four parts, detailed below, each in parallel and contrastive relationship with its adjacent part/s:

Part 1 : Look at the stars! … .Ah well! it is all a purchase, all is a prize. (II. 1 — 8)

Part 2 : Buy then! bid then! –What?—Prayer, patience, alms, vows. (l.9)

Part 3 : Look, look: a May-mess........... mealed-with-yellow sallows! (II. 10 —11)

Part 4 : These are indeed the barn.........Christ and his mother and all his hallows. (II. 12 —14)

Significantly, Parts 1 and 3 focus on the sensual beauty of the starlight night whereas Parts 2 and 4 highlight its divine dimension. The text thus features a well-knit schematised pattern of discourse, all focused on its cyclic order that alternates between the sensual beauty of the starlight night and its divine dimension. Apparently, this helps retain parallel and persistent focus on contrastive orientations of the poem, the sensual and the divine.

Yet, beyond these cyclic shifts of focus, the text leaves no one in doubt where its ultimate thematic focus lies. This explains why the poem concludes with peak focus on the divine dimension of beauty of the starlight night, not with focus on its sensual aspect, notwithstanding the latter getting elaborate description in the text right from its beginning through most part of it.

Note, the four Parts of the text are not just parallel and contrastive with their adjacent Part/s; indeed, they are all crucially interlocked in a certain sequential paradigm. So, any reversal in this paradigm would distort, even deface, their schematised discourse value in the text.

Viewed thus, Parts 1 and 4, and Parts 3 and 2, each function as contrastive pairs, with *inter se* focus, respectively, on the sensual and divine dimension of beauty of the starlight night. The foregrounded value of each of the pairs, however, varies in terms of their specific function in the text. So much so that they cannot swap their places in the text without affecting their message value. Further, Part 4, focused on the divine dimension of beauty of the starlight night, receives maximum foregrounded value, solely because of its final occurrence in the text. By sharp parallel contrast, Part 1, focused on its sensual dimension, with which the text begins, does not seem to get as much focused value:

Part 4 : These are indeed the barn ..... all his hallows. (II.12-14)
Part 1 : Look at the stars! .... all is a prize. (II. 1-8)

Next, in the same descending order of foregrounded value, Part 2 precedes Part 3 in the text. This is so because Part 3 seems like an 'add-on' to the extensive description of the sensual beauty of the starlight night, whereas Part 2 functions as a turning point in the text with changed focus on the divine dimension of beauty of the starlight night :

Part 2 : Buy then! bid then! –What?—Prayer, patience, alms, vows. (l. 9)

Part 3 : Look, look: a May-mess .... mealed-with-yellow sallows! (II.10-11)

Notwithstanding the validity of what has been stated in the foregoing paragraphs, the fact remains that the text is structured in the sequential order: Parts 1-2-3-4. This is attributable to a number of crucial overlapping factors. It is worth noting that the poem is titled **The Starlight Night**. So, it would seem highly incongruous and unacceptable if it began with Part 4, rather than Part 1, despite its ultimate core focus resting with Part 4.

More importantly, the thematic progression of the poem—from the sensual to the divine—would not have been possible if Parts 1 and 4—for that matter, Parts 2 and 3 as well— were to swap their locations in the text. The occurrence of Parts 1 to 4, which is their sequence order in the text, helps evolve a smooth, coherent and credible transition of focus from its peripheral part to its core section, precisely, from the sensual to the divine dimension of beauty of the starlight night.

The Starlight Night is an outstanding poem in its own right if only because it bears a most singular stamp of identity. This would explain why the poem has ever remained the subject matter of constant scholarly research, even a long time after it was first published. The foregoing discussion has been just a chain effort in this on-going constant pursuit, aimed at exploring the style-content matrix of the poem in perhaps a refreshing light.

The discussion above highlighted how the poem appears unique in several ways. Yet, what seems most prominent about the poem over-all is how it strikes an intricate balance between its dynamics of 'linguistic expression' and that of its 'linguistic content' (Leech. 1969/74:74). Apparently, the poem demonstrates that its "... foregrounded regularity *(parallelism)* predominates in linguistic expression, and foregrounded irregularity (deviation) in linguistic content." (*ibid.*).What needs further attention is how the poem makes discreet use of both deviation and parallelism[11], all at once, as efficacious stylistic tools to foreground the core message of the text.

Notes

1 A citadel…"is **rectangular** in shape, having four circular towers at each corner…." **Tus Citadel– Wikipedia**.

2 'delves' is used here in its archaic meaning, 'cave (s)'.

3 For details on this point, see //https://hokku.wordpress.com/2012/10/04/heaven-barn-hopkins-starlight-night/

4 'Hallows', or 'holy ones', are archaic terms of reference to saints.

5 "Obtrusive irregularity (poetic deviation) and obtrusive regularity (parallelism) account for most of what is characteristic of poetic language; but they do not both occur with equal frequency at the different levels of linguistic organisation". (Leech 1969/74:73)

6 "Although repetition sometimes indicates poverty of linguistic resource, it can, as we see, have its own kind of eloquence. By underlining rather than elaborating the message, it presents a simple emotion with force." (*ibid*: 79)

7 "Most people will agree that the disturbance of the pattern, far from being a blemish, breaks up the formality of the speech, and makes it more like a genuine expression of strong feeling". (*ibid* : 77)

8 For more on this point, see *ibid* :76-77.

9 "The assignment of significance to a parallelism rests upon a simple principle of equivalence. Every parallelism sets up a relationship of equivalence between two or more elements: the elements which are singled out by the pattern as being parallel. Interpreting the parallelism involves appreciating some external connection between these elements. The connection is, broadly speaking, a connection either of similarity or of contrast." (Leech 1969/74 : 67)

10 "The interpretation of parallelism is like the interpretation of deviation in being divisible into an *immediate* interpretation and *wider* interpretation, which takes into account its relation to other foregrounding, and ultimately to the whole work in which it appears." (Leech 1969/74 : 68-69)

11 "Obtrusive irregularity (poetic deviation) and obtrusive regularity (parallelism) ....do not both occur with equal frequency at the different levels of linguistic organisation." (Leech 1969/74 : 73).

References

Cantrall, William R (1972) : 'The artistic use of seeming contradiction'. In *Current Trends in Stylistics*. Eds. Kachru, Braj B and Stahlke,

Herbert, F.W. Linguistic Research Inc. Edmonton, Champaign. 1972.

Fowler, Roger (ed) (1970) : 'Linguistic Theory and the Study of Literature'. *Essays on Style and Language.* Routledge & Kegan Paul. 1970

________(ed) (1971) :'Some linguistic contribution to criticism'. *The language of Literature*. Routledge & Kegan Paul. 1971.

Freeman, Donald C. (ed) (1970) : ' Linguistic approaches to literature'. In self-edit. *Linguistics and Literary Style*. Holt, Rinehart and Winston. 1970.

Leech, Geoffrey N. (1969/74) : *A linguistic guide to English poetry*. Longman. 1974

________(1970) : 'This bread I break – language and interpretation'. In Freeman, Donald C (1970).

Mukarovsky, Jan (1970) : 'Standard language and poetic language'. In Freeman, Donald C. (1970).

Riffaterre, Michael (1960) : 'Stylistic context'. In *Essays on the language of literature*. Eds. Chatman, S B and Levin, S R. Houghton Mifflin. 1967.

________(1969) : 'Criteria for stylistic analysis'. In Chatman, S.B. and Levin, S.R. (1967).

Thomas, Dylan : 'Notes on the art of poetry'. In *Literary Types and Themes*. Eds. McNamee, M.B., Cronin, J.E. and Roger, J.A. Holt, Rinehart and Winston. 2nd edition. 1971

Wikipedia : Tus Citadel-Wikipedia.

https://hokku.wordpress.com/2012/10/04/heaven-barn-hopkins-starlight-night/

3

A Slumber which *did not* Seal his Spirit: Towards Peeling the Message of a Poetic Discourse

A basic distinction between literary and non-literary discourse is not necessarily, as commonly perceived, one of esoteric vis-à-vis everyday uses of language.[1] Indeed, the blurred distinction between the two, if at all, essentially lies in the former being far more intricately patterned than the latter.[2] This is so because literary discourse has to be of necessity intrinsically a "self-contained" (Widdowson 1975: 36) and autonomous piece of communication wherein the reader, being at the passive/receiving end, is denied a chance whatsoever to query the writer/poet for an answer on points of doubt, if any. A piece of literary discourse is therefore naturally designed to transmit complete import of its targeted message.

Literary discourse is moulded either by discreet selection from among the normal patterns of linguistic regularity or by creation of a micro-code of its own employing non-regular patterns of the language—linguistic oddities/ deviance—or, at times, by an admixture of both.

Frequent focus in stylistic studies on deviant structures of literary text has often led to a sweeping impression that it is deviance that typifies literary discourse. However, one would note that the choice of one mould in preference to the other—of linguistic regularity or deviance, or an admixture of both —to structure a piece of literary discourse does not make it a bit more or a bit less literary than it really is.[3] What is indeed substantially important in literary discourse is whether or not its underlying message is discreetly encoded, obviously with an eye to its aesthetic and thematic value, whatever be the mould. Equally importantly, the efficacy of literary discourse lies in that whether or not, and to what extent, it helps the reader decode the message through insightful application of his linguistic knowledge.

The foregoing perspective provides a basis for the following discussion of one of the most-celebrated poems of William Wordsworth (1770-1850), **A slumber did my spirit seal.** The poem is noted for its towering simplicity of language, or linguistic regularity, yet considered a well-wrought extraordinary piece of poetic discourse. It has a neat and simple structure that consists of only two stanzas of one sentence each, spread over a total of eight lines. The poem is also acclaimed as a masterpiece 'elegy' of the English literature, and also commended by Samuel Taylor Coleridge asa 'sublime epitaph'[4].

The discussion below is divided into two broad sections that together help offer a viable cohesive framework for the study of discourse structure of Wordsworth's poem. Section I briefly highlights certain aspects of the structure of everyday language/ non-literary discourse which seem to have a crucial relevance for discussion of Wordsworth's poem. As the following pages would show, Section II draws its functional framework of enquiry from Section I in a significant way because of its critical relevance to exploration of discourse structure of Wordsworth's poem.

Section I : The structure of non-literary discourse

The earlier reference to literary discourse being far more intricately patterned than its non-literary counterpart implies existence of a continuum between the two types of discourse structure, and not a cleavage between the two. It further implies that the language structures recurrent in non-literary discourse may well have a pre-eminent value in literary discourse, if employed in a judicious manner, for reasons of communicative focus. This point will be discussed later in Section II.

Similar to the continuum between the structures of literary and non-literary discourse does exist the one within non-literary discourse itself. This means that non-literary discourse has within it a range of structural variations, from simple terminal discourse structure **(TDS)** to complex extended discourse structure **(EDS)**, with the possibility of the former running into the latter. I shall discuss below this aspect of non-literary discourse from the angle of operator **do** as a device of information focus (see Quirk and Greenbaum 1973: 14.6), as well as in terms of the pattern of clause relation and clause sequence.

1.1 Terminal discourse structure (TDS)

Consider the following illustrations :

(1) A : Who signed the letter in absence of the Director?

B : I *did* (sign it).

(2) A : Did you meet John last evening to discuss the matter?

B : I *did* meet him last evening, *but didn't discuss the matter.*

In both the illustrations above, B's affirmation of signing the letter/meeting John, in response to A's query, follows a regular pattern of logical order and sequential clause relation. Yet, the difference between the two illustrations lies in that the interaction between A and B in (1) is a clear instance of TDS as the termination of discourse here is emphatically and unequivocally signalled in B's utterance by the operator **did.** By a marked difference, the interaction between A and B in (2) is an instance of TDS only if B's utterance includes the entire sentence, i.e. both its clauses. But B's utterance in (2) will not be a TDS if it excludes its clause in italics, despite emphatic focus of the operator **did** on its initial clause, just because, in that case, the remaining part of the sentence, i.e. its initial clause, will not provide a complete answer to A's query. Consequently, TDS in (2) may run on into EDS, as here, because numerous queries would crop up on the mission of B meeting with John. This will lead to further queries from the interlocutor, resulting in extension of discourse, i.e. EDS.

The operator **did** above reinforces clausal signal of the end of discourse by restricting information focus on positive, as contrasted with negative, assertion. The positive assertion in (1) B is thus : 'Instead of nobody signing the letter I *did* (sign it)', while in (2)B it is further narrowed down to only the act of meeting John.

1.2 Extended discourse structure (EDS)

Extended discourse structure (EDS) is a regular feature of non-literary discourse, only that it isnot considered its style marker as it is a part and parcel of common parlance, being easier to decode in a routine way than EDS of literary discourse. Nevertheless, EDS of non-literary discourse also requires special attention to decode, which is not quite unusual, whenever it features a complex structure. The following illustrations will help explain the point:

(3) (a) : His manners *did* win him my confidence.

(b) : I had no idea of his being a cheat.

(4) (a) : His failure in the exam. *did* hurt me.

(b) : I had no doubt about his success in the exam.

Both the illustrations above have each a corresponding set of identical syntactic structure, juxtaposed sequentially but not logically. The message content in both (3) (b) and (4) (b) logically precedes the one in (3) (a) and (4) (a), respectively:'no idea of his being a cheat' and 'no doubt about his success in the exam' exist prior to the one of 'winning of my confidence'/ 'the feeling of my hurt', respectively. Nevertheless, (a) precedes (b) in both (3) and (4) in the text sequentially in both the illustrations above, solely because of focal thematic value of the core message : 'the winning of my confidence'/ 'the feeling of my hurt'.Notably, (3) and (4) are both instances of EDS because their discourse message (DM) does not terminate with (b) in both (3) and (4), as in the text, but extends far beyond, *by implicature*, to the corresponding hypothetical sentences suggested below:

(3) DM 1 : My opinion about him stands revised now.

DM 2 : My trust in him is gone now.

(4) DM 1 : My opinion about him stands revised now.

DM 2 : My feeling of hurt still remains.

DM 1 in both (3) and (4) conveys identical message pattern of 'revised opinion' since both follow identical sequence of logical structure as detailed below :

Stage 1 (b) : Past opinion (no idea of his being a cheat/ no doubt about his success in the exam.)

Stage 2 (a): Event (winning of confidence/feeling of hurt)

Stage 3 (DM1) : Revised opinion

However, the discourse message gets further narrowed down in DM 2 of both (3) and (4) which is, in each illustration, different from DM 1, but not incompatible with it. The difference between DM2 of (3) and (4) lies in that in each of these illustrations, additional lexical clues help decode their core message. Thus, the feeling of loss of trust and the feeling of hurt are derived, respectively, from the lexical clues that underline pejorative/commendatory assertions in (3) (b) and (4) (b)——'no idea of his being a cheat'/ 'no doubt about his success in the exam.'

The function of operator ***did*** in both (3) (a) and (4) (a) is twofold : first, to emphasise contrastive aspects of the message : 'Instead of his manners not winning him my confidence they *did*'/'Instead of his failure in the exam not hurting me it *did*'; and, secondly, by extension, to reinforce, through lexical clues, the core message content of DM2. The affirmation in (3), 'His manners *did* win him my confidence' followed by 'I had *no idea* ...... cheat' makes it temporarily positive ——'winning of confidence' was only for a while since 'I had *no idea* of his being a cheat'. By contrast, the affirmation in (4), 'His failure in the exam. *did* hurt me' followed by 'I had *no doubt* about his success in the exam.' makes it positive but currently valid as well : 'His failure did hurt me in the past' as it does in the present, because 'I had *no doubt* about his success in the exam.'

It is in discourse perspective of non-literary discourse, precisely, its pattern of TDS vis-à-vis EDS, outlined above, attention now shifts, in Section II below, to exploration of a classic piece of literary text.

Section II : The structure of literary discourse : A slumber did My Spirit Seal

The discussion of the structure of non-literary discourse above, though only brief, has been focused and selective with specific reference to only those aspects of non-literary discourse that seem to have direct/indirect bearings on this section, concerned with the study of discourse structure of William Wordsworth's classic poem, **A slumber did my spirit seal**.

Apparently, literary discourse, despite being marked by its intricate structure, essentially shares the EDS pattern of non-literary discourse. However, its distinctive value comes out prominently only when it is far more discreetly patterned, often in nuanced ways, than the structure of the latter. It is in this perspective that the discourse structure of Wordsworth's poem, **A slumber did my spirit seal,** (text below)is discussed in the following pages from four overlapping angles, namely, clause relation and clause sequence, tense and aspect, lexical choice and thematic organisation.

A slumber did my spirit seal 1
I had no human fears : 2
She seem'd a thing that could not feel 3
The touch of earthly years. 4

No motion has she now, no force;
She neither hears nor sees:
Roll'd round in earth's diurnal course
With rocks, and stones, and trees.

2.1 Clause relation and clause sequence

Notably, **A slumber did my spirit seal** is a poem of only two stanzas, consisting of one complex sentence each, that feature a regular pattern of clause relation and clause sequence. The first stanza/ sentence thus sequentially precedes the second stanza/ sentence, both logically and temporally. The past event of sealing of spirit of the addresser, as well as his illusion of 'no human fears' and the referent seemingly being above the 'touch of earthly years', is followed up in the next stanza by the current state of the referent's *motionlessness*, as well as her ultimate *movement* with the 'diurnal' rotation of the earth, together with other manifestations of Nature — 'rocks, and stones, and trees'.The first stanza of the poem that describes the past event thus stands out in sharp contrast to the second one, describing the current state, in terms of both intra-clausal relation and intra-clausal sequence.

In the second stanza, the first two clauses (II.5-6), which describe the referent's state of *motionlessness* and *numbing of her audio-visual senses*, betokening her death, precede the clauses (II. 7-8), having reference to her current/ultimate state of *movement* with the earth, along with 'rocks, and stones, and trees'. All the clauses in this stanza thus sequentially occur, both logically and temporally.

Interestingly, considered *per se*, the first stanza displays an irregular pattern of clause relation and clause sequence. Even as the coordinate clauses in the first stanza — '*I had no human fears: She seem'd a thing .... earthly years*' (II.2-4) — precede the initial clause of the stanza, '*A slumber did my spirit seal*' (l.1), both logically and temporally, they do not occur in the text sequentially in that order Plainly, this is because the addresser's state of illusion — the state of 'no human fears', having obvious reference to the chief human fears of ageing, decay and death (II.2-4) — existed before the event of *sealing of his spirit* (l.1), it is the latter that is given thematised/ pre-eminent value in the stanza as, indeed, in the entire discourse structure of the text.

Apparently, there seems to be nothing unusual about this kind of clausal organisation inasmuch as it is a regular feature of literary discourse. What seems though most striking is the crucial function of the operator **did** in giving contrastive value to the thematised event : Instead of a slumber not sealing the addresser's spirit, it **did** (l.1). Notably, the operator *did*, however, does not function here as a constituent of terminal discourse structure (TDS) of the text as might appear initially. Indeed, it is a vital constituent of extended discourse structure (EDS) of the entire text, which has a far more important discourse value, as further discussion later would show (see 2.2).

Whether or not the affirmation of the event—sealing of his spirit— has a past/passing value for the addresser is not revealed from the pattern of clause relation and clause sequence of the text. For this, one has to look for other clues in the text for an answer (see 2.2 and 2.3).What is though significantly revealed from the clause pattern of the text is the addresser's implicit affirmation of '*no human fears*' that existed prior to the event of '*A slumber did my spirit seal*' (l.1), the thematised line of the text. In other words, the addresser was seized by *human fears* only after his spirit was sealed by a slumber.

In the first stanza, juxtaposition of the initial clause (l.1) with subsequent coordinate clauses (II. 2-4) in the text — all in the simple past——makes it amply explicit that the latter (II. 2-4) precede the former (l.1), both logically and temporally (cf. Leech 1971:20a), though they do not occur in the text sequentially in that order.This implies that the addresser's state of '*no human fears*' (l.2) spanned only until his spirit was not sealed (l.1), not thereafter when it got sealed. Significantly, such a juxtaposition of the referred clauses lends illocutionary force to the addresser's implicit affirmation of '*human fears*' (II.2-4), which follows the event of '*A slumber did my spirit seal*'. Consider below the logical and temporal sequence of the addresser's implicit affirmation of *human fears*:

Stage 1 : State of illusion: No human fears/ '*I had no human fears....*' (II.2-4), prior to Stage 2

Stage 2 : Event following Stage 1: Sealing of his spirit/ '*A slumber did my spirit seal*' (1.1)

Stage 3 : Illocutionary force of the addresser's modified perception in the aftermath of Stage 2 :

'I had no human fears' until '*A slumber did my spirit seal*', leading to implicit affirmation :

'I have human fears now.'

Notably, the sequence in which the discourse of the text evolves, from Stage 1 to Stage 3, is not the order of sequence in which they occur in the text because of the reasons spelt out earlier.

2.2 Tense and aspect

In the earlier section, the functional value of the thematised clause, '*A slumber did my spirit seal*', was discussed in terms of clause relation and clause sequence of the text.The validity and expanse of the earlier discussion is considered now from the perspective of the poem's choice pattern of tense and aspect. The narrowed focus is here precisely on how, if at all, such a choice pattern has a critical value in structuring the discourse pattern of the text.

Strikingly, the two stanzas of the poem are marked by a sharp contrast in their choice pattern of tense. The first stanza is all through in the simple past whereas the second and final one is entirely in the simple present. Apparently, this difference in choice pattern of tense seems derived from discourse requirement of each of the stanzas. While the simple past in the first stanza signals a 'completed event', or an event that 'takes place before the present moment' (Leech 1971: 18), the use of the simple present in the final stanza, with state verbs, *be*, *have*, etc., has unrestrictive reference to its infinite span of time, ranging from past to future (*ibid* : 7).

Thus, reference to *sealing of spirit* and *state of no human fears* in the first stanza, both in the simple past, points to their passing value/irrelevance to the addresser in the present as each of them is a 'completed event' in the past. Consider the following clauses of the text vis-à-vis their alternative variants, given below, in terms of discourse value of their tense and aspect:

(1) (a) '*A slumber did my spirit seal*' (Simple past): 'A slumber seal**ed** my spirit.'

No relevance in the present.

(b) A slumber does my spirit seal (Simple present): 'A slumber seal**s** my spirit.'

Continued relevance in the present.

(2) (a) 'I had no human fears' (Simple past):No relevance in the present.

(b) I have no human fears (Simple present): Continued relevance in the present.

In (1) (a), the operator **did** has a more critical functional value than what might appear initially, i.e. just as an emphasiser of the past event of *sealing of spirit of the addresser*. Indeed, as a crucial constituent of EDS of the entire text, occurring in the simple past, the operator **did** helps highlight the passing value/ present irrelevance of the past event of sealing of spirit of the addresser. This suggests that the slumber **did** seal the spirit of the addresser in the past, but it **does not** keep it sealed in the present any longer.

Apparently, the addresser's observation on the past events — *sealing of spirit* and *no human fears* —-reflects a marked shift in his perception —in retrospect/ in 'tranquil recollection'[5]–of their passing value value/ irrelevance in the present. Such a tangible shift is well reflected in the illocutionary force of the addresser's implicit *acceptance of his spirit being no longer sealed* as well as *acceptance of human fears* in the present. This observation may sound paradoxical if one looks at the poem at its face value, i.e. as a text, not as a discourse.

Consider the gradual process of discourse evolution of the text, from the addresser's perception of the past event—'*A slumber did my spirit seal*'—to his perception of its present state of reality, as detailed below :

Stage 1: 'A slumber **did** my spirit seal' : Instead of a slumber not sealing my spirit, it **did** (seal it).

Stage 2: Implication of EDS message: But the event of *sealing of my spirit* has lost its present relevance.

Stage 3: Illocutionary force of EDS message: I have a revised perspective on this past event now—

'A slumber **did** seal my spirit in the past, but it **does not** keep it sealed in the present any longer.

(Further discussion on this point in 2.3 and 2.4)

In (2) (a), the addresser's perception of the past event— '*I had no human fears....earthly years.*' (II. 2-4), described in the simple past to mark it as a 'completed event', also underscores its irrelevance to him in the present. As mentioned earlier, the past event of '*I had no human fears.......*years' (II. 2-4) precedes the past event of '*A slumber did my spirit seal*' (l. 1), both logically and temporally, though **not** sequentially in the text in that order. This lends illocutionary force to the addresser's *implicit affirmation of human fears* (also discussed earlier). Consider this process of discourse evolution, detailed below :

Stage 1:Past event described in Simple past: The event, 'I *had no human fears* … earthly years ' (II. 2-4), precedes the event, '*A slumber did my spirit seal*' (l. 1)

(Stage 2), both logically and temporally, though not sequentially in the text in that order.

Stage 2: Past event described in Simple past: The event, '*A slumber did my spirit seal*' (l. 1) (Stage 2), precedes the event, '*I had no human fears…earthly years*'

(Stage 1), sequentially in the text in that order, though not logically and temporally.

Stage 3: Illocutionary force of EDS message: The addresser is seized (made aware) of '*human fears*.......' only in the aftermath of Stage 2 experience of *sealing of his spirit,* not earlier than it.

In parallel contrast to the simple past used in the initial stanza to mark the *completed phase of the past event*, the use of the simple present in the concluding stanza brings out in sharp relief the *infinite/ timeless state of the present event.* The use of the simple present forms of state verbs in the final stanza (II. 5—8) —*has, hears, sees, (is) roll'd*—indicates infinite/timeless state of the present event that spans into the future :

No motion has she now, no force;
She neither hears nor sees :
Roll'd round in earth's diurnal course
With rocks, and stones, and trees.

The initial clauses in the final stanza—— '*No motion has she now, no force*; *She neither hears nor sees*' (II. 5-6) — may seem, at a first glance, to be a euphemistic description of the referent's death, considered only *a state of her motionlessness and numbing of her audio-visual senses*. What needs special attention though is that the addresser's observation has a restrictive reference here to the transitory moment, **now**, '*No motion has she* ***now****, no force* ....' (II.5-6).

The restrictive illocutionary force of the transitory moment **now** is elaborated in the following lines of the stanza that describe a marked and quick transition in the referent's state, from *her past state of motionlessness and numbing of audio-visual senses* (II. 5-6) to *her ultimate state of movement,* along with daily rotation of the earth and its other manifestations : '*Roll'd round in earth's diurnal course with rocks and stones and trees*' (II.7 –8). Apparently, the addresser's observation is essentially derived from his cognitive/ pragmatic awareness that, once in grave, the referent's body transits from the *state of no motion/motionlessness* to one of *timeless/*

eternal motion, along with daily movement of the earth and other manifestations of Nature, '*rocks, and stones, and trees*' :

Roll'd round in earth's diurnal course
With rocks, and stones, and trees.

Obviously, the referent's *eternal state of motion and force*, along with daily rotation of the earth, etc is indicated by the simple present only because its reference range is timeless, spanning from the past to the future. Additionally, the use of the simple present in the concluding stanza underscores, not only the current irrelevance of the past completed event — sealing of the addresser's spirit by a slumber — but the present relevance of the referent's life of eternal motion and force along with the daily rotation of the earth and other manifestations of Nature with which the referent is merged after death. This brings home the core message of the poem :The slumber which *did* seal his spirit initially *did not seal it for long*. Plainly, this is because the addresser had an abiding cognitive/ pragmatic awareness of the referent's eternal life of motion — even after her death —once she (her body) was merged with ever-moving earth and other manifestations of Nature : 'Roll'd round in earth's ……….. trees.'

2.3 Lexical choice

Although the poem is hallmarked by its over-all lexical simplicity the same is brilliantly employed to give its discourse structure a stamp of unique identity. Except the formal Latinate lexeme, ***diurnal,*** and a fairly uncommon literary lexeme, ***slumber***, both of which have a crucial function in its discourse dynamics, the lexical stock of the entire poem is drawn from the English language living speech situation.

Notably, the thematised affirmation of the event, '*A slumber did my spirit seal*', mentioned earlier, has only a past and passing value since what the addresser ultimately considers relevant is the referent's eternal state of timelessness. This discourse pattern is well reinforced in the text by a thoughtful choice of the lexeme, **slumber**, in preference to a more simple and common lexeme 'death', and for quite valid reasons.

Apparently, the key-lexeme of the text, ***slumber,*** is used, not as a euphemism for death as might overtly seem, but with specific and nuanced reference to its root meaning, a "*period or occasion of sleep or repose; freq. a light or short sleep*" (italics mine) (SOED : 2014), whose connotation suitably fits in with the discourse pattern of the text. This validates the reason why the referent's death is glossed in the text as *her state of motionlessness and numbing of audio-visual senses*, rather than plainly referred to as her death:

No motion has she now, no force;
She neither hears nor sees :

It is worth noting that the referent's ***slumber***, described as ***her state of motionlessness and numbing of audio-visual senses,*** having connotation of its root meaning, logically coheres with the next lines that refer to her transition to ***the timeless state of mobility and force,*** along with daily rotation of the earth, etc:

Roll'd round in earth's diurnal course,
With rocks, and stones, and trees.

Such an abstract/cognitive view of the referent's death (II. 5 — 8), perceived as her ultimate state of timeless mobility and force along with '*diurnal course*' of the earth, etc, strikes the addresser only after he is starkly disillusioned with his past perceptions of '*no human fears*' and the referent being beyond the '*touch of earthly years*', both of which have implicit reference to ageing, decay and death. The addresser's state of illusion in the past, described in the following lines, has thus clear implicature of his acceptance of '*human fears*', which stands out in marked contrast to his earlier illusion of '*no human fears*' (discussed earlier) :

I had no human fears :
She seem'd a thing that could not feel
The touch of earthly years.

The lexemes, ***seem'd*** and ***thing***, only underscore the addresser's state of illusion about the referent's profile. In the clause, 'She *seem'd* a *thing……years*', the emphatic focus is on the addresser's illusion about the referent's *real* self, possibly because of her singular extraordinariness. Notably, the addresser's illusion about '*no human fears*' (II.5-8) remained until, indeed emanated from, his illusion of the referent being immortal : 'She ***seem'd a thing***' that was beyond the '*touch was of earthly years*'—ageing, decay and death. This has implicature of the addresser's affirmation of '*human fears*', which followed the death of the referent (discussed earlier).

The past and passing value of the traumatic event of the referent's death is also revealed through a collocative clash — unusual collocation—between the lexemes, ***slumber*** with ***sealed***, which do not normally co-occur with each other. The lexeme, ***seal*** (verb), which normally refers to such activities as "*to close an envelope, etc. by sticking the edges of the opening together*"; "*to close a container tightly or fill a crack, etc.…*" (italics mine) (OALD: 1394), at once conjures up the reversative lexemes 'unseal/ unfasten'.This goes to underscore that the usual follow-up of something being ***sealed***— as contrasted with 'closed' —implies the eventual possibility of it being ***unsealed*** later. Such is *normall*y not the case with the lexeme, 'closed'.The 'sealing' of spirit of the addresser, like its agentive subject ***slumber***, carries the usual implicature of a momentary event, having normal possibility of it being unsealed later.

The addresser therefore views the referent's death only as a ***slumber*** — a momentary event — that ***sealed*** his spirit in the past only for a while, which got eventually '**unsealed**' later. Plainly, this is related to his cognitive awareness that the referent's body, once in grave, transited from ***slumber*** (in its root meaning, cited above) to the timeless state of mobility and force along with the daily rotation of the earth and its various manifestations, '*rocks, and stones, and trees*'.

The crucial choice of an offbeat and rather exotic lexeme, ***diurnal***, also seems to have a vital discourse relevance. The lexeme has a dual reference, one to its usage in astronomy where it means "taking one day/day and night both", and the other to its usage in biology where it means "(of animals) active during the day"/ day time as opposed to "nocturnal"/ night time (OALD : 447). Transparently, ***diurnal*** is used in the text here in astronomical sense of the term, having reference to cosmic and stellar movement of the earth, day and night. The lexeme thus is a prudent choice to describe the ***referent's timeless state of stellar mobility day and night*** *along with diurnal movement of the earth.* The choice of the lexeme, **diurnal**, thus seems indeed a superb way — perhaps inimitable – by which to immortalise the memory of the referent:

Roll'd round in earth's diurnal course
With rocks, and stones, and trees.

2.4 Thematic organisation

In the earlier sections, the discourse structure of the text was considered from various complementary angles, each of which having pointed focus on its core pattern of discourse dynamics.

The thematic structure of the poem, comprising two sub-sections, or two one-line stanzas, seems discreetly designed to unfold a pragmatic, indeed holistic, vision of the referent's death. The first stanza deals with the *completed phase* of the event of the referent's death and the trauma it caused the addresser whereas the second and final stanza, describing its *timeless phase,* elaborates his cognitive awareness of the event and the great solace that he draws from it. Notably, both the two phases of the event are neatly strung together in the text coherently to form a seamless continuum of thematic evolution.

The *completed phase* of event of the referent's death and the trauma it caused the addresser has reference to his two-phase state of illusion. In the first phase, the addresser makes an emphatic assertation of his trauma following the referent's death : '*A slumber did my spirit seal*'. This is followed in its next phase by his emphatic declamation of '*no human fears*' : '*I had no human fears …….years.*' The paradoxical implicature of both these assertions, or his two-phase state of illusion, in the first stanza, lies in that they are both eventually nullified by the addresser in the next and final stanza of the poem (discussed in earlier sections).

Significantly, what is thematised in the text is the addresser's state of illusion, his emphatic declamation of his spirit being sealed by a slumber. But, then, this state of illusion is accorded a past and passing value by the addresser ultimately. The utterance, '*A slumber did my spirit seal*', thus, conveys a paradoxical discourse message in the text, singularly because it occurs as a constituent of its EDS (cf. 1.2), that stands out in sharp contrast to its face discourse value if the same utterance were to occur as a constituent of a TDS (cf. 1.1). The bottom-line message of the utterance, discussed earlier, is therefore :Instead of a slumber not sealing the spirit of the addresser, it *did seal it*, though only initially and for a while. However, the event lost its current relevance to the addresser after he was through a state of reflection on it later. This state of awareness is neatly enunciated in the final stanza of the poem (cf. 2.2).

The description of *timeless phase* of the referent's death in the final stanza logically coheres with the addresser's earlier affirmation of the past and passing value of the referent's death, only that it is viewed here in a wider pragmatic and holistic perspective. The addresser's state of awareness of *timeless phase* of the referent's death comes through in two stages. In the first stage of awareness, the addresser makes out the referent's death as a mere ***slumber***, 'light or short sleep' (*ibid*), featuring 'No motion ….. no force', etc :

No motion has she now, no force;
She neither hears nor sees; (II.5-6).

In the next stage of ultimate awareness, the addresser views the referent's death in a pragmatic and cognitive perspective, considering it merely her transmutation— after her body's merger with the earth/ Nature —to the *timeless state* of eternal life and mobility along with 'diurnal' movement of the earth (II.7-8):

Roll'd round in earth's diurnal course
With rocks, and stones, and trees. (II.7-8)

Noticeably, the poem is streamlined by a neat pattern of thematic evolution, from illusion to awareness, culminating in a cognitive/holistic perspective of the referent's death. In the process, it displays its down-to-the-earth realistic orientation towards life. Thus, while human fears, having obvious reference to those of ageing, decay and death, are affirmed by the addresser in no uncertain terms, the referent's death is not (II.5-8).

The transparent message that comes out of the poem ultimately is thus not one of loss, mourning and disillusionment, but, on the contrary all through, progressively one of recovery, resilience and cognitive/holistic perception of a transmuted reality —the referent being vibrant and alive, even after death, because of her eternal mobility along with 'diurnal course' of the earth. The declamation, '*As lumber **did** my spirit seal*', thematised in both the title and beginning line of the poem thus plainly implies only an *initial and transitory* assertion of a slumber sealing the spirit of the addresser, which got ultimately **unsealed** the moment the addresser had the cognitive acumen to perceive the transmuted reality of the referent's eternal life and mobility, despite her death.

Notes

1 This chapter is a revised version of my paper presented at the *National Seminar on Stylistics, Semiotics and the Teaching of Literature*, Central Institute of English & Foreign Languages (now rechristened Central University of English & Foreign Languages), Hyderabad, India. 1990.

2 In the Preface to the Lyrical Ballads, Wordsworth affirmed, among other things, that the language of poetry should be the language "really used by men", but it should be "a selection of such language."

3 Though it is common to find violations of linguistic rules in literature it is neither a necessary nor a sufficient condition for a discourse to be literary that it should be deviant as text." (Widdowson 1975: 37)

4 "Upon receiving Wordsworth's letter containing a copy of 'A slumber ...', **Coleridge** described the work as a 'sublime epitaph'." https: //www.wikipedia.org.

5 Cf. Wordsworth's famous definition of poetry as "the spontaneous overflow of powerful feelings *recollected in tranquillity* (italics mine)"

References

Coleridge, Samuel Taylor: 'A letter to Wordsworth by Coleridge'. https// www.wikipedia.org.

Leech, Geoffrey N (1971) : *Meaning and the English Verb*. Longman. 1971.

OALD (2015) : *Oxford Advanced Learner's Dictionary*. Oxford University Press.

Quirk, R & Greenbaum S (1973) : *A University Grammar of English*. Longman. 1973.

SOED (1973) : *The Shorter Oxford English Dictionary*, Vol. II. Clarendon Press.1973.

Widdowson, H G (1975) : *Stylistics and the Teaching of Literature*. Longman. 1975.

Wordsworth, William (1798/1800) : *Preface to the Lyrical Ballads*. (1798/1800).

4
Lexical Style of Indian Newspaper English

Nativisation of the English language in India, like elsewhere globally where English is widely used as a non-native language, is an expanding and absorbing area of linguistic study if only becauseexplorations in the dynamics of nativisation of the language unfold multiple facets of linguistic creativity. This focused study of the lexical style of Indian newspaper English, which approximates normal Indian English (IE) communication, would seem relevant inasmuch as it examinesfrom functional perspective some key facets of the dynamics of IE[1].

Lexical studies of IE were earlier largely focused on its formal deviance (from British English (BE)) rather than the functional value of its lexical structures, thus ignoring the core dynamics of nativisation of the English language in India. What is more, the focus initially remained largely tilted in favour of IE literature from which the data were drawn either extensively (Kachru 1962 1965, 1966, 1973, 1975) or exclusively (Dubey 1978), rather than normal IE speech situation in which diverse day-to-day IE communication requirements are met. Even though the two sources of data marginally overlap, IE literature is specially noted for lexical innovations bearing the 'singularity' (Crystal and Davy 1969: 66, 76-77) of the author's style, and not the Indianness of IE in general.

Plainly, the so-called IE lexical items from IE literature, such as 'cow-dust hour', 'spoiler of my salt', and 'well-oiled road', appear unusual even to IE participants, and may well be considered an author's coinages, which have little linguistic relevance in normal IE communication. This should explain the welcome shift of interest to functional aspects of IE in general (cf Daswani 1972, 1978; Parasher 1979; Kachru 1982), and to functional aspects of its lexical structures in particular, as the following discussion will show.

As the lexical structures of Indian newspaper English extensively share structures with normal IE communication, their in-depth study seems to be well pointed to suggesting what really typifies the IE lexical structures in general. More precisely, it suggests how their distinctive choice pattern, through their efficacious reflection of the modern Indian socio-cultural reality, saliently features IE as a nativised language having its distinctive stamp of autonomy.

The lexical structures of Indian newspaper English are register-bound. This implies that the register of editorials (ED), for instance, would differ from that of matrimonial advertisements (AD) with respect to their lexical structure because of their varied linguistic functions, even though both are generally oriented towards normal IE communication. There are, of course, variations within the lexical structures of the same register; for instance, the ED texts of national and provincial dailies are marked by their own distinctiveness, which are traceable to situational variables and/or the performing skill of the participants.

The lexical structures of Indian newspaper English will be examined below in terms of the nodal concept of 'constraints'—socio-cultural and linguistic—under which the language functions, indeed gains its functional viability in IE communication. Such a framework of study seems to be in order as it perhaps offers a most viable functional perspective on the lexical style of Indian newspaper English. Significantly, this study of the strategies commonly used to overcome these 'constraints'—borrowings of native lexical items and replenishment of the lexis of the language through semantic shifts—not only brings out their native functional value that essentially characterises IE, but also shows how their distinctive choice pattern underlies the crucial efficacy of IE as a nativised language.

Constraints in Non-Native English: Implications and Applications

The use of a non-native language (English) to meet native (Indian) communication requirements is faced with constraints which are mainly of two types, socio-cultural and linguistic. Since language has a sociological ecology (Haugen 1971), and since no two cultures are alike, transmission of socio-cultural messages in a non-native language is certain to cause problems in terms of linguistic communication. The problems may derive from purely socio-cultural factors of the society (in the present instance, Indian society) in which the participants have to use the language (here, English), or from inherent limitations of the non-native language (English) to capture and convey the nuances of native (Indian) culture, or from the performing skill of the (Indian) participants. The problems stemming from the first two factors, which are universally applicable, may be broadly studied in terms of socio-cultural and linguistic constraints, respectively. However, the problem localised to the individual participants need not be discussed exclusively, since the participants' performing skills are highly variable and relative to their place on the cline of bilingualism, and in a way linked to the factors just mentioned.

Socio-cultural constraints are operative in a language in those lexical items which are culture-specific and code-bound. This implies that these lexical items acquire their specific semantic value from native culture precisely because they are not effectively expressible in similar terms in the non-native language. Consider, for instance, the lexical items *girl friend* and *dharna* from BE and Hindi/IE, respectively. These items are so very specific to the two cultures (British and Indian, respectively) and imply a lot more than their core (dictionary) meaning that their translated version would provide only a partial clue to their real/connotative meaning. For precise communication, such native lexical items are therefore integrated into the structure of the non-native language. I shall examine this lexical aspect of Indian newspaper English in the section on loan lexical items.

The use of non-native language in native communication, however, also entails linguistic constraints which, though related to the socio-cultural factors of native communication, in fact underscore the limitations of the lexical structures of the non-native language as a message-carrier. To overcome such constraints, the participants adopt various linguistic devices (Halliday 1978: 195-197) to add new meanings to the non-native language and thus develop its lexical register to cater to native communication requirements. A common linguistic device used for this purpose in Indian newspaper English/IE communication, is extension/ reinterpretation of the semantic content of the existing BE lexical items. The Indianness of such semantically-extended lexical items reveals itself by the fact that, though these items have the structure of BE, they will nevertheless be semantically opaque in BE unless the receiver is well acquainted with Indian socio-cultural reality.

Some illustrations of typical IE lexical items, widely recurrent in the register of Indian media English/Indian politics/overall IE communication as also marked by extension/ reinterpretation or semantic shift of the existing BE items, are discussed below to amplify the point.

The IE items, vote bank/vote bank politics, though coined after ‘clearing bank’, ‘merchant bank’, ‘blood /sperm/organ bank’ (LDCE 2012 : 116), etc., would seem opaque to the native speaker of the language, just because of their semantic shift in IE, unless he is aware of IE speech situation.

The item *vote bank* has a specific reference in IE to a religious minority/ some under-privileged sections of the Indian electorate who largely vote/transfer their votes *en bloc* in line with absolute/ blind loyalty to their religion/ caste, like a ‘bank of votes’, in favour of whichever political party seeks them solely on the same token. The item *vote bank politics* has thus unambiguous reference to an

Indian brand of realpolitik, rather than politics of principles and values. Herein, flouting the law, some political parties blatantly wheedle the Indian electorate, especially of a religious minority/ some under-privileged sections of the society, into voting in their favour in the name of their religion/caste as this proves to be the best expedient means to secure their block votes/*vote bank*. The IE coinages, *vote bank/vote bank politics*, however, come with a strong pejorative implication in IE speech, being despised as a form of retrogressive politics.

Likewise, the items, *secular/secular political party*, extensively recurrent, and also controversial, in IE speech, have undergone semantic shift in the Indian context, with two contrary slants, depending mostly, if not always, on one's political orientation/ expediency/ mindset. It seems, therefore, relevant to consider first the dictionary meaning of *secular/secularism* before carrying this discussion any further.

In LDCE (2012 : 1574), the item *secular*is explained as being "not connected with or controlled by a church or other religious authority", whereas secularism refers to "a system of social organisation that does not allow religion to influence the government, or the belief that religion should not influence a government". OALD (2015 :1399) explains *secular* as being "not connected with spiritual or religious matters", or "(of priests) living among ordinary people rather than in a religious community", and *secularism* as "the belief that religion should not be involved in the organisation of society, education, etc."

However, in IE speech, the items, secular/secular political party, have undergone the following two contrary slants of semantic shift that deserve a special note :

(a) One slant of semantic shift that marks secular/secular political party, currently widespread in IE general parlance, appears overtly crafted and usage-promoted by a section of people and political parties. Given this slant of semantic shift, *secular/secular political party* imply being pro-religious minority, even at the cost of overlooking genuine concerns and interests of the religious majority. Such a semantic shift nullifies in no uncertain terms the dictionary meaning of secular/ secularism cited above.

Apparently, this slant of semantic shift stems from *block votes/vote bank* (discussed earlier) leverage of the religious minority, quite crucial for victory/loss of a political party in elections. Indeed, this critical leverage of vote bank is exploited by either side – the concerned section of the electorate and the concerned political party/ parties—as *quid pro quo*, to serve their mutual vested interest. The lofty tags, 'secular'/'secular political party', brandished about by some people/political party, are indeed a subterfuge to gain respectability for promoting their nefarious brand of realpolitik.

(b) The other section of people/political parties, with a contrary socio-political orientation/ mindset, sticks to the standard dictionary meaning of secular/secularism. Their notion of *secular/secular political party* implies being fair and equitable to all sections of the society, whether religious minority or majority, and, more significantly, brooking no room for interference of religion in government and other areas of public life. Their notion of *secular/ secularism*, however, accords primacy of place to the Hindu religion and culture in national life, explicitly because India is the homeland country of its origin where it is followed by an overwhelming majority of the natives, without being biased at all against any other religious section.

Note, given the perverted semantic shift of secular/ secular political party in IE general parlance, the usage of these items to refer to people/political party (parties) in (a) has made these items highly controversial in IE speech. For this obvious reason, a trend in IE speech is catching up of late to call those in (a) *pseudo-secular*, instead of *secula*r. I shall examine this lexical aspect of Indian newspaper English later in the section on semantic shifts.

Loan Lexical Items and their Stylistic Implications

The occurrence of loan lexical items in a language generally signals some or all of the following possibilities: (a) The language (native/non-native) has proved to be ineffective in conveying aspects of, or messages from, a culture alien to it, with the greater degree of polarity culture leading to higher frequencies of loan lexical items; (b) the language suffers from limitations in meeting the surging demands of specific communications, as in the fields of science, technology, etc.; (c) the performer's individual linguistic repertoire is inadequate for him to exploit the available lexical resources of the language; and, (d) the performer, in sheer compliance with the fashion of the day, sticks to the prevailing 'linguistic etiquette'[2] of the speech community.

The observance of linguistic etiquette of the day is a global linguistic phenomenon that spans socio-geographical locations of speech communities. In the third world speech societies where English is used as a second/foreign language, as in IE/pan-India communication, the performer often opts for terms of politeness, address, etc. in English, such as *please*, *thank you*, *sorry*, *sir, madam/ma'am*, *mum/mummy/mom*, *papa/dad*, *uncle*, *cousin*, etc, just to keep pace with the linguistic etiquette of modern-day life, despite conventional terms being already existent in their native lexical repertoire. I shall not discuss here the possibility under (b), which has relevance for specific uses of language, or that under (c), which varies with the individual performer, or that under (d), which is separately dealt with later in Chapter 7. I shall, for the present, restrict attention to the possibility under (a) because of its relevance for normal IE speech to which Indian newspaper English approximates.

Considering the divergence between Indian and British cultures and the possibility under (a) above, one might naturally expect a high incidence of loan (native) lexical items in Indian newspaper English/IE. Noticeably though, the facts point to the contrary. My data[3] (see Table 1) recorded a bottom-low frequency (0.58%) of loan (native) lexical items per 100 words in Indian newspaper English, which outright cancel the sweeping assumption made under (a) above. This is by no means to undermine the limited functional value of native lexical items in normal IE communication, as will be evident from the discussion that follows.

The occurrence of native lexical items in Indian newspaper English, reflecting pervasive constraints of the Indian socio-cultural factors on IE in general, is generally related to situational requirements of communication rather than registral (sub-registral) variations in the texts (NS, ED, IT, AD). This means that the native items occurring in LT or AD (the register of non-journalists), for instance, may well appear in NS or ED (the register of journalists), if the situation or context so demands. The following native items (in italics) may thus appear in texts/sub-registers other than the one to which they are assigned below:

LT: *dharna* (SL), *mandis* (HT), *jhopadpatti/jhuggi jhonpari* (HT), *gur* (HT).

NS: *zilla parishad* (HD), *Lok Sabha* (HT, HD, and TI), *Rajya Sabha* (HT).

The four sub-registers of Indian newspaper English tend to serve specific situational requirements of communication, and therefore their pattern of choice for native lexical items varies accordingly. One would thus find in AD the highest frequency of native items per 100 words (6.75%), with NS (0.59%), LT (0.26%) and ED (0.06%) trailing far behind. Apparently, this shows only a pattern slant, not necessarily the registral features of the relevant sub-register *per se*. Thus, when the situational compulsions are insurmountable, even ED, which normally tend to refrain from using native items, opt for them for focused discourse value, as the following illustration would show:

ED: Can there be anything more pathetic than the *Hamari Bachchiyan Wapas Do* ("Give us back our daughters") demonstration ?

constraints, thus frequently opts for native items in order to effect clear communication. This explains why AD recorded the highest frequency of native items in Indian newspaper English. The native items are, however, by no means the prominent markers of the lexical style of Indian newspaper English in general, appearing as they do in miniscule proportions (0.58%). So, I shall now turn to a more interesting area of the lexical structures of Indian newspaper English.

Semantic Shifts and their Stylistic Implications

Being highly context-governed, a language undergoes restrictions and extensions of meaning, depending on who says what, when and where. Though such restrictions and extensions of meaning of lexical items seem fairly natural, even go unnoticed in native communication where socio-cultural contexts are well known to the participants, they acquire stylistic significance with respect to a non-native language used in native communication, as in India, where contexts are known only to the natives. The tendency to refurbish lexical items of a non-native language with new meanings to serve native communication requirements, though linguistically viable and highly productive, may, however, entail extensive code-confusion.

Semantic shifts of lexical items are a general feature of IE. Yet, in Indian newspaper English, they appear foregrounded in one of its sub-registers, that of AD, with multiple stylistic implications. Apparently, the lexical items of AD, designed to provide a crystal clear perspective of a wide range of complex Indian social meanings, have to be of necessity more ingeniously tailor-made than those of NS, ED and LT, largely because the latter are concerned with a broad spectrum of Indian life to deal with.

For the present, I shall examine such items from AD, sampled from IE newspaper English, that undergo marked semantic shifts in terms of economic and aesthetic/social value judgements of the native participants, and offer their plausible interpretations, together with their stylistic implications in the context of modern-day Indian society.

Economic value judgements

Besides religion and caste, a major decisive factor in arranged Indian marriages is the economic status of the bridegroom, bride, and/or their parents. Marriages in India, an overwhelming majority of them being arranged ones, are thus generally solemnised, not as a sequel to emotional attachment and all that courting involves, but primarily by pragmatic considerations of sound economic eligibility/condition of the bridegroom and bride, particularly of the former, and/or their parents. Consider the following clipped illustrations from AD :

(i) *well-placed* (1) match (HT);

(ii) *Senior Scale Railway Accounts Officer* (2) (HD);

(iii) *employed for MBA* (3) (HD);

(iv) *Already resident in England* (4) (TI);

(v) *having own flat with telephone in a posh locality of South Calcutta* (5) (ST);

(vi) father *settled* (6) in Delhi (ST);

(vii) *well-established* (7) *W.B. Kayastha groom, only child* (8), *permanent lecturer* (9) (HD);

(viii) *divorcee* (10), *independent* (11) (TI);

(ix) *well-placed* (12) spinster invites proposals from *well-placed* (13) bachelors (TI);

(x) Sindhi ... *well-placed* (14)...*alone* (15) looking for *a bride with a male child* (16) (TI);

(xi) .....officers.....who are *well-settled* (17) (TI);

(xii) parents *well-settled* (18) seeks *decent* (19), *well-*

Table 2b: Frequency distribution (%) of the superordinate term WPS

	Break-up of frequency of WPS		
Total no. of texts examined	**Well-placed, well-settled, settled, well-established (WES)**	**Hyponymous lexical sets (HLS)**	**Overall frequency of WPS**
24	42.50	16.67	59.17

In BE, the reference to *well-placed* match (1) and *parents well-settled* (18), in the context of marriage, would hardly make much sense, nor would the items *alone* (15) and *independent* (11). However, in the context of arranged Indian marriage, the items *only child* (8) and *alone* (15) carry crucial implications. Whereas *only child* (8) implies that the referent is the sole heir to the family property, as also free of any family encumbrances, *alone* (15), in the context of arranged Indian marriage, refers to the person who either does not have a family or is no longer a member of a joint family — thus free of any socio-economic encumbrances — rather than one who is alone, say, in a room (cf Longman 2012 : 46 : "if you are alone in a place, there is no one with you = by yourself"). These items thus undergo semantic shifts in IE to reflect the fast-changing socio-economic value system of the modern-day Indian society.

The advertiser, specially those wishing to highlight sound economic status of the bridegroom/bride, often makes a detailed reference to the nature of his/her employment. Hence, (2) makes a specific reference to economic profile of the referent as someone drawing a high salary and enjoying quite a few fringe benefits, as in Indian railways benefits, not available in other services.

Likewise, *permanent lecturer* (9) and *employed girls* (23), contrasted with 'temporary lecturer' and 'unemployed girls', respectively, highlight the sound financial standing of the bridegroom/bride. The same is true of the lexical item, *employed for MBA* (3), which means that the person is lucratively employed.

The lexical item (4), *already resident in England,* implies that the person enjoys a better living condition than is available in India, while the item (5) goes to an extreme to mention that the person not only owns a flat in the megacity of Calcutta (renamed Kolkata) but owns it in a plush locality within the larger posh locality of South Calcutta, and has also a residential telephone connection — no longer considered a prized possession – as well. Economic considerations in arranged Indian marriages are further focused in the items *decent* (19) and *decent marriage* (21), which, marked by semantic shift in the Indian context, suggest, respectively, that the bridegroom, being looked for, should come from a very rich family, and that a huge dowry would be offered to him/his parents in the marriage.

Aesthetic/social value judgements

Social and aesthetic value judgements are indeed a highly subjective matter which vary from person to person in the same society. To comment on them is to enter a delicate area of human susceptibilities.Yet the task seems engaging and immensely worthwhileas one seeks to decipher them objectively by means of lexical clues. The items below, marked by semantic shift in AD/IE, provide a fairly objective and overall perspective of the social norms and concepts that grip the modern-day Indian mind.

(xv) *stable charactered* (24) .... spinster invites ... proposals from *stable charactered* (25) ... bachelors (TI);

(xvi) *highly respectable* family (26) (HT);

(xvii) *respectable* family (27) (ST);

(xviii) A *tall* (28), *fair* (29) . . . bride (ST);

(xix) *fair* (30), *handsome* (31), *slim* (32) (ST);

(xx) *slim* (33), *wheatish* (34), *155 cms* (35), belonging *respectable* UP family (36) (HT);

(xxi) Maharashtrian girl . . *working* (37), *home-loving* (38), *kind nature* (39), *sweet natured* (40) (TI);

(xxii) *sweet tempered* (41) girl (IN);

(xxiii) for an *attractive* (42), *broad-minded* (43) . . send *full particulars* (44) (TI);

(xxiv) send *all particulars including day, month of birth* (45) (TI);

(xxv) Alliance . .for a *respectable* (46), *good-looking* (47), *fair* (48), *slim* (49)....*162 cms* (50) (ST);

(xxvi) *Good-looking* (51), *fair* (52), *tall* (53) ... seeks matrimonial alliance with *respectable* (54) ..... (ST);

(xxvii) a *clean shaven engineer* (55) (TI);

(xxviii) *tall* (56) . . . *fair* (57) girl (IN);

(xxix) *tall* (58) . . . girl (T1);

(xxx) a *very beautiful* (59), *tall* (60) ... bride (ST);

(xxxi) *Actually fair-complexioned* (61), *beautiful* (62), *tall* (63) girl (ST)

(xxxii) A *beautiful* (64), *charming* (65)...*moderately modern* (66), *sincere* (67).... girl (TI);

(xxxiii) *Exceptionally beautiful* (68), *homely* (69) spinster (TI);

(xxxiv) *150 cms* (70), *non-working* (71), *well-trained household affairs* (72) (TI);

(xxxv) *working girls* (73) (ST);

(xxxvi) Sindhi *vegetarian* (74) (TI).

Perspective of Social Values in Modern Indian Society

Consider the item *divorcee* (10), for instance, as used in BE and IE. Whereas in the former it means as stated, it comes with a pejorative implication in overall IE communication. This is so because Indian marriages are looked on, ideally and normally, as a lifetime affair, but if divorce caused a break-up–occasionally in the past, but more frequently in present times—it is not generally viewed kindly in the Indian socio-cultural context. Thus, the item has undergone a distinctive semantic shift in AD/ IE.

Interestingly, Indian society, especially in upscale towns and cities, finds itself at a crossroads today. While it has moved fast ahead of the socially 'sex-segregated' life style of earlier times that frowned upon mingling of opposite sexes in social company, it has not yet quite discarded its critical – even cynical — view of such 'free' socialisations between men and women out in the society. This is borne out by the typical semantic shifts that mark the IE items *sincere* (67) and *stable charactered* (24) and (25).

The nearly-synonymous items, *sincere* (67) and *stable charactered* (24) and (25) in AD/IE, connote, respectively, a life-partner who will remain absolutely loyal to the spouse in marriage all his/her life, and to the one who will retain an impeccable moral character, despite his/her free socialisation with the other sex.

Some other typical AD/IE lexical items, marked by semantic shift, stem from the same admixture of modern Indian craving to embrace all the best in modern life globally while retaining/aspiring after core values of Indian morality. This explains the recurrence of such un-British lexical items in AD/IE as *broad-minded* (43), *working girls* (73) and *home-loving* (38), all having reference to the kind of bride being searched, which roughly convey the same meaning, when appearing in collocation, as implied by the item *moderately modern* (66).

Concept of Respectability in Modern Indian Society

Along with the requirement of rectitude of the spouse in arranged Indian marriages is the overriding core concern of the modern Indian society for *respectability* of the families of the bride and the bridegroom. The recurrence of *respectable* as a node of collocation in (26), (27), (36) and (54) in AD/IE brings out this point most clearly.

The concept of *respectability* though appears to be a rather amorphous notion in the modern Indian society, being open to diverse interpretations by its different sections. For instance, the family of a tycoon may seem to some people in India to be more respectable than that of a teacher of eminence, while the reverse may appear true for others. Yet, going by the economic pull in arranged Indian marriages the notion of *respectability* in the Indian context acquires a specific implication.

beautiful Indian woman, which of course includes her being *tall*, *wheatish* and *slim*.

The items *very beautiful* (59) and *exceptionally beautiful* (68) thus convey a superb notion of a beautiful Indian woman that will admit these three physical attributes and many more which are recoverable from the Indian context alone. The item *good-looking* (47) and (51) would mean, in the Indian context, an average beauty, and not a more-than-average beauty as in BE. This explains why *good-looking* collocates with *fair* (47), (48) and (51), (52) rather than with *beautiful* (62) and (64), which collocates with *actually fair-complexioned* (61) and *charming* (65).

Some Other socio-Cultural Dimensions of Arranged Indian Marriages

As suggested earlier, the modern Indian society is an amalgam of conservative Indian moral and social values on the one hand, and the fast-evolving value system of the so-called 'free society' of the modern-day world, on the other. Such a socio-cultural scenario has given rise to a number of lexical items in AD, typical of IE, which will not fit into the pattern of social meanings of British culture/ BE.

The items, *working* (37), *working girls* (73) and *non-working* (71) have a crucial implication in the Indian context as some people, depending on their social and cultural orientation, would, or would not, accept a bride for marriage if she has, or does not, have a job. In conservative sections of the modern Indian society, women are supposed to take care of household chores while men attend to the business outside. Thus, the items *well-trained in household affairs* (72), *home-loving* (38) and *homely* (69) acquire specific connotations in the Indian context, being an unequivocal assurance that the bride would/should make herself a perfect housewife.

Indian marriages being generally a lifetime affair, the advertisers often make a special mention of their food habits to specify who should/should not consider oneself to be the suitable respondent. Such semantic shifts in lexical items play a vital function in typifying IE speech. The lexical item *vegetarian* (74) has thus a special meaning in the Indian context. The *vegetarian* meal, in IE, consists of cereals, milk, vegetables, fruits, etc., but excludes meat, even fish and eggs that constitute a part of the vegetarian meal in BE. The semantic shift in the item here is thus far too crucial to overlook in BE, as also in IE.

The Indian belief in astrology and astrological predictions is quite deep-rooted, pervasive, and intangible, although not many Indians would like to acknowledge it formally. In arranged Indian marriages, therefore, special care is taken by the bridegroom/bride, or their parents, to get the horoscopes of the prospective bridegroom and the bride astrologically scrutinised to ensure beforehand whether the proposed marriage will work out to success or not. The ultimate decision on marriage thus crucially rests with the outcome of such a scrutiny. The lexical items *full particulars* (50) and *all particulars including day, month of birth* (45) –having reference to precise date, time and place of birth of the bride/groom — which may seem opaque in BE, have a vital import in IE, being a request for horoscope details of the bridegroom/bride for astrological scrutiny.

The foregoing discussion broadly shows the extent to which the lexis of Indian newspaper English/ IE, or perhaps of any non-native language variety, may undergo explicit or implicit semantic changes under the socio-cultural constraints of the native situation vis-à-vis the inherent constraints of the non-native language. While constraints of both types have their overall impact on the lexis of Indian newspaper English/IE, they tend to vary according to situation types/registral variations, rather than performing skill of the participants.

Noticeably, constraints of both types are overcome in AD/ IE more often by endowing available items of the (non-native) language with new (native) meanings than by easier recourse to borrowing of items from the native culture/communication. Native items, though, remain indispensable in certain socio-cultural contexts, as in AD/IE, or, are opted for exclusively because of stylistic reasons, as in IE commercial advertisements.

Indeed, the polarity between language and culture, as in non-native IE communication, is best bridged through semantic shifts of lexical items in the non-native language, reinforced by their pattern of collocations, through maximal exploitation of the available lexical resources of the (non-native) language and minimal recourse to loan of items from native language and culture. The bottom-low frequency of native lexical items in Indian newspaper English, which closely approximates the 'living' IE communication, is a clear pointer to this tendency.

Significantly, lexical creativity of Indian newspaper English/IE lies in its efficacy to reflect, despite constraints of both types, a fairly realistic picture of the modern-day Indian socio-cultural reality— its variegated socio-cultural-aesthetic notions and leanings. However, IE's typical flavour as a nativised variety of language comes out best where both these constraints not only seem visibly formidable but are also overcome most effectively, as in AD.

Interestingly, this study of the lexical style of Indian newspaper English/IE, incidentally offered some revealing insights into certain facets of the modern-day Indian society, specially its notions of *respectability*, *Indian beauty* and the *economics of arranged Indian marriages.* A word of special note ought to be added here by way of putting things in a perspective. Indian notions of *respectability*, *Indian beauty* and the *economics of arranged Indian marriages* came as enlightening research finds in course of this study, though in the passing, but most notably, entirely by empirical and objective means of lexical clues.

Notes

1. This chapter is a revised version of my paper published in *World Englishes*, Vol.10. No. 1, Pergamon Press, Oxford. 1991.
2. The label 'linguistic etiquette' refers to the practice in any speech community of organising linguistic action so that it is seen as appropriate to the current communicative event. The scope of phenomena assembled under this label is thus much broader than what is suggested by the dictionary definition of etiquette, which restricts the term to denote "the formal rules of proper behaviour"

(Longman Dictionary of Contemporary English 1978: 373). For detailed discussion on linguistic etiquette, see Kasper, G (2017).

3. The data of this study comprise news stories (NS), editorials (ED), letters to the editor (LT) and matrimonial advertisements (AD), from four leading national dailies of the country, namely, *The Hindustan Times*, New Delhi (HT), *The Times of India*, Bombay (now renamed Mumbai) (TI), *The Statesman*, Calcutta (now renamed Kolkata) (ST) and *The Hindu*, Madras (now renamed Chennai) (HD), and two leading provincial dailies from the state of Bihar (since closed), namely, *The Indian Nation*, Patna (IN), and *The Searchlight*, Patna (SL). The two reputed and long-established provincial dailies of their time, like most other provincial dailies across the country, closed down their publication as most of the national dailies, including the ones mentioned above, grabbed their regional/local media space with simultaneous publication of their own provincial/local editions. Nevertheless, the provincial/regional editions of these national dailies somewhat continue to be marked by their distinctive regional, linguistic-stylistic identity from their parent national editions, though to a limited extent. Note, the data of this study, though sampled in 1981, seem still relevant in real-time context today as they have been currently collated with the changing patterns of IE newspaper English of the day, as also the perennial flux of language fads and innovative variations that normally impact a language over a period of time.
4. The lexical item *wheatish*, an IE coinage, explored in the earlier version of this study (Dubey 1991: 28), which did not find entry in the dictionary earlier (cf. LDCE 2004 and 2012; OALD 2004) has now been incorporated in the dictionary as an IE adjective. (cf. OALD 2015 : 1776).

References

Bazell, C E, Catford, J C, Halliday, M A K and Robins, RH eds. (1966) : In Memory of J R Firth. London: Longman.

Kasper, G (2017) : '*Linguistic Etiquette*' in The Handbook of Sociolinguistics. Ed Coulmas, Florian. Wiley-Blackwell Publishing Ltd, Oxford, UK. 2017.

Crystal, D and Davy, D (1969):Investigating English Style. London:Longman.

Daswani, C J (1972): '*Some theoretical implications for investigating Indian English*'. In Mohan (1972).

_____(1978) : '*Pidginisation in a multilingual society: the case of Indian English*'. In the Proceedings of the 5th AILA Congress. Montreal.

Dil, Anwar S (ed.) (1971) :The Ecology of Language : *Essays by Einar Haugen*. Stanford, CA: Stanford University Press.

Dubey, Vinod S (1978) : '*A stylistic analysis of* Mulk Raj Anand's *Seven Summers : A dialectal approach*'. Unpublished MA thesis. Department of Linguistics, University of Wales, Bangor, UK. 1978.

____(1991): '*The lexical style of Indian newspaper English*'. World Englishes, Vol.10, No.1, Pergamon Press, Oxford. 1991.

Halliday, Michael A K (1967) :Grammar, Society and the Noun. London: University University College. London.

_____(1978) : Language as Social Semiotic: *the Social Interpretation of Language and Meaning*. London: Edward Arnold.

Haugen, Einar (1971) : The ecology of language. In Dil (ed.) (1971).

Kachru, Braj B (1962) : '*Analysis of some features of Indian English: a study in linguistic method*'. Unpublished PhD thesis, Department of Linguistics, University of Edinburgh.

____(1965): The Indianness in Indian English.Word, 21 (3), 391-410.

____(1966) : '*Indian English: a study in contextualisation*'. In Bazell et al.

Kachru, Braj B. el al. (1973) : Issues in Linguistics: Papers in Honor of Henry and Renee Kahane. Urbana. IL: University of Illinois Press.

____(1973) : '*Toward a lexicon of Indian English*'. In Kachru et al. 1973.

Kachru, Braj B (1975) : '*Lexical innovations in South Asian En*glish'. International Journal of the Sociology of Language, 4, 55-74.

Kachru, Braj B ed. (1982): The Other Tongue:English across Cultures. Urbana, IL : University of Illinois Press.

______(1982) : '*Meaning in deviation: toward understanding non-native English texts*'. In Kachru ed. (1982).

LDCE (1982, 2004 and 2012): Longman Dictionary of Contemporary English. Longman:London.

Mohan, R (1972): Indian Writing in English. Orient Longman. New Delhi.

OALD (2004 and 2015) : Oxford Advanced Learner's Dictionary. OUP.

Palmer, F R (1976): Semantics:*a New Outline*. Cambridge University Press, Cambridge

Parasher, S V (1979):'*Certain aspects of the functions and forms of Indian English : a sociolinguistic study*'. Unpublished PhD thesis, CIEFL, Hyderabad.

5
Lexico-morphological Dimension of Indian English

Indian English (IE) has drawn scholarly attention worldwide as a nativised variety of the English language for its prolific linguistic creativity, as also for its widening user range through expanding presence of IE speech community globally.[1] This is reflected in periodic reference to/entries of IE lexical items/coinages in research studies and standard dictionaries.

There are several aspects of IE linguistic creativity that make it a distinctive nativised language variety, namely phonetic-phonological, lexical and syntactic. Yet, what makes it more so is its hallmark lexical structure, especially its intricate semantic aspect, that serves as a viable message carrier of native communication requirements in the non-native language. It has therefore long since received central focus of attention in pioneering studies in IE (cf. Kachru 1962, 1965, 1966, 1973, 1975 and 1983).

Nevertheless, IE lexis also stands out markedly different—and often overtly –in the patterned ways British English (BE) lexical items are ingeniously re-structured /nativised in IE through lexico-morphological changes. Interestingly, this aspect of IE linguistic creativity has largely gone unnoticed by a majority of its everyday non-native Indian users themselves, being taken for a regular feature of the language (BE). The native (BE) speaker would, however, make a sharp note of these IE items, structured through lexico-morphological changes, just because they appear so very overtly deviant from BE, often resulting in communication gap to him.

Earlier, in chapter 5, I essentially addressed myself to a discussion of some of the core semantic patterns of nativisation of IE lexical structure. What follows here is a close study of some of the key patterns of lexico-morphological strategies that are generally employed to nativise it.

IE pattern of nativisation of its lexical structure through application of lexico-morphological strategies appears somewhat largely independent of its semantic and collocative patterns of nativisation (cf. Dubey 1989: 86-121). The lexical items nativised through lexico-morphological changes would thus seem typical *Indianisms* as they are generally overtly marked structurally. More so, because their occurrence in pan-IE speech is wide and extensive that cuts across registral and regional variations of the language. Further, they are not limited to Indian newspaper English (INE) as such from which the data of this study are sampled, but, quite validly, extend beyond to everyday IE speech.[2]

Interestingly, while INE largely approximates IE speech, IE speech community that constitutes overwhelming section of INE's regular readership often derives their language inputs, role-models of the language from INE to a considerable extent. Either way, both INE and IE speech community together play a participative and crucial role in the build-up of IE speech, though, of course, in varied proportions. A prior reference to this aspect of IE speech would thus seem relevant before this discussion moves any further.

The data of this study show that some of the most prominent lexico-morphological strategies, normally employed in nativising the lexis of INE/ IE, include those of *deletion* and *productivity*. The occurrence of these strategies of nativisation in INE is, by and large, confined to the registers of LT, AD and NS, whereas, by contrast, the register of ED shows their rate of occurrence at a minimum level.

IE choice of lexico-morphological strategies of nativisation of the lexical structure of the language would thus seem to be in inverse proportion to performing skill of the participant in the target language. This implies that the participant's ascending performing skill in the language is generally, if not always, indicative of progressive decline in recourse to these strategies of nativisation, and vice versa. This explains why LT and AD record frequent occurrence of these strategies of nativisation of IE lexis while NS/ED generally—not always—record their relative absence.

Noticeably, these strategies are generally opted for far more regularly in NS/LT/AD of provincial dailies, irrespective of registral variations, and more in the regional editions of national dailies than in their national editions. Nevertheless, what is worth noting here is that the occurrence pattern of these lexico-morphological strategies in IE largely mirrors the *living IE speech* if only because it is pooled in by an overwhelming section of everyday users of the language.

Deletions

Quite often a language undergoes linguistic economy/deletion for reasons of fast communication/linguistic laziness, etc. For instance, in BE, one often hears such requests in a tea-shop/restaurant : 'Two teas, please.' instead of a longer version, 'Two cups of tea, please.' However, in non-native IE speech, the reasons for linguistic economy range from fast communication/linguistic laziness, etc to a sheer lack of performing skill of the participant in the target language. Whatever be the reasons that occasion deletions, IE lexis is distinctly impacted/nativised in the process over a period of time.

The choice of *deletion* at various levels of linguistic structure is a commonplace universal trend. While such a choice in the context of native language facilitates fast communication, the choice of deletion in nativised IE speech often makes it stylistically distinctive, even semantically opaque, to the native speaker of the language, unless he is acquainted with nativised IE speech. The following sample illustrations of lexical deletions, having proximity to living IE speech, are all taken from INE :

Data from LT

i. for getting the *degree* earlier it needed a political 'pairavi'	: degree (certificate)
ii. *hardship of Chapra*	: *hardship of* (the residents of) *Chapra*
iii. Samastipur-Banmankhi passenger	: *Samastipur-Banmankhi passenger* (train)
iv. Hindi version certificate	: *Hindi version* (of the) *certificate*

Data from NS

v. Electricity Board failed to meet situation created by *poor generation*	: poor (power) generation
vi. Exchange of firing between *two parties*	: two (political) parties

In the sample illustrations above, the lexical items featuring deletion are italicised while their deleted portion is given opposite to each in brackets. Lexical deletions of the types in (i), (ii), (iii), (iv) and (vi) seem to be fairly integrated with IE lexis as indicated by their recurrence and widespread distribution in IE speech. The type of deletion in (v) has not yet found its overall acceptance in IE speech, even as it remains a marked feature of IE lexis.

Of all the items cited above, the ones in (v) and (vi) may cause real communication hurdle to the native speaker, unless he is aware of IE speech situation. In (v), *poor generation* would imply in British English (BE), 'generation': 'all people of about the same age' (Longman 2009/2012 :727) who are 'poor', which is quite contrary to the intended meaning here. (Refer to the deleted portion of the item, given opposite to it within brackets, that offers a clue to the intended meaning.)

In (vi), the lexical item *two parties* would seem semantically opaque to the native speaker because of deletion of 'political' from in between 'two' and 'parties', to which the item has implicit reference. Note, in BE, among other meanings, 'party' has reference to: (a) 'a political organisation with particular beliefs and aims, which you can vote for in elections: I have always voted for the Labour Party. /He failed to win the party's nomination for President./ The conference is open to all party members.', (b) 'a group of people who go somewhere together or do a job together: a party of tourists/A search party…' (Longman 2009/2012: 1270). Going by the context of situation of the text, the native speaker is likely to opt for (b), its alternative meaning in the dictionary, 'a group of people…/ A search party…', to decode message of the text suitably, in preference to its meaning in (a) 'a political organisation..'.

Plausibly, in terms collocation expectancy/restriction, an 'exchange of firing between two parties/two groups of people/two search parties' is conceivable and likely whereas an 'exchange of firing between two political parties' is arguably an extreme possibility, and thus ruled out. However, in IE general parlance, 'party' as such often implies its dictionary meaning in (a) unless otherwise denoted by the context of situation. The item *two parties* in the text above has thus implicit reference to *two (political) parties*, and the 'exchange of firing', has, indeed, factual reference in the text to—though it may seem preposterous to assume so—'exchange of firing between two (groups of) political parties. 'Party', as a word/ lexical item *per se* is thus an instance of typical Indianism in that while it helps speedy communication in IE speech, it is likely to cause real communication hurdle to the native speaker (unless he is aware of IE speech situation).

The stylistic significance of lexical deletions in IE speech lies in the degree to which they are nativised, and not necessarily in the degree to which they hinder communication to the native speaker. Thus, lexical deletion of 'political' from in between *two parties* is a clear instance of typical Indianism, since it is fully nativised in overall IE speech, whereas the one in *poor generation* is not as thoroughly accepted/nativised in IE speech even as lexical deletions in both these items may cause real communication hurdle to the native speaker.

Similarly, the lexical deletions in (i), (ii), (iii) and (iv) are instances of typical Indianism through their overall integration with

IE speech, even as the items marked by these deletions may seem somewhat strange, despite being fairly intelligible to the native speaker.

The deletion in (iv) is marked by a process of transformation, involving deletion of grammatical morphemes of the qualifier in the embedded phrase from which it is derived. Here, a part of qualifier of the embedded lexical structure, *certificate*, shown in (iv)[a], assumes the slot of Head of the noun phrase (NP) in the transformed lexical structure, together with deletion of the grammatical morphemes, *of* and *the*, as shown in (iv):

(iv) *Hindi version certificate* : *Modifier Head*

(iv)[a] *Hindi version of the certificate* : *Modifier Head* Qualifier

Despite structural variation between them, both (iv) and (iv)[a] share identity of information focus on *certificate*. While (iv) does so by deleting 'of-genitive structure' (see Quirk and Greenbaum 1973: 4.71), (iv)[a] retains end-focus on *certificate* by positioning it finally as Head of the noun phrase, omitting in the process grammatical morphemes of low information value. It seems that the function of deletion here entails information focus as much as verbal economy as both are here inextricably intermixed with each other.

Apparently, the overall trend of deletions that emerges from the cited illustrations above largely points to a general pattern of verbal economy being subservient to information focus. This IE pattern of lexical deletions is overwhelmingly shared by the rest of the sample illustrations as well.

In (ii), a part of Qualifier, 'of the residents', remains implicit/ deleted from in between '*hardship*' and '*of Chapra* (a town)'—*hardship* (of the residents) *of Chapra*—as the name of the town, functioning as a metonym for its residents, gives it focused information value, besides effecting verbal economy. This seems to be quite in line with metonymic style often followed in journalese :'*New Delhi* has declined to sign the NPT ...' instead of '*The Government of India* has declined...'.

In (iii), it is Head, 'train', which is deleted, because of its minimal information value in the context of the situation, while its Modifier 'passenger', having priority information value, is retained and focused. Consider the difference between 'Samastipur-Banmankhi *passenger* (train)' and 'Samastipur-Banmankhi *express* (train)' with/without 'train', in terms of their information value.

In (v) too, deletion is employed to effect information focus. Here, a part of Modifier, 'power' (in brackets), in *poor* (power) *generation*, remains implicit/deleted because of its limited (presumed) functional value in the context of the situation. What gets focused value instead is its remainder, i.e. the existing text, *poor generation*: (incomplete) Modifier + Head, *poor* (power) +*generation*, with primary focus on Modifier, *poor*.

Similarly, in (vi), a part of Modifier, 'political', remains implicit/deleted from in between, *two* and *parties*— *two* (political) *parties*—because the restrictive focus on *parties*, carries with it, in IE general parlance, implicit reference to its Modifier, 'political'. As suggested earlier, 'party', in IE general parlance, generally implies 'a political party', unless signalled otherwise from the context of the situation.

However, in (i), the pattern of deletion is much different, and for a valid reason. Here, despite central focus on 'certificate' (Head), the document/certificate of award of the *degree*, the very word remains implicit/deleted while its Modifier *degree* (not *diploma*), which has contrastive value, receives focused value. This is so because the lexical item *degree*, marked by semantic shift, is polysemous in IE speech, having reference to 'the qualification of a degree obtained by a student who successfully completes a university or college course' (OALD 2015: 404), as well as the document/certificate of award of the degree.

The discussion above would show that the choice of lexical deletions in IE speech is not erratic or random. On the contrary, it is patterned, ingeniously and intricately, with a clear eye to the functional orientation of nativised IE speech. Consequently, IE lexical deletions have largely followed a similar pattern overwhelmingly, i.e. deletion of the lexical item/ a part thereof, not for verbal economy but for its low information value. Interestingly, this pattern is shared by a majority of IE speech community, having varied levels of proficiency in the language.

Productivity

Productivity/creativity is a regular feature of language that makes it dynamic and viable in course of time. In native language context, linguistic productivity seems so much of a natural and continuous process that it usually goes unnoticed, unless the innovations, introduced in the language, are incredibly new or vastly amazing. However, productivity/creativity in IE speech at various levels of linguistic structure has positioned it as a major nativised variety of the language globally, if only for its functional orientation and pragmatic perspective.

Productivity in IE speech in this study has restrictive reference to productivity of its lexical structure, precisely, two types of its lexico-morphological productivity, viz. the **–ing- type productivity** and the **-ed type productivity**. Both these types of lexical strategies are usually employed to build up IE lexical structure, and both of them are its stylistic markers. Even as there seems to be no specific reason that would account for their recurrence in IE speech, their pattern of recurrence and wide distribution in IE speech mark them out as distinctive features of IE lexical structure.

Significantly, the recurrence of the two types of productivity in IE lexical structure shows that their ascending choice largely, though not invariably, corresponds with the participant's descending order of performing skill in the language, and vice versa. The data of this study show that frequent choice of these strategies of lexical productivity in INE/IE is particularly restricted to the register of non-journalists, though, significantly, it is not exclusive of the register of journalists. That journalists also do opt for these two types of lexical productivity, though infrequently, is a pointer to their sweeping range of nativisation in IE speech. Noticeably, the two types of lexical productivity involve both their structural and semantic aspects.

Productivity : *-ING Type*

The choice of bound morpheme ***-ing*** to structure lexical items is an instance of free variation in IE speech in so far as it is, by and large, not conditioned by semantic or structural compulsions of the given lexical items. However, it is variable in occurrence pattern in terms of performing skill of participants. The choice of ***–ing***-type lexical productivity is a typical ingredient of IE lexis since both journalists and non-journalists contribute to it, though in varying measure. While LT and AD, the registers of non-journalists, record overwhelming preference for *-ing* type lexical creativity extensively, NS and ED, the registers of journalists, are marked by their infrequent and restrictive pattern of occurrence. The following sample illustrations from national dailies that comprise the register of journalists (NS/ED) as well as that of non-journalists (LT/ AD) would amplify the point :

i. There were reports of *booth-captur**ing**/land-grabb**ing.***[3] All the relevant parts of the lexical items are given in italics, partially in bold italics. (NS)

ii. *Shift**ing*** of blame… is of no avail. (LT)

iii. I request the Chief Minister… to play the national anthem before the *start**ing*** of …film… (LT)

iv. Rail track, rail coaches… and the *brak**ing*** system… are all scientifically designed… (LT)

v. graduate girl… smart-*look**ing*** (AD)

vi. … home-*lov**ing***… (AD)

vii. for Bombay-based…girl…*non-work***ing …** (AD)

viii. … *work**ing*** girls… (AD)

ix. Rainy season witnesses *water-logg**ing*** on the main road… (LT/NS/ED)

x. … the *water-logg**ing*** culminated in the *tumbl**ing** down* of the houses… (LT/NS/ED)

In (i), the choice of ***-ing*** morpheme to structure lexical items is free of any constraint, structural or semantic. The lexical coinages, *booth-captur**ing*** and *land-grabb**ing**,* widely recurrent in IE, are preferred in INE/IE speech despite regular structures with identical meaning being already available in the language : 'booth-capture' and 'land-grab' (noun + noun). In both the clipped illustrations, the choice of *-ing* morpheme to suffix each of them does not result in a change of their grammatical category/word class, neither in creation of a new word. They are thus instances of *free variation*, purely volitional/free of any constraint, and yet typical Indianisms in this sense of the term.

The clipped illustrations from (ii) to (v) reinforce the trendy pattern of IE lexical productivity discussed above. All the lexical items in (ii) to (v) opt for***-ing***-suffixed lexical structures in preference to the available lexical items of the language, which are either without this suffix or with a different one, as*–er* in (v).Note, all the clipped illustrations from IE, alongside their corresponding BE items, listed below, stay put to the same word class and same meaning:

	IE	**BE**
(i)	*booth-captur**ing***/land-grabb**ing** (N)[4]	booth-capture/land-grab (N)
(ii)	*shift**ing*** (N)	shift (N)
(iii)	*start**ing*** (N)	start (N)
(iv)	*brak**ing** system* (N)	brake system (N)
(v)	smart *look**ing*** (N)	smart look**er** (N)

Inasmuch as***-ing-***suffixed lexical items, cited above, do not involve a change in their core word class, or a coinage of a different word within the same word class, or a semantic difference, they are all instances of IE *-**ing**-typezero-inflectional productivity*.

Interestingly, the pattern of option of***-ing-***type zero-inflectional productivity is shared by journalists as well as non-journalists, though in varied proportions, which thus marks it out as a general feature of over-all IE lexical structure. The variant pattern of occurrence of this type of IE lexical productivity is largely linked with performing skill of the participant in the language. The sample illustrations below would suggest that non-journalists, with a *generally* lower level of performing skill in the language as compared with journalists, tend to opt for this type of lexical creativity more often than journalists.

In illustrations (vi) to (viii), the same pattern of lexical creativity is adhered to, though with a crucial difference. Whereas all the –**ing**-suffixed lexical items herein do not entail a change of their word class, they undergo crucial change in meaning in IE speech vis-à-vis their corresponding lexical items in BE :

	IE	BE
(vi)	*home-lov**ing*** (Adj.)	loving (Adj.)
(vii)	*non-work**ing*** (Adj.)	working (Adj.)
(viii)	*work**ing** girls* (N)	working mother (N)

The hyphenated lexical items in (vi) and (vii), *home-lov**ing*** and *non-work**ing***, respectively, structured after *–**ing**-*type IE lexical productivity, apparently follow similar BE lexical pattern and meaning as in 'loving' and 'working', and thus do not seem to constitute nonce formations at all. Yet, what makes both the lexical items gain their specific semantic value in IE speech is their hyphenated structure. In IE, *home-lov**ing***, with reference to a girl, implies that 'the girl would make herself a good housewife/ home-maker rather than one who just enjoys being at home, as in BE'. Similarly, *non-work**ing*** implies in AD/IE that 'the girl is not in employment, neither perhaps is inclined to be in one'. The item thus holds pivotal importance in AD/ arranged Indian marriage as it unequivocally signals the girl's marriage eligibility or otherwise for the prospective groom.

Likewise, the lexical item *work**ing** girls* in (viii) is structured after BE item 'working mother', and given the context of the text, it oughtn't to leave an iota of doubt in one's mind about its implicit meaning. To this extent, there seems to be nothing distinctive about this IE item. Yet its typical value as an Indianism emerges should the native speaker opt for its dictionary meaning (cf OALD, 2015 : 1800), stripped of the context of the text here[5].

Apparently, the choice of ***-ing***-suffixed IE lexical coinages in (vi) to (viii) seems to be free of semantic and structural compulsions, much like in (i) to (v), and appear even substitutable by their synonyms/near-synonyms available in the language. However, IE option pattern of **-ing**-suffixed lexical items in (vi) to (viii) falls into a separate class since each of the items has, as suggested above, a nuanced semantic value in IE speech. Thus, *home-lov**ing*** is preferred to 'domestic', *non-work**ing*** to 'unemployed', and *work**ing** girls* to 'job-holder girls', for instance. The lexical items in (vi) to (viii) may therefore be considered as instances of IE-***ing***- type *optional-derivational lexical productivity*.

In variation with-***ing***-type lexical pattern discussed above, the one followed in (ix) and (x) is somewhat complex. In (x), IE option of ***-ing***-suffixed lexical structure in *tumb**ling*** (+) *down of the houses*, reinforces the pattern of the preceding similarly-structured lexical item, *water-logg**ing***, in the same sentence, more so as it is in marked preference to an everyday synonym in the language, 'collapse'. It is worth noting that IE –**ing**-type trendy pattern of lexical productivity apart, what really goes into structuring of the item is its specific functional value. The lexical item (the water-logging culminated in) *the tumb**ling** down of the houses,* an NP structure, precisely matches with the connotation of VP structure: 'come tumbling down' (LDCE 2009/12:1896)[6], rather than 'tumble-down' (AdjPhr)[7]. Since the context of the text has reference to sudden falling down of the houses, 'come tumbling down' rather than 'tumble-down/ dilapidated houses', the IE lexical item derives from the former in preference to the latter. This results in IE –**ing**-type lexical innovation, (…the water-logging culminated in) *the tumbl**ing** (+) down of the houses* as contrasted with 'tumble-down' houses. The lexical item *tumbl**ing** down*......may thus be considered an instance of IE-***ing-****type replacive-derivational lexical produc*tivity.

A most prominent instance of all the *-ing*-type Indianisms discussed above is *water-logging* in (ix) and (x), which recurs commonly in IE speech irrespective of performing skill of the participant. This is despite the fact that the data of this study incidentally records its restrictive occurrence in the register of LT.

Water-logging is a typical *Indianism* in that it has long since been in wide distribution in IE speech, even as it did not find a dictionary entry earlier.[8] The *-ing*-type lexical productivity in *water-logging* is of a complex sort. The item is structured by clipping-*ed* constituent of the existing item *water-logged*, followed by suffixation of *-ing* morpheme in its place along with creation of a non-existent base/root word 'water-log'. Were it a case of routine suffixation as from'water-logged' to*'water-logged *ing*', not involving creation of a non-existent 'base word', 'water-log', the identification of the word class of *water-logging* would not have posed any etymological problem. But given the structure of the word, its word class in IE speech is identifiable with reference to its functional value in the syntactic structure of IE/the language. Note, the functional value of the word in IE syntactic structure is that of S or O_d, as an NP/N, which is derived, as here, from the embedded NP structure that contains existent item of the language, *water-logged* as an Adj. The illustrations below would bring out the point :

(ix) Rainy season witnesses *water-logging* (NP/N&O_d) on the main road......the *water-logging* (NP/N&S) culminated in the tumbling down of the houses...

Note, *water-logging* (N), as illustrated above, is derived, for instance, from NP structure :*water-logged* (Adj) area/room (NP), etc as shown in (ix)[a] and (x)[a] below :

(ix)[a] Rainy season witnesses *water-logged* (area) (NP) on the main road.

(x)[a] ...the water-*logged* (area) (NP) culminated in the tumbling down of the houses......

The functional value of *water-logging* (N) is thus derived from *water-logged* (Adj) in embedded NP structure whereas the lexical structure of the word involves its morphological re-structuring, or back formation, from *water-logged* to'water-log', and morphemic replacement of *-ed* by *-ing* :*water-logg**ed*** by *water-logg**ing***. Both ways, the structure of *water-logging* is derivational in nature, involving morphological re-structuring, syntactic transformation (from Adj. to NP (S/O_d)) and change of word class, from *water-*

logged (Adj) to *water-logging* (N). *Water-logging* is therefore a typical instance of IE *replacive-derivational productivity*.

Productivity : *-ED* Type

The preponderant choice of *-ed* suffix to form adjectival lexical items is a feature markedly restrictive in INE to the register of AD. However, its recurrence in over-all IE speech underlines it as being a stylistic marker of everyday IE speech. The *-ed*-suffixed items, like *-ing*-suffixed ones discussed above, are also typical *Indianisms*, but they have not yet found entry in the lexicon under the given structure, word class and sense in which they appear in IE.

Note, *-ing*-type and *-ed*-type IE lexical productivity stand out distinct from each other in that the former is generally independent of structural and semantic compulsions, being more of a linguistic fad than a real necessity, while the latter seems crucially conditioned by communication requirements. The option of *-ed*-suffixed items, as shown in AD, is explicitly intended to gain both structural economy and information focus. In the process, these items usually—not invariably—undergo a change of word class and semantic shift to suit the Indian context. While some of these *-ed*-suffixed items are typical Indianisms which may appear, in BE, structurally odd, even semantically opaque, others, already in the lexicon, acquire stylistic significance simply because their recurrence, marked by creativity, rein-forces IE's pattern of overwhelming preference for *-ed*-suffixed adjectival items.

All the *-ed*-suffixed adjectival items in the data of this study showed an all-out pattern of derivational productivity, involving a change of word class, from (V)→(Adj) and (N)→(Adj), in that choice order. The pattern of their derivational productivity, though marked by a range of variations, falls into two broad categories, featuring (a) normal/probable lexical productivity, and (b) distinctive lexical productivity/creativity featuring structural oddity and semantic opaqueness vis-à-vis BE. The items in the former category gain their stylistic value in terms of their over-all recurrence in IE speech, largely because they are routinely modelled on the pattern set by the items in the latter category. Consider, first, the following items from (b), the latter category, which are typical *Indianisms*, both structurally and semantically:

Data from AD :

*(i) employ**ed*** in Delhi

*(ii) employ**ed*** in England

*(iii) stable character**ed**...* spinster...*stable character**ed*** bachelors

Data from NS/ED :

(iv) bond***ed*** labour

All the -ed-suffixed items above are typical Indianisms, aimed at structural economy and information focus. Their structure evenly prefers derivational pattern, (V)→ (Adj), as in (i) and (ii), and (N)→ (Adj), as in (iii) and (iv).

In (i) and (ii), the item '*employed*' (Adj.) implies in IE 'being in employment', precisely, 'a job holder', as against 'being *unemployed*' (Adj.).The word is an instance of IE derivational lexical productivity in two ways. In the first place, it seems directly sourced from BE item, *unemployed* (Adj), and coined through clipping of its prefix *-un*, which results in the word being a typical IE coinage, having a specific meaning in IE speech, 'a hob holder', and patterned on a notional illustration: 'unavailing' (Adj)→ 'availing' (Adj.) (?).

Secondly, the functional value of *employed* in IE speech, as in (i) and (ii), is further highlighted when the item is considered in terms of a prepositional verb, 'employed in', that follows it. Note, the prepositional verb 'employ in' always anticipates a direct object (O_d) as in the sentence 'She was employed in watering the garden' (Longman 1982:359). So, the omission of O_d in (i) and (ii) renders '*employed*' structurally odd and semantically opaque in BE. However, in both the illustrations, *employed* acquires specific functional value in IE speech since the preposition 'in'which follows it functions here as a constituent of the adjunct of place, '*employed* in Delhi'/ '*employed* in England', instead of the prepositional verb, 'employ in'.

Thus, in AD, indeed in over-all IE speech, the IE item *employed* is structured to highlight one's state of being 'in employment'/'a job holder', as contrasted with one's state of 'unemployment'. Apparently, the *Indianism*, *employed* (Adj.), derives from the Indian priority concern for employment, precisely 'holding a job', whatever be its nature/ profile.

Next, the Indian over-all concern extends to the place of employment that promises better living conditions as in a metropolitan city, an affluent country, etc. This explains why *employed* in IE tends to prefer/ is often followed by an adjunct of place, as 'in Delhi/in England', etc, rather than an O_d as in a prepositional verb construction.

In (iii), *-ed* suffixation helps narrow down focus on adjectival clusters, '*stable character**ed***...spinster..*stable character**ed*** bachelors', through their attributive position in the lexical items. The *-ed*-suffixed adjectival clusters, in their fronted attributive position, serves to focus on the disposition/character of the 'spinster'/ 'bachelors'.Consequently, this results in these items being typical *Indianisms*, marked out for their structural oddity and semantic opaqueness vis-à-vis BE.

In BE, 'character' (N) does not accept *-ed*suffixation.But in IE, as in (iii), 'character' (N) is adjectivised by means of -ed-suffixation to form the adjectival cluster, '*stable character**ed***'. The choice of adjectival cluster in the attributive position is intended, not merely for structural economy but essentially to ensure focus in the entire lexical item on the front-positioned adjectival cluster, '*stable character**ed***...spinster', '*stable character**ed*** bachelors'.

Apparently, the text focuses on the morality profile, precisely, 'stable character'/moral integrity of the advertiser (spinster), as also the preconditioned eligibility requirement of the respondents (bachelors), i.e. their 'stable character'/ moral integrity'. This explains why the adjectival cluster, 'stable charactered' is fronted in attributive position in both the lexical items to give it focused attention. Consider the thematised information value of *-ed*-suffixed lexical items in (iii) as contrasted with (iii)[a] below, a variant illustration of the same lexical item that employs an of-genitive case construction :

(iii) 'stable *charactere**d*** ...spinster'...'stable *charactere**d*** bachelors'

(iii)[a] '...spinster of stable character'... 'bachelors of stable character'

The of-genitive case constructions suggested in (iii)[a] are a normal feature of language, structurally as well as informatively. However, they are marked by a longer structure and neutral end-focus in the NP structure. By contrast, *-ed*-suffixed adjectival clusters in (iii) result in a shorter NP structure; consequently, and more importantly, their fronted attributive position accords them prime attention value in the NP structure.The *-ed*-suffixed adjectival clusters in (iii) feature derivational lexical productivity of IE, and they are thus typical instances of *Indianism*.

In (iv), the lexical item *bond**ed** labour*, though structurally analogous to BE items 'bonded wood' and 'bonded goods' (Longman 1982: 109), semantically stands out different as an *Indianism*. In IE, it implies 'a labour who is bound by a bond to serve his master practically all his life, or until he repays him his outstanding loan with interest'. The IE recourse to *-ed* suffixation to structure *bonded labour*, in preference to available, albeit archaic, BE lexical items, which do not have *-ed* suffixation, such as 'bond man, bond servant, bond slave', etc. (CODCE 1977: 110) is thus a departure from BE usage. The item is thus marked out as an instance of IE lexical creativity.

The item, *bond**ed** labour*, is a typical *Indianism* in several ways. First, the item conveys a meaning quite a few shades different from the one associated with the existing items in the lexicon, 'bond man/servant/slave' (Oxford 1977:110; cf.the gloss of *bonded labour* given earlier). Secondly, it involves a change of word-class, from 'bond' (N) $\rightarrow$' bonded' (Adj.).Thirdly, the-*ed*-type derivational productivity of *bond**ed** labour* shares *-ed*-type lexical-pattern congruity with IE speech in general.

Inasmuch as *-ed*-suffixed items in (i) through (iv) undergo lexico-morphological re-structuring and ingenious change of word class to serve IE's vital communication requirements, they are all typical instances of IE *positive/creative type derivational lexical productivity* (details to follow). It would be relevant to add that further exploration of more such instances of Indianisms featuring IE *positive/creative type lexical creativity* (not covered within the data of this study), would help access more such widely-used instances of IE positive/creative lexical productivity.

IE's pattern of lexical productivity, just discussed, is reinforced by recurrence of quite a few other instances of IE lexical items available in the data of this study, which are also formed with *-ed*-suffixed adjectival clusters. However, being a shade structurally different from the foregoing illustrations, they are discussed separately below as instances ofIE *normal/probable type lexical productivity*. IE items, having *-ed*-suffixed adjectival clusters that follow IE *normal/probable type lexical productivity* are quite recurrent in IE speech, if only because they are routinely structured after existing BE items. Their distinctive Indianism, nevertheless, lies in their nuanced lexical creativity and semantic shift. Indeed, the functional/creativity value of such *-ed*-suffixed adjectival clusters would appear to be much similar to those in (i) through (iv) as the following sample illustrations would show :

Data from AD

(v) *well-plac**ed*** groom

(vi) *career-orient**ed**...* girl

(vii) *broad-mind**ed**....*girl

(viii) *open-mind**ed*** family:

(ix) *convent-educat**ed**...*girl

(x) *Bombay bas**ed*** girl

All the *-ed*-suffixed items above have a derivational structure, and all but those in (vii) and (viii) involve a change of word class. The derivational items, *broad-minde**d**...girl* (vii) and *open-minde**d** ...girl (viii)*, structured after BE usage, are a combining form within the same word class, (Adj.) → (Adj.). Nevertheless, they acquire stylistic derivative significance in IE because of their semantic shift in native context, as also for sharing share pattern congruity with other *-ed*-suffixed adjectival clusters in IE speech.

Both the items, *broad-minde**d**......girl* and *open-minde**d**....... girl*, also structured after BE usage, broadly carry identical implication in IE, that 'the girl... (is) free of restrictions and taboos of conservative Indian society by which most Indians are bound' (Dubey 1989 : 102; 1991: 26-27). This is widely different from what 'broad-minded...' and 'open-minded...' imply in BE, respectively: 'being tolerant or liberal in thought or opinion' and 'with open mind, unprejudiced' (CODCE 1977: 124, 767)/ 'willing to listen to other people's opinions and accept behaviour that is different from our own' and 'willing to listen to, think about or accept different ideas' (OALD 2015: 187, 1080). Both the items in (vii) and (viii) above are thus instances IE derivational lexical productivity.

In (x), the adjectival cluster in *Bombay-base**d** girl*, again structured on the combining form of BE, 'London-bas**ed** firm...', etc (LDCE 2004:108), is marked though by a change of word class (N) → (Adj.). More notably, the cluster, being front-focused in the lexical item, reflects a nuanced semantic shift to underscore the cosmopolitan ambience of the referent's city of residence, i.e. Bombay. By this token, the advertiser/referent girl stipulates a pre-condition that the respondent must match up with this foremost criterion of marriage compatibility, i.e. temperament and adaptability to reside in the mega-cosmopolitan city of Bombay (after marriage with her). The item is thus an instance of IE derivational lexical productivity, involving semantic shift as well as change of word class.

The lexical items *well-plac**ed**...groom* in (v), *career-orient**ed**... girl* in (vi) and *convent-educat**ed**...girl* in (ix), having *-ed*-suffixed adjectival clusters, are all characterised by IE derivational productivity, and all are marked by a change of word class. Note, *-ed*-suffixed adjectival clusters, *well-plac**ed***, *career-orient**ed***, *convent-educat**ed***, have long since had widespread distribution in IE speech across a spectrum of users of the language with varied levels of proficiency in the language. However, these Indianisms, despite being widely used in IE speech for decades, and cited in much earlier studies as typical Indianisms (Dubey 1989:133-34; 1991: 23-27), have not yet received the attention of the lexicographer (cf. LDCE 1982, 2004 and 2012; OALD 2015).

In *well-plac**ed** groom* and *career-orient**ed**...girl*, the *-ed*-suffixed adjectival clusters have a two-fold derivational function in forming the lexical items. First, it changes the word class of relevant part of the lexical items:'place' (V) → 'plac*ed*' (Adj);'orient' (V) →'orient*ed*' (Adj). Secondly, the *-ed*-suffixed items, combined with words, 'well' (Adj.) and 'career' (N), result in typical Indianisms, with/without a change of word-class, as in *well-plac**ed*** (Adj)→ (Adj), and *career-orient**ed*** (N)→ (Adj.), respectively.

Interestingly, the items, *well-plac**ed** groom* and *career-orient**ed** girl*, feature semantic shift in IE speech. In IE, *well-placed groom* implies that 'the groom holds a well-paid position in a reputed organisation/office, etc' whereas *career-oriented girl* comes with a specific connotation that 'the girl is solely devoted to her chosen/ targeted professional career and is, more importantly, totally unsuited for the role of a housewife'.

In *convent-educat**ed** ...girl* (ix), the existing *-ed*-suffixed word in the language, 'educated' (Adj.), is combined with 'convent' (N) to structurean IE adjectival cluster *convent-educat**ed***, which involves a change of word class : 'convent' (N)→ (Adj.)The item, widespread in IE speech, also comes with a typical semantic shift in native parlance. It carries implicit connotation in IE that the referent, *convent-educated girl*, is proficient in spoken English by dint of her education at a convent (school), which is, in IE, synonymous with an English medium school. Note, in native socio-cultural context, the girl's fluency in spoken English is considered an essential requirement in (arranged) Indian marriage, especially in the middle class/upper crust Indian family. The item, '*convent-educat**ed** ...girl*' thus carries a distinctive semantic shift in AD/IE speech.

Consider the instances of *-ed* type IE *positive/ creative lexicalproductivity* below as contrasted with those featuring *-ed* type IE *normal/ probable lexical productivity* in terms of their possible/ implicit predicative structure and interpretation :

Predicative structure/Interpretation

(a) IE -ed type positive/ creative lexical productivity

(i) *employ**ed** in Delhi* : 'employed (in/as ??) in Delhi'

(ii) *employ**ed** in England* : 'employed in/as ??) in England,

(iii) *stable character**ed**...spinster ...stable character**ed** girl*: 'spinster/bachelor having stable (normal/balanced ??) character'

(iv) *bond**ed** labour* : 'labour bonded (like wood/goods (??)'

(b) IE -ed type normal/probable lexical productivity

(v) *well-plac**ed** groom* : 'groom placed well (in life)/ groom occupying a high position'

(vi) career-orient**ed** ... : 'girl oriented to her career'/'career girl'

(vii) broad-mind**ed**...girl : 'girl who is liberal in thought or opinion'

(viii) open-mind**ed**...family : 'family having open/ unprejudiced mind'

(ix) convent-educat**ed** girl: 'girl educated at a convent school'

(x) Bombay-bas**ed** girl: 'girl residing in Bombay'

It would seem easier to predict/interpret in BE, with reference to their predicative structure, *broad/hazy* meaning of all the IE adjectival clusters in the lexical items, (v) through (x), than that of those in the items in (i) through (iv), even though all these items are instances of typical Indianisms of IE *-ed* type derivational lexical productivity.

The discussion above points to a pattern contour of convergence of BE and IE, as well as that of contrast between them. IE items in (v) through (x), formed with *-ed*-suffixed adjectival clusters, are all patterned after BE usage and feature *normal* (BE)/*probable* (IE) *type lexical productivity*. They may thus all be classed together because of their common derivational structure and semantic clarity of meaning, though quite *broad* and *hazy*, vis-à-vis BE. In this sense, they feature affinity/ convergence with BE, but only to an extent. Note, the IE items in (v) through (x) only broadly, *not precisely,* unfold their meaning in BE in terms of their implicit predicative structure (discussed above). By contrast, the same is not the case with IE items in (i) to (iv) which are marked by both structural oddity and semantic opaqueness vis-à-vis BE. They are thus considered instances of IE *positive/creative type lexical productivity*.

The difference between *probable* and *positive* types of IE *-ed* suffixed lexical productivity is essentially one of nuanced difference of structure and meaning between them. Though both types of *-ed*-suffixed lexical productivity characterise over-all IE speech, it is *positive/creative type lexical productivity* that marks it out more distinctly and is relatively more pervasive in IE speech than *normal/probable type lexical productivity*. For this reason, its contribution to IE lexical structure is considered both creative and generic. This is reflected in widespread distribution of such *-ed*-suffixed IE lexical items, *employ**ed***, *bond**ed**labour*, *well-plac**ed***, as also *well-settl**ed***, well- establish**ed**, etc (cf Dubey 1991: 23-27) that help reflect a whole vista of the variegated Indian socio-cultural reality efficaciously, notwithstanding IE being a nativised language.

Irrespective of nuanced difference between the two types of IE lexical productivity, all the lexical items in (i) to (x) remain, however, instances of IE lexical productivity. What classes them all together is their common pattern of option for semantic shift, their widespread distribution and long-time usage in IE speech. This aspect of IE, therefore, needs special attention of the lexicographer inasmuch as the functional implication of the cited instances/ sample illustrations of IE lexical items is not just restricted to everyday IE speech within the country but, quite often and most glaringly, extends much beyond to the global context as well.

One would observe that *lexical deletions and productivity: -ing* and *-ed types* are among the hallmarks of IE lexical structure. But all the instances of their occurrence do not qualify them as being a constituent of IE lexical structure to the same extent. In terms of their structure and meaning, some of these instances seem to be more distinctive and more widespread in IE speech than others.

Apparently, two major criteria that account for variation in their rate of acceptance in IE speech are, in that order: first, how ingeniously such IE lexical items are structured so as to serve vital communication requirements of IE speech community as also how crucially they help reveal the native socio-cultural meanings; and/ or secondly, their frequency of recurrence and expanse of their acceptance in over-all IE speech, even over a period of time and largely bereft of linguistic creativity.

This would explain why IE items marked by lexical creativity, such as of *replacive-derivational* and *positive-derivational* types that vitally contribute to over-all IE speech, namely *water-logg**ing***, *employ**ed***, *bond**ed** labour*, etc, are more thoroughly nativised in IE, irrespective of the level of the participant's performing skill in the language, than those lacking in lexical creativity such as of *zero-inflectional or quasi-optional- inflectional types*, viz *shift**ing***, *start**ing***, *brak**ing***, *home-lov**ing***, *non-work**ing***, etc, which are largely, if not invariably, restricted to IE speech of the participants lacking in requisite performing skill in the language.

It is thus easier to predict, in pan-IE speech, occurrence of Indianisms reflecting lexical creativity than of those marked by its (complete/ relative) absence. However, IE items falling in the latter category, which are initially restricted to sociolect of the participants having inadequate performing skill in the language, sometimes make their entry into pan-IE speech gradually in course of time, sheerly by their extensive recurrence. IE lexical items *booth-captur**ing***, *land-grabb**ing***, *ensur**ing***, *smart look**ing***, etc are all typical Indianisms in this sense of the term. It needs a special mention that such typical Indianisms are now largely shared by a wide spectrum of pan-IE speech community having varied levels of performing skill in the language, that includes journalists as well as non-journalists.

Like derivational productivity, especially of a positive type, lexical deletions, employed for structural economy and information focus, are no less a typical feature of IE speech. Some of the instances of IE lexical deletions, deftly employed to gain information focus, are more speedily and thoroughly nativised in IE speech than those marked by little or no functional value.

The following instances of lexical deletions in IE speech, employed for both structural economy and information focus—already discussed above— have largely been integrated with everyday IE speech: *degree* (implicit reference to the certificate of award of the degree), *passenger* (implicit reference to a passenger train), *party/parties* (implicit reference to political party/parties), *poor generation* (implicit reference to poor/insufficient generation of power).Note, the implicit reference of each of the instances of deletions above has restrictive reference to the context of the cited texts. It needs to be added that deletions employed in IE speech, with little functional value, get rejected soon or fade off in course of time.

Looked at in a global and pragmatic perspective, the nativised IE lexical items acquire added functional value in real-time communication in English internationally. This is because, with increasing number and widespread presence of IE speech community globally, these nativised IE lexical items –and perhaps many more in the offing—would normally spill over in the speech of IE speakers with other non-IE users of the language. This is likely to entail communication hurdle/breakdown to the interlocutor. The functional implication of such nativised IE lexical items thus cannot possibly be ignored or undermined in everyday communication in English internationally. This lexical dimension of IE therefore needs special attention of the lexicographer.

The foregoing discussion has been done in a functional framework, with central focus all along on lexico-morphological strategies of nativisation of IE lexical structure, as well as on the core IE participant-contributors who employ these strategies of nativisation to the best of their varied levels of performing skill in the language. Such an orientation of the study has helped explore not only some very interesting and commonly used instances of nativised IE lexical items, but, more significantly, the very core dynamics of their shaping patterns of nativisation as well. Interestingly, in the process, this study has also touched upon some revealing aspects of modern-day Indian socio-cultural-economic reality, which quite a few native Indians themselves may not perhaps be quite aware of, or would like to acknowledge them frankly.

Notes

1 This chapter is a revised version of my paper published in *Indianisation of English Language and Literature*, ed. Pathak. R S Bahri Publications, New Delhi. 1994.

2 The data of this study consist of a representative sample from news stories (NS), editorials (Ed), 'letters to the editor' (LT) and matrimonial advertisements (AD), taken from four national and two provincial English dailies (both since closed) in India.

3 All the relevant parts of the lexical items are given in italics, partially in bold italics.

4 **Abbreviations**: N (noun), NP (noun phrase), V (verb), VP (verb phrase), Adj (adjective), AdjPhr (adjective phrase), S (subject), O (object), Od (direct object).

5 OALD (2015:1800) defines **working girl** as " *noun* (*informal*) **1** *(becoming old-fashioned*) a PROSTITUTE. People say 'working girl' to avoid saying 'prostitute'. **2** (*sometimes offensive*) a woman who has a paid job".

6 "**come tumbling down**: if something comes tumbling down, it falls suddenly to the ground: *Removing the debris could cause the rest of the building to come tumbling down*." (LDCE 2009/12:1896)

7 "tumble-down" has reference to " (of a building) old and in a poor condition so that it looks as if it is falling down/**dilapidated**" (OALD 2015 : 1682).

8 The item *water-logging*, a typical *Indianism* of IE speech, found first mention in Dubey (1983; 1989 : 130). Note, *water-logging* does not have an entry in OALD (2000/2004 and 2015) and LDCE (1982). However, this Indianism found entry much later in LDCE (1995/2004), though without reference to the word being an Indianism, a typical coinage of IE speech, as suggested earlier (*op. cit.*).

References

Dubey, Vinod S (1989): *Newspaper English in India*. Bahri Publications. New Delhi. 1989.

________(1991):'*The lexical style of Indian English newspapers*'.*World Englishes*. 10/1. Pergamon Press. Oxford. 1991.

CODCE (1977) : *The Concise Oxford Dictionary of Current English*. OUP. 1977.

Kachru, Braj B (1962) : '*Analysis of Some Features of Indian English : A Study in Linguistic Method*'. Unpublished PhD dissertation, 1962. Edinburgh University.

________(1965) : '*The Indianness in Indian English*'. *Word* 21/3. 1965.

________(1966): '*Indian English : A Study in Contextualisation*'. *In Memory of J R Firth*. Eds. Basell, *et al.,* Longman.1966.

________(1973) : '*Toward a lexicon of Indian English*'. In Kachru, Lees, Malkeel, Pietrangeli and Saporta eds. *Issues in Linguistics:Papers in Honor of Henry and Renee Kahane*. Urbana: University of Illinois Press. 1973.

________(1983): The Iindianisation of English : The English Language in India. New Delhi : OUP. 1983.

LDCE (1982, 1987 and 2004): *Longman Dictionary of Contemporary English*. Longman.

LDCE (2012): *Longman Dictionary of Contemporary English*. Longman.

OALD (2015) : *Oxford Advanced Learner's Dictionary*. OUP.

Quirk, R & Greenbaum, S (1973): *A University Grammar of English*.

6
Discourse as Weapon: The Dynamics of Election Advertisements

Notion of discourse

The notion of discourse has over the years undergone a drastic reinterpretation in linguistic literature in both orientation and scope.[1] The term **discourse** is no longer identified with formal features of inter-sentence linkage (cf. Harris 1952: 357;Widdowson 1979: 92) or inter-textual cohesion.On the contrary, it is currently viewed functionally in terms of over-all textual coherence—with or without cohesion[2]—and communication acts performed by sentences in combination to characterise a "piece of language as a whole as a kind of communication" (Widdowson 1979: 98). The central concern of discourse thus lies with communication as such, with the process of creation or negotiation of meanings *per se*. Since language is the primary and vital means of human communication, discourse generally, though not always, implies the process of communication by means of language.

The extended implication of discourse has also undergone enlargement of its scope to cover both spoken and written texts and, beyond these, to both verbal and visual channels of communication.[3]

That the very process of communication is initially set in motion during early childhood, verbally—at the phonic/speech level—as well as visually—through gesture, posture and facial expression—only goes to underline the crucial function of both verbal and visual channels of communication. Indeed, our cultural evolutiontoday is characterised by "simultaneous use of verbal and non-verbal communication", as reflected in "plays, films, television, strip cartoons ... most advertising" (Vestergaard and Schroder 1985: 13), photographs, sketches, hoardings and such other visual channels of communication. It is therefore "quite artificial to conceive of discourse in exclusively verbal terms", especially when even visual texts are " visually perceived by interpreters." (Fairclough, 1989 : 27)

Approaches to discourse

Language as discourse has been considered here mainly from three different, yet overlapping, orientations of inquiry, all of which are relevant in one way or the other for exploration of discourse dynamics of election advertisements in this study in its totality, namely, social, pragmatic and psychological.

Language is basically a sociological phenomenon. No language can occur without a speech community, and therefore language is considered a "social semiotic" (cf. Halliday 1978). Considered thus in terms of "social practice" and " the whole process of social interaction" discourse involves "social conditions of production and social conditions of interpretations." (Fairclough 1989 : 24-25)

The pragmatic angle envisages discourse as a creation of "presuppositions of a pragmatic kind or implications"—the relation between what is said and what is meant, based on linguistic and extra-linguistic context of utterance, "which can override those presuppositions which are associated with linguistic forms." (Widdowson 1979: 128-9)

The psychological approach to discourse, enunciated by Sperber and Wilson (1986), views discourse in terms of the *Theory of Relevance*. They conceive of communication in terms of the complementary concepts of " association and inference" involving the speaker —the signal that he has something to communicate— and the addressee—the logical process that enables him to derive meaning: "... the communicator produces a stimulus which makes it mutually manifest to the communicator and the audience that the communicator intends, by means of his stimulus, to make manifest, or more manifest to the audience a certain set of assumptions." (Sperber and Wilson 1986 : 63)

Note that the use of terms " manifestness" and " assumptions" by Sperber and Wilson in preference to the stronger and more categorical terms, 'knowledge' and 'proposition', suggests that communication is a matter of relevance —one of degrees of communication or ambivalence—manifestness or more manifestness— and degrees of commitment to truths (assumptions, not propositions). Sperber and Wilson elaborate this further with reference to what they call the " extent conditions of relevance", detailed below:

Extent Condition 1 : *an assumption is relevant in a context to the extent that its contextual effects in that context are large.*

Extent Condition 2: *an assumption is relevant in a context that the effort required to process it in that context is small.*

Discourse structure of election advertisements

Election advertisements are a type of display advertisements designed to grab instant and overpowering attention of the addressee. They typically feature thus mixed discourse structure that exploits both verbal and visual channels of communication. The choice is not, as might seem, for reasons of 'aesthetisation' of the advertised message of the text[4] *per se*—for sprucing up its lay-out—but essentially for "mutually reinforcing" the message of the visual and the verbal that are too intricately coalesced to be disentangled from each other (Fairclough 1989:49)[5], without of course impacting its underlying core message value and thrust.

Election advertisements are also a kind of public communication, though of a uniquely complex type. The participants involved herein are not just amorphous addresser-addressee with an assigned communicative purpose as in public notices, newspaper stories, articles, etc. They indeed make up a complex set of interlocutors, having to communicate at once between themselves—the rival political parties—also with, more crucially, an anonymous third participant, the target public readership/ electorate. Whereas the public remains all through at the receiving end in the role of a passive participant, the rival political parties, by contrast, address each other by turn, at times even simultaneously, as in parliamentary debates, radio/TV interviews, discussions, etc, notwithstanding the fact that the public remains all through the ultimate focal target/ arbiter in their mind. This matrix of addresser-addressee relationship involving a range of diverse communicative roles, functions and targets, thus makes election advertisements a most interesting and enterprising type of public discourse.

Election advertisements are also a distinctive variety of media discourse.[6] This is so because it is designed for mass audience, for an "ideal subject"and "actual reader", the latter having to negotiate a relationship with the "ideal subject"in order to make communication possible (cf. Fairclough 1989: 49). All this endows these advertisements with immense discourse value and high stakes for both the addresser and the addressee. For these reasons, the ultimate make-up of election advertisements, both their visual and verbal components, is meticulously crafted.

Discourse as weapon : The dynamics of election advertisements discourse

Prior to a discussion of discourse dynamics of election advertisements, precisely, how discourse is deftly manoevred as a weapon in the raging war of election advertisements, it would be worthwhile to reflect on the following quote from George Bernard Shaw's celebrated classic, *Arms and the Man* (1894: 34), wherein, in response to Raina's poking comment: "*And you're nolonger a soldier, Sergius*", Sergius comes out with the following brilliant retort:

Soldiering, my dear madam, is the coward's art of attacking mercilessly when you are strong, and keeping out of harm's way when you are weak. That is the whole secret of successful fighting. Get your enemy at a disadvantage; and ... on any account, fight him on equal terms.

Though Sergius' witty remark above is intended to debunk the 'romantic' view of war, it lays bare in the process the stark truth of any warfare, specially, the secrets of 'successful fighting', like the one fought through election advertisements.

Unequal discourse situation

The copywriter of election advertisements perhaps knows it only too well that a battle, most of all the royal and riveting battle of power politics, or the battle of the ballot, is never—and ought not ever to be—fought on equal terms, and never really ever fought to be lost. Consequently, election advertisements typify a unique instance of *unequal discourse situation*.

Election advertisements, in the first instance, fall into *mono-type discourse texts*, such as pamphlets, books, advertisements in the media, both electronic and print, etc that preclude instant/ simultaneous face-to-face interaction with the interlocutor/ target audience. This gives rise to an *unequal discourse situation* wherein election advertisements grab a *vantage position vis-à-vis* their target audience in the 'war' of election advertisements discourse. The copywriter has thus ample freedom/opportunity to choose the message content and format of the election advertisement text, steer the course of its agenda and modulate its tone and tenor with changing necessity. More crucially, it enables him to strategise, from a vantage point, the timing and sequence pattern of its publication. In this situation, he has the leeway to exploit his best communicative skills and resources, both verbal and visual, to the maximal advantage of his client political party, all at his convenient terms and pace.

Parallel discourse situation

The unequal discourse situation of election advertisements just discussed also often leads to somewhat *parallel discourse situation* as distinct from unequal discourse situation. Herein, the 'real' subjects—rival political parties–attempt to communicate with each other through election advertisements, even while remaining at cross-purposes, so as to gain an upper hand in the raging one-up manship war of politics. In normal discourse situation, the following type of communication between the interlocutors is bound to collapse as meaning cannot be easily negotiated between the texts A and B below :

> A : ***Now is the time to make your choice***
> ***APPEASEMENT OR EQUALITY*** (Plate 1)
> B: **HOW CAN THOSE WHO DO NOT BELIEVE IN THE BROTHERHOOD OF MAN SPEAK OF RELIGION?** (Plate 3)

Discourse in the instance above is obviously not possible in normal communication situation since A and B, the rival political parties, have both contrary messages to communicate. Yet, in election advertisements, as here, this exchange of utterances would make discourse possible to the 'real' subjects involved, the rival political parties, as well as to their ultimate target, the 'ideal' subjects/ the electorate, just because of its sheer functional value. The instance of parallel discourse above is indeed an exchange of allegations and counter-allegations by the warring political parties.

See-saw type of discourse situation

Despite added advantage available to political parties from unequal/parallel discourse of election advertisements their position of strength remains rather precariously constrained by four major factors, listed below, that operate all at once. These factors are critical enough to reverse the vantage position of a political party *vis-à-vis*its political adversary, the real subject (s), as in a see-saw, in case it fails to take them into account and swiftly manoeuvre the course of discourse in its favour.

First, in the battle of the ballot, a lot depends on the timing and sequence order in which the texts of election advertisement are brought out, and on who first initiates the agenda of discourse and who finally winds it up, and how.

Secondly, high stakes are involved depending on who, in a given context, is the priority target in mind in the discourse of election advertisements, whether the 'ideal' subject or the 'real' one, or both together.

Thirdly, it relates to the priority choice of communicative/ speech acts, viz. expressive, directive, informational, interactional, etc. (cf. Vestergaard and Schroder, 1885: 16-18; Searle 1969 1971), that the copywriter sets to himself in the election advertisement. A choice or combination of choices based on these factors turns the discourse of election advertisements into a potent weapon of offence or defence, in varying degrees of exposition.

Finally, it is the copywriter's by no means less significant choice of the visual—sketch/image—to 'anchor' the election advertisement in real-time context of situation that has critical functional value. This is so because the visual helps "relay (s)" (cf. Barthes 1964) a reciprocal relation between the visual and the verbal to reinforce the discourse message of the text. Whether the visual chosen has iconic, indexical or symbolic value (cf. Pierce 1960: 156-73)[7] and whether it has denotative or connotative implications (cf. Barthes 1964), and, yet more, the location where it is positioned in the framework of the text, lend together a cumulative effect on the dynamics of election advertisements discourse.

The weapon in use

Interestingly, only two national political parties of India, Congress (I) and BJP, apparently major contenders for power, joined the fray of election advertisements discourse on the eve of mid-term elections to four state and one union territory assemblies in India in November 1993[8]. More interestingly, the two political parties set out on this course simultaneously, i.e. on 1st November 1993, though it was Congress (I) that finally called a stop to the exchange of election advertisement discourse on 7th November 1993. In all, six **moves** were made, four by Congress (I) and two by BJP, or six election advertisements appeared in the national English dailies over a span of one week. These moves are discussed below with reference to **four stages of evolution of the election advertisement discourse.**

Stage I : Move 'A' by BJP

Stage I is set off by BJP through Move 'A' (see Plate 1) that defines its agenda of election advertisement discourse, giving it a vantage position. Apparently, this explains why it evokes a strong counter-response by the rival political party, Congress (I), through its Move 'C' at Stage II (see Plate 3). Being the initiator of discourse, BJP thus grabs both time and discourse edge over the rival political party to delimit and fore-set the course of election advertisement discourse to its maximal advantage.

Apparently, Move 'A' by BJP is an act of skilful manoeuvring aimed at striking a balance between two types of target readership —the 'ideal' and the 'real' subjects—only to ensure that both the targets are hit, squarely and surely.

The deictic anchorage of personal pronouns (see Plate 1)—'*your choice*', '*the great cultural heritage that binds us as one*, '*question before you*', '*Let's go*' has all unambiguous reference to the 'ideal' subject, the reader/electorate, whereas the utterance, '*You can declare*', has specific reference to the 'real' one, the rival political party. This deictic anchorage of personal pronouns at once serves the dual purpose of striking an informal/intimate rapport with the reader/electorate, while frontally attacking the rival political party in no uncertain ways.

Significantly, Move 'A' initiates the agenda of election advertisements discourse through a complex choice of the verbal and the visual channels that mutually relay and reinforce the core message of the text. Verbally, the thematised topic of discourse (in bold prints at the top of the text), "...*your* ('ideal' subject's) *choice* (between) *Appeasement or Equality*", is only front-sliding/thematisation of a section of the main text of the advertisement:

"The question before you is not just BJP or the rest. It's Equality or Appeasement, Integrity or Corruption, Peace or Panic, Niti (morality) or Aniti (immorality)."

However, the illocutionary value of this thematisation, equating BJP with '*Equality ...Integrity...Peace...Niti* (morality' comes out by implicature[9]. This is evident from the way the reference to BJP is deftly juxtaposed with a string of options in the text body in that order, both semantically and sequentially: 'BJP or the rest' is immediately followed by a parallel set of juxtapositions "It's Equality or Appeasement, Integrity or Corruption, Peace or Panic, *Niti* (morality) or *Aniti* (immorality)."

The reference in the text to '*Rise and restore the national honour before it's lost forever*' carries the implicature that the rival political party is to blame squarely for the loss of national honour. This is underscored by how the discourse gradually evolves on the following line : "*Rise and restore the national honour...The question before you is not just BJP or the rest. It's Equality or Appeasement .....Let's go with the BJP. The only party with ... patriotic fervour.*"

Move 'A' is noticeably marked by a set of directive communicative acts, neatly placed at the beginning of the text of election advertisement, mid-way in the text and finally at its end. The utterances, "*Now is the time to make your choice*" (at the top of the text), "*Now is the time to act.*" (mid-way in the text), "*Let's go with the BJP*", " *TODAY, FIVE STATES : TOMORROW, THE NATION : VOTE BJP*" (lower down in the text) have all together illocutionary value of candid declarations and spirited invocation. What stands out, discourse-wise, prominently noticeable here is the discreet order in which they occur sequentially in the text so as to gradually sway the mind of the 'ideal' subject/ electorate in favour of the supplicant political party.

Visually, the choice of conventional image of a balance, positioned at the top of the text (Plate 1), to reinforce verbal message of the advertisement acquires added 'symbolic'/conventional implicature as distinct from natural or 'motivated' connotation.

In the iconic image of balance of justice, the balance is shown

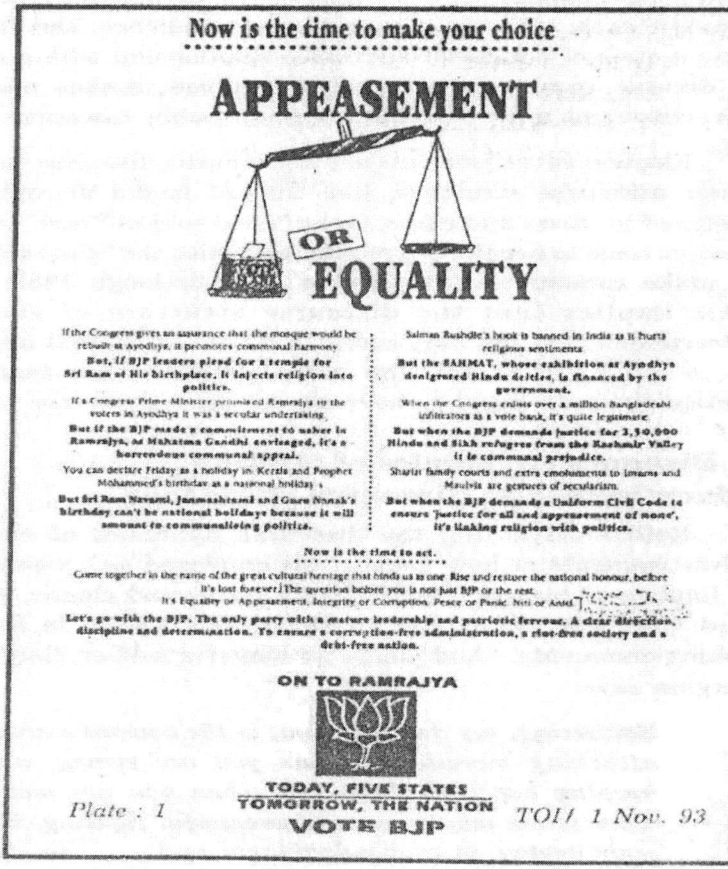

Plate 1

heavily tilted in favour of **APPEASEMENT** (printed in bold capitals at the top of the image) as against **EQUALITY** (printed in bold capitals at the bottom of the image), for, as described in the text, '*vote bank*' politics. This is further amply illustrated by the iconic image of a ballot box with a ballot paper half-inserted into it and placed at the bottom left side of the balance. The image thus carries the implicature of a fervent invocation to the 'ideal' subject/ electorate to make a choice between appeasement (inequality) and equality: **APPEASEMENT OR EQUALITY**. This is further underscored by the utterance half-way down the text: '*Now is the time to act.*' Move 'A' is thus a well-crafted instance of rival-bashing-cum-self-laudatory communicative act.

Stage I : Move 'B' by Congress (I)

Plate 2

Move 'B' by Congress (I) (see Plate 2) is, obviously, an instance of terminal discourse since it evokes no response from the rival political party, BJP, at any point of time in the later stages of the on-going discourse of election advertisements (Stages II–IV). As stated earlier, the discourse of election advertisements involves the 'real' subject— the rival political parties, the 'actual' participants of the discourse—and the 'ideal' subject—the formidable addressee electorate and the everyday readership who participates in it avidly, though only passively. Thus, even as Move 'B' by Congress (I) synchronises with Move 'A' by BJP in point of time (their publication date in the national dailies being the same, i.e. 1st November 1993) its functional value stands rather blunted because of its restrictive limit to the communicative act of exposition or exhortation only, rather than spanning over to that of offence and defence, a hallmark of BJP's Move 'A'. Congress (I)'s Move 'B', therefore, evokes zero response by the rival political party at any of the later stages of election advertisements discourse.

What needs a special note is that Congress (I)'s Move 'B' is also noticeably shorn of illocutionary force that normally features the formidable discourse of election advertisements. Further, since its ultimate target, the 'ideal' subject, the addressee electorate, as also the general readership has little role in steering/shaping the discourse course of election advertisements for obvious reasons, Congress (I)'s Move 'B' thus turns out to be a dud squib of election advertisement.

Stage II : Move 'C' by Congress (I)

Following abysmal failure to evoke a response to its earlier Move 'B', Congress (I) restructured afresh its discourse pattern of election advertisements in its next Move 'C' (see Plate 3). Move 'C' thus proceeds to evolve a markedly different course in the on-going discourse of election advertisements, ushering a transition from Stage I to Stage II.

BJP's Move 'A', as suggested earlier, was plainly a rival-bashing-cum-self-laudatory communicative act. Obviously, Congress (I)'s Move 'C' is a rather belated response to BJP's Move 'A', made over a gap of three precious days. Nevertheless, Congress (I)'s Move 'C', appears to be a concerted all-out vitriolic response to BJP's Move 'A'. What prominently makes it different though from its earlier Move 'B' is how Congress (I)'s Move 'C' carves out now a fresh agenda of election advertisements of its own choosing —clearly a strategic means of self-defence—instead of giving a head-on rebuttal of the inventory of charges listed in Move 'A' by the rival political party. Notably, such a tactical retreat by Congress (I) carries, by default, the apparent implicature of Congress (I)'s abject helplessness to fend off the charges against it by the rival political party.

Looked at from another perspective, Congress (I)'s Move 'C' is an instance of parallel discourse. It derives its functional value from unleashing a barrage of snide allegations against the rival political party, while, most glaringly, ducking a straight counter-response to the latter's offensive in Move 'A'. In the normal course, it would be imperative for the respondent, i.e. Congress (I), to counter squarely, item-wise, the charges of 'appeasement', etc levelled against it by the rival political party.

However, Congress (I)'s Move 'C' is essentially an ingenious attempt to deflect the agenda of election advertisements discourse set by the rival political party. It opts therefore for a parallel discourse of election advertisements to serve its own political agenda and political expediency. This explains why, in line with its core political agenda, it chooses to highlight the term '*religion*' in its Move 'C', "HOW CAN THOSE....SPEAK OF RELIGION?", as a retort to BJP's Move 'A', "APPEASEMENT OR EQUALITY". Were it not precisely so, there is hardly any rationale behind specific mention of the term RELIGION out of context in its Move 'C'.

In Congress (I)'s Move 'C', the thematised sentence in bold prints and within a highlighted box at the top of the text, "HOW CAN THOSE .... SPEAK OF RELIGION ?", and the one that immediately follows it in smaller bold prints below, '*Which religion is not based on the brotherhood of man?*', are instances of indirect speech act (cf. Searle 1979), or of what Sadock (cf. 1974) calls "whimperatives" or "declarations", wherein questions get the elocutionary value of a declarative pronouncement: '*Those who do not...cannot speak of religion*', and '*Every religion is based on ....*'

The indirectness of speech act is further reinforced equally indirectly by the choice of a demonstrative pronoun of distant (cf. Quirk and Greenbaum 1973: 4.90) and exophoric reference, *those,* to refer to the opponent as many as three times in the text: "*How can those…..*", "*the face of those...*" and "*every Indian to resist those……*" The exophoric potential and elocutionary value of *those* is interpretable in either of the two diametrically opposite ways.

First, *those* functions in normal communication as a word of polite and oblique reference, and therefore, even without a clue to its discourse value, the "reader (would) construct(s) a context of situation in order to supply it for himself (Halliday and Hasan 1976: 18)".But, in the given context of the raging battle of election advertisements, such an interpretation is a remote possibility.

Secondly, and quite plausibly, the elocutionary value of *those* lies here in being a word of impolite/disparaging reference to the rival political party. Indeed, *those* used as a pronoun of oblique reference seems to be an acerbic way to denigrate the public image of the opponent political party. This would not have been possible had the rival political party been referred to by its name.

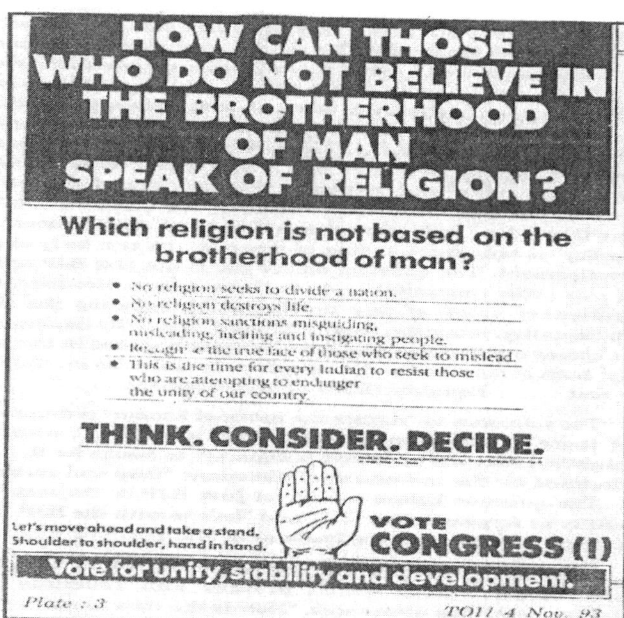

Plate 3

What immediately follows in the text is a rhetorical question : "*Which religion is not ... man*?" Notably, '*religion*' occurs again, as a refrain, in three out of five declarative statements, neatly itemised below, but all of which seem, at best, instances of subdued and snide verbal offence and retaliation against the rival political party. (see Plate 3)

What follows at the bottom of Move 'C' text is a string of directive speech acts : "*This is the time for every Indian to resist those who are attempting to endanger the unity of our country*"; "*THINK. CONSIDER. DECIDE.*"; "*VOTE CONGRESS (I)*"; "*Vote for unity, stability and development*". All of these directive speech acts emphatically warn, exhort and seek the support of the target readership, the 'ideal' subject/electorate, in the forthcoming elections. Whether or not, and to what extent, such platitudinous directive speech acts would evoke the desired response from the 'ideal subject'/electorate, even without mention of valid rationale to support them, of course remains a matter of wild guess.

A notable feature of Congress (I)'s Move 'C' is the striking omission of an image from its text, except, of necessity, that of the party symbol. True, inclusion/ exclusion of an image from the text is the copywriter's absolute discretion. But, in the context of the ongoing mixed verbal-visual pattern of election advertisements discourse, the routine iconic image of the party symbol apart, the omission of an evocative image, such as that of a balance as in Move 'A' by BJP, comes with a rather negative implicature. Overtly, such an omission from the text of Move 'C' cannot be explained away in terms of space constraint, neither in those of the copywriter's free volition, etc.

Apparently, Congress (I)'s Move 'C' (see Plate 3) reflects the political party's disinclination, aversion or sheer inability to counter, with a more overpowering symbolic image, the elocutionary force of BJP's centrepiece eye-catching image of the balance with a ballot paper half-inserted into it (see Plate 1). This perhaps explains why Congress (I)'s Move 'C' opts for a small-sised text, more as a compulsive necessity than a free choice.

The text of Congress (I)'s Move 'C' is, nevertheless, compact and streamlined that ensures maximal focus on its key political agenda of '*religion*'. The brief text makes reference to '*religion*' quite a number of times. The refrain of '*religion*' is strikingly noticeable in both its banner headline, '*HOW CAN THOSE..... SPEAK OF RELIGION?*' and its sub-headline, '*Which religion is not ... man*?', as also in the text that follows it. However, the implicature that clearly emerges here is that Congress (I)'s recourse to its core agenda of '*religion*' seems indeed a fragile ploy of self-defence in the face of BJP's opening vehement salvo in Move 'A'.

Stage III: Move 'D' by BJP

Plainly, BJP's Move 'D' (see Plate 4) is a forthright and reasoned response to Congress (I)'s Move 'C' (see Plate 3). Since it is BJP's crucial Move —that tuns out to be its final one as well, as the political party withdraws from the ongoing discourse of election advertisements thereafter—it appears more forthright, frontal, scathing and decisive than its earlier Move 'A'.

The agenda of election advertisements discourse, initiated by BJP's Move 'A', is not only firmly pursued in its Move D but fortified more solidly and vigorously by giving it a sharper cutting-edge. Obviously, BJP felt emboldened by Congress (I)'s abysmal failure in Move 'C' to counter BJP's inventory of charges, made against it in its Move 'A'. By ducking those charges, meekly or otherwise, Congress (I) indeed proffered its political adversary, BJP, a wide leeway by default. So much so, even Congress (I)'s ploy of building up a parallel discourse in Move 'C' as a strategy of offence-cum-self-defence-cum-self-projection proved to be a damp squib.

Significantly, BJP's Move 'D' retains the overall discourse format of its initial Move 'A', as it sensed that the core points of agenda, set out in its earlier Move 'A', had hit the political rival squarely and surely. Nevertheless, the discourse format of Move 'D' is distinctly different from that of its earlier Move 'A' in significant ways.

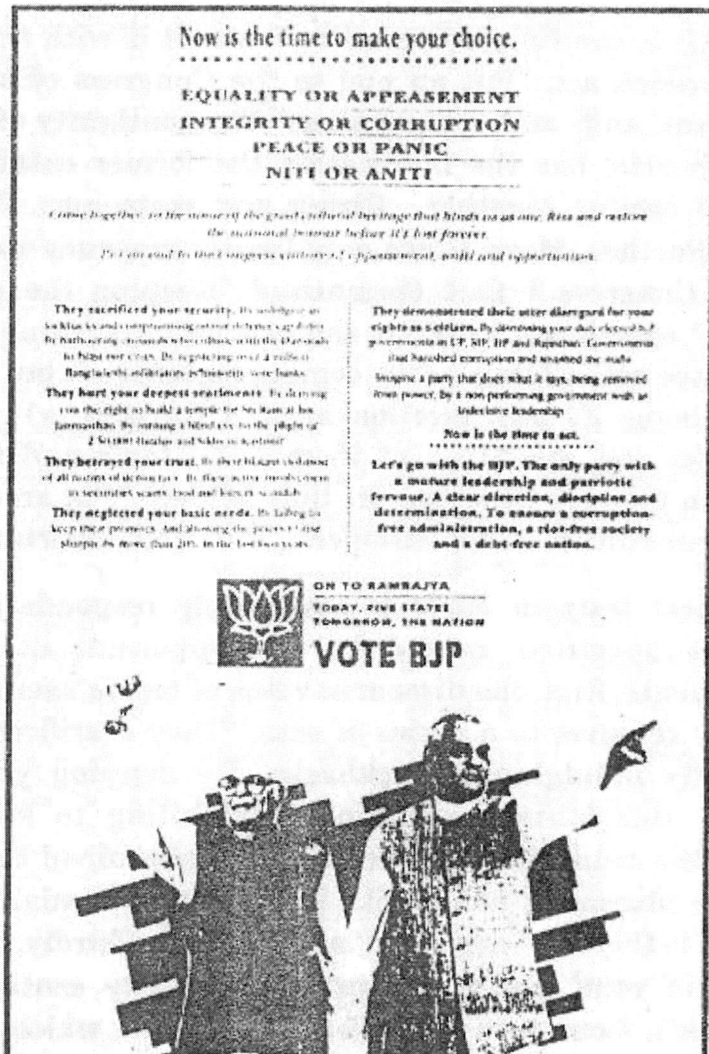

Plate : 4 *TOI/ 6 Nov. 93*

Plate 4

The sequential order of the thematised topic of discourse in Move 'A', '*APPEASEMENT OR EQUALITY*' is reversed and rephrased in Move 'D' as '*EQUALITY OR APPEASEMENT*' while the remaining part of the thematised topic of the text of Move 'D' is lifted *verbatim* from the text of Move 'A'. BJP's Move 'D' thus appears more neatly streamlined and sharply focused than its earlier Move 'A' :'*EQUALITY OR APPEASEMENT /INTEGRITY OR CORRUPTION/ PEACE OR PANIC/NITI* (morality) *OR ANITI* (immorality)'.

In line with its coherent pattern of discourse continuity, BJP's Move 'D' carries over a number of directive speech acts from its earlier Move 'A', though with their marked relocation in the text body. The directive speech act that makes banner headline of its earlier Move 'A', '*Now is the time to make your choice*', is retained *verbatim*, again in the same slot as the banner headline of Move 'D' text. Noticeably, more such directive speech acts— (i) and (iii) below—from Move 'A', are incorporated *verbatim* in the text of Move 'D', and given prominent placement for heightened overall focus:

(i) '*Come together in the name of the great cultural heritage that binds us as one. Rise and restore the national honour, before it's lost forever.*'

(ii) '*Put an end to the Congress culture of appeasement, aniti* (immorality) *and opportunism.*'

(iii) '***Let's go with the BJP. The only party with a mature leadership and patriotic fervour. A clear direction, discipline and determination. To ensure a corruption-free administration, a riot-free society and a debt-free nation.***'

One would note that some of the directive speech acts of BJP's Move 'A' got scoffs in Move 'C' by Congress (I). Taking due note of them, BJP's Move 'D' comes out with a well-crafted quick and pointed response to those charges of the rival political party. Its text is thus formatted with utmost attention to minute details. This would explain why BJP lifts a central part of the text from its earlier Move

'A' *verbatim* (see (i) and (iii) above), and places it higher up in the text to ensure that it gets sharper cutting-edge and added overall functional value.

The directive speech acts in (i) are followed by the directive speech act in (ii), which is a new addition to Move 'D' text. The functional value of the directive speech acts in (i) lies in sounding a wake-up call to the 'ideal' subject/electorate to rise up and protect the national unity and national honour. The functional value of the directive speech act in (ii) that follows it is more formidable and frontal. Not only does it refer to the rival political party specifically by the name, which underlines the aggressive tenor of the counter-attack, but, more significantly, it gives a clarion call to the 'ideal' subject/electorate to '*Put an end to the Congress culture of appeasement, aniti and opportunism.*'

The contiguity of the series of speech acts, (i) and (ii), has the implicature that the former, (i) entails the latter (ii). This 'implicates'[10] that by '*Come (coming) together in the name of the good cultural heritage that binds us as one. (and)Rise (Rising) and restore (restoring) the national honour before it is lost forever*' (i), the 'ideal' subject/electorate is urged to (because it can) '*Put an end to the Congress culture of appeasement, aniti (immorality) and opportunism*' (ii).

BJP's Move 'D' is indeed a sharp rebuttal of Congress (I)'s Move 'C', a goal well achieved through discreet formatting of its text. The text thematises four key points of its election advertisements discourse, mentioned at the top of the text and enumerated in a choice order of prominence:'*EQUALITY OR APPEASEMENT/ INTEGRITY OR CORRUPTION/ PEACE OR PANIC/NITI (MORALITY) OR ANITI (IMMORALITY).*' This seems to be a deft way to counter and debunk the rival political party's core agenda of '*religion*' brandished in its Move 'C':'*HOW CAN THOSE.... SPEAK OF RELIGION?*', '*Which religion...... brotherhood of man?*', '*No religion seeks.....*', '*No religion destroys...*', '*No religion sanctions...*'

In stark contrast to Congress (I)'s priority focus on the divisive political agenda of '*religion*', BJP's Move 'D' highlights its overriding political concern for unity :'*Come together in the name of the great cultural heritage that binds us as one.*'

By not mentioning the word '*religion*' even a single time in the entire text —-a subtle and smart move to slight and trash in one go the rival political party's much-flaunted political agenda of '*religion*'—BJP's Move 'D' not only shifts the limelight of election advertisements discourse away from '*religion*' but restores it back onto its own core political agenda of '*unity*', etc: '*Come together in the name of cultural heritage that binds us as one.*'

Notably, BJP's Move 'D' makes a focused reference to Congress (I)'s emotive agenda of '*sacrifice*'[11], often raised periodically in the public domain to curry favour of the electorate. The text of Move 'D' therefore contains a series of declarative statements, noted below, all aimed at blunting the opponent's possible discourse edge over use of the term '*sacrifice*', and many more such emotive talking points:

'*They sacrificed your security... By indulging in kickbacks... By denying you the right....By this blatant violation....By failing to keep....*'

The connotation of the term '*sacrifice*' is also downplayed and derided by collocating it with such incompatible words as '*security*', '*kickbacks*' '*hurt*', '*denying*', '*betrayed*', '*neglected*' and '*failing*'.

BJP's Move 'D' also debunks Congress (I)'s emotive plank of '*sacrifice*' by means of deictic anchorage of '*your*', instead of '*our*': *your security*/ sentiments/*trust*/*needs*. Plainly, all these declarative speech acts are addressed straight to the 'ideal' subject/electorate, rather than the 'real' one, the rival political party.

The text of BJP's Move 'D' contains, like that of its Move 'A', an image as well, in addition to that of the party symbol, which comes with a symbolic value. The image, printed in bold and placed at the bottom of the text, is, this time, that of its dual leadership, Atal Bihari Vajpayee and Lal Krishna Advani. The joint image of the top dual leadership underlines, in no uncertain way, the ethics of collective and transparent leadership that sets it apart from other political parties. The image of the two leaders, known for their leadership quality and staunch nationalism, also reinforces the verbal message of the text, printed in bold and placed mid-way on right side of the text :'**Let's go with the BJP. The *only party with a mature leadership and patriotic fervour.***' (the italics mine)

Stage IV : Move 'E' by Congress (I)

Going by the tenor of discourse, Congress (I)'s Move 'E' (see Plate 5) appears to be a terminal move, intended to conclude the ongoing discourse of election advertisements. Apparently, this is so because Congress (I)'s earlier offensive in Move 'C' evoked a belated response from BJP's Move 'D'.

Notably, BJP's Move 'D' text, a sharp retort to Congress (I)'s Move 'C' text, appeared in the newspaper, coincidentally, alongside Congress (I)'s Move 'E' text, on the same date, i.e. 6th November 1993. Naturally, Congress (I)'s Move 'E' does not (for it could not) take notice of BJP's Move 'D'.Nevertheless, it follows a discourse pattern markedly dissimilar from its earlier Move 'C'.

Congress (I)'s Move 'E' is, in the main, expressive, similar to its Move 'B', not offensive or denunciatory like its earlier Move 'C'. Its discourse pattern thus typifies expository speech acts.

With the 'real' subject, the rival political party, presumably out of the fray of election advertisements discourse—since BJP' Move 'D' text did not appear in the newspaper earlier than the publication of Congress (I)'s Move 'E' text—Move 'E' by Congress (I) apparently seems slated to be its Move finale. Move 'E' thus virtually effects a final encounter between Congress (I) top leadership and the 'ideal' subject/ electorate. The text therefore contains the image of its top leader, P V Narasimha Rao, then-prime minister (PM) of the country, placed at top-left vantage position in the text. Since the image is that of none else than the ruling PM of the country it intrinsically endows it with deep symbolic connotation.

The discourse value of the visual in the text is to help the 'ideal' subject/electorate readily identify and connect with the real addresser, the ruling PM of the country. More than its evocative implications, the image underscores self-projected credentials of strong leadership of the party securely ensconced in one individual.

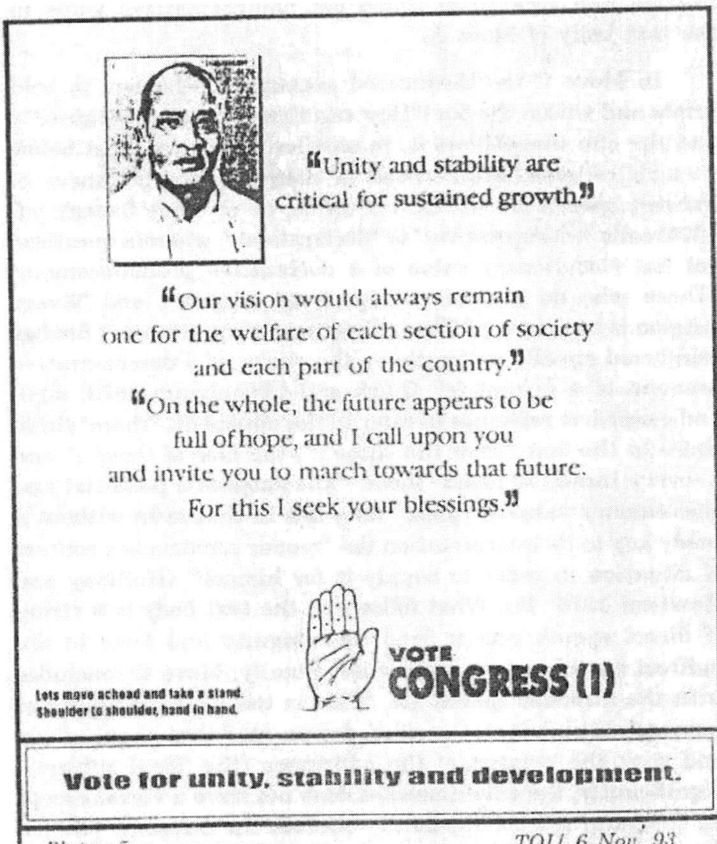

Plate : 5 *TOI/ 6 Nov. 93*

Plate 5

The text of Move 'E' (Plate 5) is however too brief, and is entirely restricted to a handful of famous pronouncements by the PM, cited within quotes. Naturally, they carry added elocutionary value in the context of instant discourse of election advertisements:

(a) **"Unity and stability are critical for sustained growth"**

(b) **"Our vision would always remain one for .... each section of society and each part of the country."**

(c) **"On the whole, the future appears to be full of hope, and I call upon you and invite you to march towards that future. .... For this, I seek your blessings."**

The implicature of these declamations by Congress (I) top leadership in (a) and (b) above is to raise the pitch of exhortation to the 'ideal' subject/electorate to vote for it in the elections in the name '**unity and stability**' of the country.

Notably, the directive speech act, '**Vote for unity, stability and development**', placed at the bottom of the text, is preceded by another directive speech act, a common refrain of election campaigns, '**VOTE CONGRESS (I)**' /VOTE **....**The recurrence of both these speech acts together in that sequential order as a footer in both the texts of Congress (I)—Move 'C' and 'E'—leads to the transparent implicature that '**VOTE CONGRESS (I)**'virtually amounts to '**Vote for unity, stability and development**'.

Move 'E' is an all-out ultimate attempt by Congress (I) to strike a personal rapport with the 'ideal' subject/electorate, all designed to wheedle them over to its side electorally. Hence the strategic choice of deictic anchorage of personal pronouns, spread across the entire text. The recurrent choice of quite a number of personal pronouns in the text, '**Our** vision', '**I** call upon **you** and invite **you** ...For this **I** seek **your** blessings' goes to reinforce this discourse pattern.

Move 'E', as mentioned earlier, seems, in the first instance, slated to be Congress (I)'s terminal move in the ongoing discourse of election advertisements. However, the choice of attitudinal disjuncts (underlined) in the utterance, 'On the whole, the future appears to be full of hope.....', gives away the implicature that the statement is more revealing than just being a summing-up comment. Indeed, the attitudinal adjuncts send out the unambiguous implicature that the statement clearly reflects a 'degree of doubt or lack of reality in what is said' on the part of the speaker (Quirk and Greenbaumm 1973: 8.50).

Further, the reference to '*On the whole, the future appears to be full of hope and I call upon you......to march towards the future*' also carries a negative implicature that the utterance is not only hypothetical but tamely apologetic too, as apparent from repetition the word, '*future*', twice over in the same sentence. What is more, it conveys a tacit admission that it has little discourse value in the present context, which is, obviously, what the copywriter obviously never intended!

The discourse tenor of the utterance also conveys an additional implicature that Congress (I), finding itself on back foot in the face of onslaught of charges levelled against it by BJP, opts to display, as a strategic ploy, its 'towering' hope in the 'nebulous' future.

Move 'E' was obviously slated to be Congress (I)'s final move in the ongoing discourse of election advertisements. Obviously, BJP did not choose to respond to it, possibly because Congress (I)'s Move 'E' contained all through expressive speech acts, expository as well as directive, that warranted little political response.

Stage IV : Move 'F' by Congress (I)

Provoked by BJP's Move 'D', Congress (I) re-joins the discourse of election advertisements by its Move 'F' (see Plate 6), contrary to its earlier overt signal in Move 'E' to conclude it finally. Congress (I)'s Move 'F', seemingly an afterthought, is thus a compelling necessity, as no political party would ever countenance its rival political party to walk away with a blistering attack on it without a reprisal.

Congress (I)'s Move 'F' eventually turns out to be its final Move to counter the attack of the rival political party. As this move is not responded to by another move by the rival political party, it offers Congress (I) fortuitous edge, if at all, over its political opponent in having the last word.

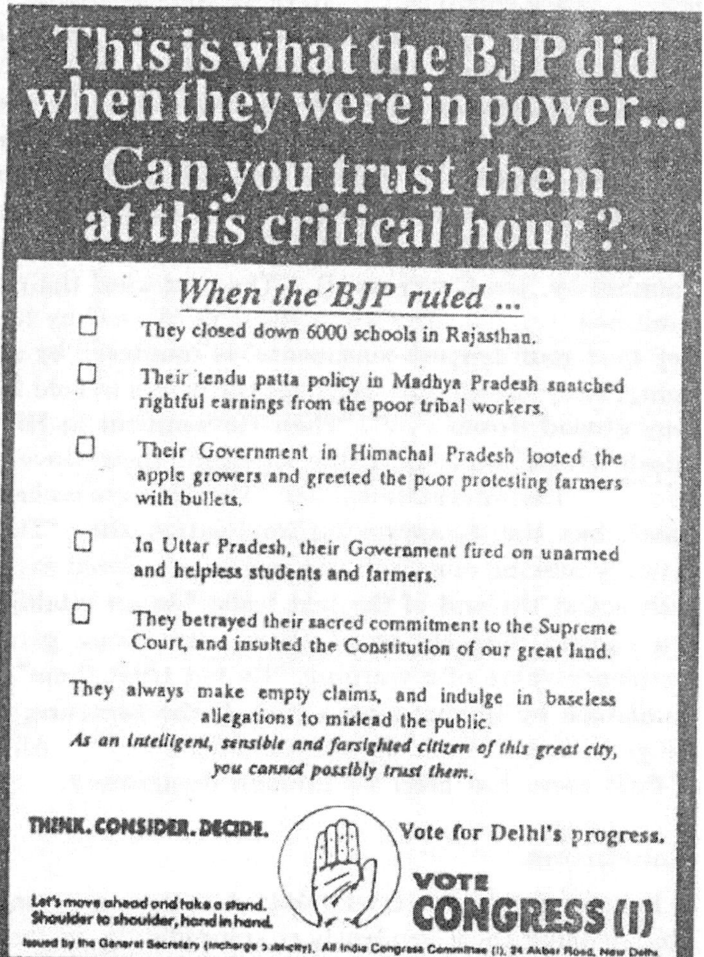

Plate : 6 *TOI / 7 Nov. 93*

Plate 6

The thematised sentences in bold fonts in box at the top of the text of Move 'F', '**This is what the BJP did when they were in power......**', '**Can you trust them at this critical hour?**' serve as a preamble to the speech acts enumerated in the main text below (cf. Leech and Thomas 1989:23). Also, the cleft-sentence structure (cf. Quirk and Greenbaum 1973: 14.5) of the header, '**This is what the BJP did when they were in power**....", helps narrow down parallel and contrastive focus on the speech acts that follow in the text. The functional value of the sub-header, '**When the BJP ruled**...', occurring in between the header and the main text below, lies in further sharpening this narrowed-down focus. The header and the sub-header of the text therefore seem a discourse necessity for, in their absence, the series of speech acts in the text, cited below, would have lost their discourse value:

> '*They closed down .....schools in Rajasthan.*'
> '*Their tendu...policy in Madhya Pradesh snatched rightful earnings...*'
> '*Their Government in Himachal Pradesh looted....*'
> '*In Uttar Pradesh, their Government fired...*'
> '*They betrayed their sacred commitments to the Supreme Court...*'
> '*They always make empty claims, and indulge in baseless allegations....*'

The adverbial clauses, '....*when they were in power*...', '*When the BJP ruled*', function as adjuncts to the thematised clause of the header, '*This is what the BJP did* ....'. The functional value of these clauses, having identical message value, is to fortify contrastive focus on specific instances of omissions and commissions of the rival political party when it was in power in the past.

The rhetorical interrogative, paired with the thematised declarative sentence of the header, '*Can you trust them at this critical hour?*' carries two-part implicature: (a) 'You cannot trust them . . .', and (b), 'In case you happen do so, you ought not to do so at least *at this critical hour.*' The two-part implicature of the sentence has the illocutionary force to ensure that the 'ideal' subject/ electorate does not perchance switch over allegiance to the rival political party, at least '*at this critical hour*' (on the eve of elections).

The rhetorical interrogative also reveals additional implicature of Congress (I) being in great jitters on the eve of elections, or else there is no reason why at all it should go overboard to this extreme extent of cajoling/begging the 'ideal' subject/electorate with pointed focus on '*at this critical hour*' (of elections).

The information speech acts in the main text have all the illocutionary value of castigating the rival political party :

'*They closed down 6000 schools in Rajasthan.*

....

They always make empty claims...... mislead the public.'

The said objective of Congress (I) is signalled right at the top of the text through thematised sentences in the header and the sub-header : '*This is what the BJP did...... Can you trust them........ hour*?'. The lexical texture of the text is therefore accordingly structured along the same line. The nodal word of discourse, *trust*, which recurs several times in the entire text, overtly/virtually highlights the focal discourse point of Move 'F' :

(i) 'Can you *trust* them....?' (in the header)

(ii) 'They closed down .....schools in Rajasthan.'

(iii) 'Their.....policy in Madhya Pradesh snatched rightful earnings from the poor .....'

(iv) 'Their Government in Himachal Pradesh *looted* (robbed) the apple growers and *greeted* the poor protesting farmers *with bullets*.'

(v) 'In Uttar Pradesh, their Government *fired* on unarmed... students and farmers.'

(vi) 'They *betrayed* their sacred commitment to ....'

(vii) 'They always make empty claims ....' (viii) 'As an intelligent ....citizen....you cannot possibly *trust* them.'

The illocutionary value of the nodal word *trust* that occurs first and last in the text, cited above, has, however, contrastive implicature of loss of trust, as distinct from trust itself, as apparent in (i) '*Can you trust them...?*' and (viii) '*As an intelligent...*

citizen....you cannot possibly trust them'. In the remaining clipped illustrations from the text as well, the focus remains centred around loss of trust, though virtually.

In both utterances, (vi) '*They betrayed their sacred commitment* (i.e. their trust)...' and (vii) '*They always make empty claims* (i.e. habitually betray their trust)', the emphatic focus remains, by implicature, on *loss of trust* of the people. Notably, the reference to loss of trust, by implicature, overtly/covertly, several times over in the text, carries the illocutionary force of a directive speech act, strongly asking the 'ideal' subject/electorate not to vote for the rival political party ever.

Consider the implicature of loss of trust in the following clipped illustrations from the text, along with their illocutionary value, detailed below :

(ii) '*They closed down....schools in Rajasthan.*'

Implicature: Closure of schools, a retrograde decision by any count, is an ample reason for loss of trust of the people in the rival political party, then ruling the state of Rajasthan.

Illocutionary value : The declarative sentence, an information act, acquires the subtle illocutionary value of a directive speech act.

Illocutionary force : The declarative sentence carries the illocutionary force of an exhortation to the 'ideal' subject/electorate not to vote for the rival political party in the elections again.

(iii) '*Their ...policy in Madhya Pradesh snatched rightful earnings from the poor.........*' Implicature : Snatching of rightful earnings of the poor, an anti-welfare measure, is a potent reason for loss of trust of the people in the rival political party, then ruling the state of Madhya Pradesh.

Illocutionary value : Consequently, the declarative sentence has subtle illocutionary value of a directive speech act.

Illocutionary force : The declarative speech act thus carries the illocutionary force of an exhortation to the 'ideal' subject/ electorate not to vote for the rival political party in the elections again.

Apparently, Move 'F' by Congress (I) is an all-out retaliatory assault on BJP, backed by a set of wide-ranging specific charges against the political opponent. Its sole objective is to outright denigrate and demolish the public image of the rival political party. So much so, quite glaringly, Move 'F' totally blanks out reference to its much-espoused and repeat political agenda of '*religion*' from the very ambit of election advertisements discourse.

Implicature: The blanking out of its much-espoused agenda of '*religion*' from the discourse ambit in its Move 'F' carries the manifest implicature of Congress (I)'s abject retreat from its core political agenda of '*religion*'.Its additional implicature is that Congress (I)'s total retreat from its core political agenda of 'religion' in its Move 'F' plainly uncovers its tacit acknowledgement/ acceptance of its discourse fault lines.

Illocutionary value: Notably, such a retreat by Congress (I) in its final Move 'F' comes tagged with the illocutionary value of a real political price, a negative implicature that the party has junked, indeed been made to junk, its core refrain agenda of '*religion*', at the end of election advertisements discourse.

Plainly, the 'ideal' subject/watchful electorate, if not the 'real' one, knows it for certain what implicature to deduce from this evolving discourse pattern of election advertisements. This is simply because he is commonly gifted with an uncanny sense to decipher by himself the implicature, as here, of why BJP never altered the basics of its core discourse agenda of election advertisements, in both its Moves, 'A' and 'D', whereas Congress (I), by parallel contrast, had to revise/retreat from its discourse agenda of election advertisements, right from the beginning, in each of its four Moves, 'B', 'C', 'E' and 'F'.

The raging battle of election advertisements discourse, with its Moves and counter-Moves, would have perhaps gone on and on if only there were no deadlines to keep for electioneering. Nevertheless, the foregoing discussion, even within the restrictive range of its data, seems to offer insightful view of how election advertisements discourse is—perhaps may be—manoeuvred, prudently or otherwise, as a virtual **weapon**—indeed a double-edged weapon—by the rival political parties in the high-stake battle of the ballot.

Which of the political parties wins or loses in the discourse battle of election advertisements depends critically on the illocutionary force of each of their Moves, more so, on its coherence and clarity. A range of ancillary factors of course do contribute to it in a major way, though not exclusively and conclusively, much like in a war. These determining factors, among others, are: Who starts off with the first Move and who concludes it with the final one, as in a see-saw, *in the real sense of the term*; whose agenda has a sharper cutting edge in the *real* context of situation; who employs it as a weapon of offence, defence, or both; who deftly remodels his discourse strategy in time in line with the evolving pattern of on-going discourse, etc.

Ultimately, it is the 'ideal' subject/electorate, gifted with an uncanny sense of judgement, who determines which political party has the upper hand in the ongoing discourse of election advertisements. Nonetheless, an incisive view of the dynamics of how he goes about doing this surely derives from the principle of **Relevance**, precisely its *extent conditions 1 and 2* (*op. cit.* Sperber and Wilson 1986), as also from Grice's **Cooperative Principle**, precisely, its *Maxims of Quantity*, *Relation* and *Manner* (Grice 1975: 45-46).[12]

The 'ideal' subject/electorate is tasked to not only negotiate between contrary orientations of election advertisements discourse—their strengths and weaknesses— but, far more importantly, sift through their polemics a verdict of his own free will and perception. Apparently, he does so with reference to the degrees of 'manifestness or more manifestness' of the communicative acts of the addresser (the concerned political party) and to the degrees of the latter's commitment to truths (assumptions, not propositions) (*op cit.* Sperber and Wilson (1986). His independent verdict on the ongoing discourse of election advertisements thus essentially derives from the principle of relevance, which is"basically a trade-off between informativeness" and "process ability" (Leech and Thomas 1989: 27), as well as from the degrees of critical balance maintained in the ongoing discourse structure between the Maxims of Quantity, Relation and Manner (Grice 1975).

Notes

1 This chapter is a revised version of my paper, published in **Issues in Stylistics**, Eds. Sharma, D D & Kumar, Ashok. Gurukul Publications, Lucknow. 2000.

2 For difference between cohesion and coherence in discourse, see Widdowson (1979 : 96-97).

3 "When we think of written, printed, filmed, or televised material, the significance of visuals is far more than obvious. Indeed, the traditional opposition between spoken and 'written' language has been overtaken by the events, and a much more helpful terminology in modern society would be spoken as opposed to *visual* language." (Fairclough 1989 : 27-28)

4 cf. "Not only does advertising help make products appear as aesthetically pleasing as possible, the advertisement becomes an aesthetic object itself."

5 "... since all discourse producers must produce with some interpreters in mind, what media producers do is address an ideal subject, be it viewer, or listener, or reader." (Fairclough 1989 : 49)

6 The term discourse is used here as a cover term having reference to both the individual texts of election advertisements in isolation, as well as the entire corpus of texts of election advertisements of this study that constitute the running discourse structure of election advertisements at both micro- and macro-levels.

7 Pierce (1960: 156-73) identifies three types of relation between a sign and its object, namely, the iconic (where the relation between sign and object is natural or motivated), the indexical (where the sign occurs in close association with object, as in metonymy), and the symbolic (where the relationship between sign and object is largely based on convention).

8 The entire body of election advertisements that appeared in *The Times of India*, New Delhi, from 1st to 7th November 1993, forms the corpus of this study.

9 The technical term 'implicature', coined by H P Grice (1975), has reference to the intended/ 'implicated' exhaustive meaning of the utterance, as distinct from its linguistic meaning that "radically undermines the message conveyed and understood." (Horn & Ward, 2005)

10 As Mey (2009 : 365) opines, "In Grice's approach, both 'what is implicated' and 'what is said' are part of speaker meaning. 'What is said' is that part of meaning that is determined by truth-conditional semantics, while 'what is implicated' is that part of meaning that cannot be captured by truth conditions and therefore belongs to pragmatics. Several types of implicature are distinguished ....The most widely accepted type of implicature is the *conversational implicature*." The term 'implicature' has thus reference to the pragmatic meaning of an utterance/communicative act in any form, conversational or otherwise, to the speaker/ addresser meaning rather than its linguistic meaning.

Both the words, '*implicate*' (verb) and '*implicature*' (noun) from which '*implicate*' is derived as a back-formation, have associative and restrictive reference in Pragmatics.

11 Congress (I) has often raised in the public domain the issue of '*sacrifice*' it has made for the nation, which has specific reference to the assassination of its leader and former prime minister of India, Indira Gandhi while she was still in office.

12 "Make your conversational contribution such as is required, at the stage at which it occurs, by the accepted purpose or direction of the talk exchange in which you are engaged. One might label this the maxims and sub maxims, the following of which will, in general, yield results in accordance with the Cooperative Principle. Echoing Kant, I call these categories Quantity, Quality, Relation, and Manner. The category of QUANTITY relates to the quantity of information to be provided, and under it fall the following maxims: 1. Make your contribution as informative as is required (for the current purposes of the exchange). 2. Do not make your contribution more informative than is required. Under the category of RELATION I place a single maxim, namely, 'Be relevant.' .... Finally, under the category of MANNER, which I understand as relating not (like the previous categories) to what is said but, rather, to HOW what is said is to be said, I include the super maxim – 'Be perspicuous' – and

various maxims such as: 1. Avoid obscurity of expression. 2. Avoid ambiguity. 3. Be brief (avoid unnecessary prolixity). 4. Be orderly." (Grice 1975: 45-46)

References

Barthes, R (1964): *Image, Music, Text* (Translation by S. Heath). Collins: Fontana. 1977.

Fairclough, N. (1989): *Language and Power.* London and New York. Longman.

Grice, H P (1975): 'Logic and conversation.' In P Cole and J Morgan ed. Syntax and Semantics 3: Speech Acts. New York. Academic Press. 1975.

Halliday, M A K and Hasan, R (1976): *Cohesion in English.* London : Longman.

Halliday, M A K (1978): *Language as social semiotic: The social interpretation of Language and meaning.* Edward Arnold. London. 1978.

Harris, Z (1952): 'Discourse analysis'. *Language*, 28.

Leech, G N (1966): *English in Advertising*. London: Longman.

_________ (1974):*Semantics*. Harmondsworth: Penguin.

Leech, G N and Thomas, J (1989) : 'Language, meaning and context: pragmatics'. In Collinge, N (ed.) *An Encyclopedia of Language*. London : Routledge.

Mey, Jacob L (ed.) (1998/2009) : *Concise Encyclopedia of Pragmatics*. 2nd edition. Oxford : Elsevier.

Hartshorne, Charles and Weiss, Paul (eds) : 'Elements of Logic'. *Collected Papers of Charles Sanders Pierce*. Vol. 2 (1932/1960). Cambridge : Massachusetts.

Quirk, R and Greenbaum, S (1973): *University Grammar of English.* London : Longman.

Sadock, J M (1974) : *Towards a Linguistic Theory of Speech Acts*. New York : Academic Press.

Searle, J R (1969) : *Speech Acts. An Essay in the Philosophy of Language*. CUP.

_________(1979) : *Expression and Meaning: Studies in the Theory of Speech Acts*. CUP.

Shaw, G B (1894) : *Arms and the Man*. London : Orient Longman. 1975.

Sperber, D and Wilson, D (1986) : *Relevance: Communication and Cognition*. Oxford: Basil Blackwell.

Vestergaard, Torben and Schroder, Kim (1985): *The Language of Advertising*. Oxford: Basil Blackwell.

Widdowson, H G (1979): *Explorations in Applied Linguistics*. OUP. 1980.

7

Towards Englishisation in India: From Code-switching to Code-intrusion

In abstract sense, the term *code* implies dynamic pattern of exchange of mean in—g sin a speech society, reflecting in the process its socio-semiotic reality (Halliday 1978:22).[1] As the exchange of meanings, or constellation of meanings, between people — primarily a language activity —occurs only in a 'social environment' (Haugen 1972:126), code is deemed "more than lexical, grammatical or phonological systems and structures" of language (Gregory and Susanne 1978: 75) that constitute it.

Elaborating the term code, Crystal (1985/1989:52) remarks: "The general sense of this term – a set of conventions for converting one signalling system into another – enters into the subject-matter of SEMIOTICS and COMMUNICATION theory rather than LINGUISTICS." However, he adds (*op cit.* 53), "...the most widespread use of the term was in the theory of communication codes propounded by the British sociologist, Basil Bernstein..." His distinction between ELABORATED and RESTRICTED codes was part of *a theory of the nature of social systems, concerned in particular with the kinds of meanings people communicate, and how explicitly they do this, using the range of resources provided by the language* (italics mine)" (*op cit.* :53). A part of the quote in italics has relevance inasmuch as it underscores the core concern of this study.

In sociolinguistics, the term code is "mainly used as a neutral label for any system of communication involving language" to distinguish it from "such terms as dialect, language or variety, which have a special status in their theories" (*op cit.*: 53).Notably, the term is a variable concept envisaging "any number of speech codes", and is free from value judgements since "there is no reason for believing that any one code is better than another" (Bernstein 1971:173).

Indian Speech Community

India, a subcontinent, is a land of diverse cultures and multiplicity of languages, yet the country exists as a cohesive nation, its far-flung geographical area and massive number of languages and dialects notwithstanding.[2] This places India in an enviable linguistic status very few countries of the world are placed in. What is particularly significant though in the Indian context is how most people across the vast country, from remotest geographical locations and speaking diverse mother tongue(s) (L_1), have devised a functional pan-Indian code of communication, becoming thus participants of the *Indian speech community.*

Code of Indian Speech

Code being a 'neutral' term (cf. Fishman 1972:22; Halliday 1978: 183), the label ***Indian speech code*** aptly betokens the overall communication code of the entire Indian community in pan-Indian 'context of situation' (cf. Malinowsky 1923; Firth 1957, ch. 14; Ellis 1966; Kachru 1966; Halliday 1978: pp. 2 and 28-29), which cuts across their disparate L_1 identities and geographical locations.

Indian speech **(IS)** subsumes overlapping choice of codes, or hybridisation of codes of different Indian native languages/ dialects, comprising two or more languages/dialects. The choice in language dependency in Indian speech occurs not only in terms of a bipolar contrast between the *inner circle* of Indian languages, such as Hindi/Punjabi, Hindi/Bangla, Hindi/Kannada, etc and the *outer circle* of non-Indian/second (foreign) language, precisely, English (cf. Kachru 1978), but in those of a complex configuration of both circles of languages, such as Hindi-Kannada-English, Telugu-Tamil-English, Kannada-Malayali-English, thus forming a typical code of *pan-Indian speech.*

Interestingly, Indian speech is marked by a linguistic paradox. Even as the contribution of Indian native languages remains massive and paramount in shaping the code of Indian speech what makes it so very typical is the crucial role of English in weaving together the Indian native languages in a cohesive and coherent code of pan-Indian speech.[3]

English occurs as a common constituent language of Indian speech in a major way across the country. This implies that English may co-occur in IS with an overwhelming majority of Indian native languages whereas the diverse native Indian languages may co-occur with only a few Indian native languages at best at a time. For instance, while, in the normal course, co-occurrence of Kannada with Assamese/Gujarati, or Kashmiri with Bodo/Telugu, etc seems a remote possibility, the co-occurrence probability of English with a vast majority of Indian native languages, including those just referred to, is maximal.

Such a pan-Indian speech scenario has now catapulted English to an ascendant position in Indian speech, culminating in its large-scale Englishisation. What is particularly significant about it is that this has happened—is still happening—quite unobtrusively and imperceptibly. And, notably, there seems to be no let-up in sight in near future from this relentless trend.

Englishisation of Indian Speech

Startling though it may seem, the process of Englishisation of IS gathered rapid pace since *after*-Indian independence in 1947, and the reasons for this stem from a variety of complex factors, including political. Englishisation of IS also appears impacted in no small measure by dominant functional role of English internationally that has coincided with manifold expansion in international and intranational travel and trade, fast growth in communication network world-wide, etc etc. These factors, though interesting in themself, are not discussed here because they are outside the focused area of this study. Instead, attention is confined to the dynamics of Englishisation of IS—the core patterns of how Indian speech has undergone large-scale Englishisation over a period of time —as well as its perennial fall-out on Indian speech/Indian native languages.

Englishisation of IS has occurred in multiple ways, and the process has been apparently seamless and unending. This makes a special case for in-depth study of its organic pattern of evolution.

The dynamics of Englishisation of IS is looked at here in a broad framework of inquiry : how it has evolved in phases, beginning with an open/voluntary incorporation of English in IS, culminating in its rather closed/involuntary or irreversible choice. Such a dynamic pattern of Englishisation envisions four phases of code-contact linguistic behaviour, namely, *code-mixing*, *code-borrowing*, *code-switching* and *code-intrusion*, all of which are functionally independent of each other, and not always occur in the sequential order mentioned here. This implies that, in a given code contact situation, the occurrence of any one of the four types of linguistic behaviour does not precondition or preclude the occurrence of the remaining three.

The four phases of code-contact linguistic behaviour in Indian speech are only broad categorisations, variable according to speech context at a given point of time. Further, there is always an ample room of overlap of instances of occurrence between these four types, even their slide from one category to another in course of time.

Code-mixing

Code-mixing is the initial and crucial stage of response to a code contact situation (cf. Ure 1972)[4]. It stipulates two or more languages/dialects to function as one text unit. It tends to be fairly open-ended, having no constraints on the linguistic pattern—

lexical, syntactic, etc—to go by, unless register-bound[5]. For this solitary reason, it is quite simple to employ in normal speech, and, most notably, linguistically highly productive.

Code-mixing of English in native Indian languages has been discussed in the literature at length earlier from various angles — pragmatic, linguistic, attitudinal and stylistic [cf. Kachru 1969, 1978 (a) and 1978 (b)]. Attention in this study, however, shifts to a rather unexplored dimension of the dynamics of code-mixing of English in Indian speech, precisely, the pattern of code-mixing of English in Indian languages as such.

This study is centred around **sample instances** of code-mixing of English in IS that feature an overall coherent pattern of Englishisation of IS prominently. What is more, all such instances of Englishisation are drawn from 'immediate situation' (Ellis 1966) of everyday Indian speech that have largely gone unmarked, even by the IS participants themselves.

Listed below are sample instances of English words and phrases, as well as English numerals and abbreviations **(EWPNA)**, commonly code-mixed in IS, whether as an isolated utterance or as an integral constituent of connected speech. They have been italicised/underlined/highlighted[6], wherever necessary, to bring out the expansive range of their occurrence as well as widespread distribution in Indian speech. A brief assortment of such EWPNA, occurring in a variety of IS registers, is noted below by way of illustration:

(1) Terms of addressing: *Mum/mom/mummy, papa/dad/daddy, uncle/uncle* ji, *auntie/auntie* ji, *sir/sir* ji, *madam/ma'am, madam* ji, *granny. Doctor* Saheb, *Professor* Saheb, *Registrar* Saheb, *Judge* Saheb, *Magistrate* Saheb, *Minister* Saheb, *DM/Collector/SP*/SDO/*BDO/CO/Manager/Engineer/ Compounder/Driver/Inspector* Saheb, *Master* (school teacher) Saheb/ji, *Ticket* Babu, *Train* Babu, *Guard* Babu, Hero. Interestingly, the relationship terms, *uncle/uncle* ji and *auntie/auntie* ji, have undergone extension of meaning, being now commonly used in IS as polite terms of addressing even strangers in a formal situation.

(2) **Forms of greetings/partings :***Hello (while receiving a call or drawing one's attention), High, Good morning, good evening, good night, ok, thank you, welcome (in response to 'thank you'), Nice to meet you, bye-bye, bye, see you, take care*, flying kiss, three cheers. thumbs up, congratulations/ congrats! well done!

(3) **Exclamation sounds, words and phrases:** *Ow*! *Wow*! *Shit*! Cheers! Three cheers! Thumbs up! congratulations/congrats! well done!

(4) **Relationship terms:** *Father, mother, uncle, aunt/auntie, cousin, nephew, niece, grandfather, grandmother, grandson, granddaughter, neighbour, landlord, tenant, doctor, nurse, patient.*

(5) **Terms of designation:** *Doctor, compounder, professo*r, *peon/orderly, security guard/officer, watchman, marshal, registrar, judge, magistrate, minister, prime minister (PM), chief minister (CM), MLA, MP, DM, collector, SP*, SDO, *BDO, CO, manager, engineer, Pilot, co-pilot, air-hostess*, d*river, inspector, master/*school teacher, *ticket collector (TC), travelling ticket examiner (TTE).*

(6) **Names of political parties:** *All*-Assam Gana Sangram Parishad, Janata Dal *(United*), Mizo *National Front,* Bhartiya Janata *Party*, Indian *National Congress, Nationalist Congress Party*, Communist *Party of* India, *All* India MIM, *All* India Trinamool *Party*.

Brand names of newspapers, magazines in Hindi and other native Indian languages: Nav Bharat *Time*s, Navodaya *Times*, Parichaya *Times*, *Daily* Punjab *Times*, New Delhi *Times*, Sandhya *Times*, Ranchi *Express, Mumbai Mirror*, Maharashtra *Times*, Imphal *Free Press*, Mumbai *Mirror*, Gujarat *Today*, Kerala Kaumadi *Flash*, Rozana *Spokesman*, Munsif *Daily*, *The* Inquilab, Navneet (Hindi *Digest*), Hindi *Express*.

(7) **Names of Indian Apps :** *Koo App*, *Mastodon*, *Paytm*, *Zomato, Swiggy*, *Phone* pe, Ola, *Bookmy show*, *flipcart*, *Redbus*, *OLX*, *MakeMyTrip*, *Hotstar*, *Map My* India, *Share Chat*, *Bigbasket*, *Dailyhunt* (news aggregator), *Myntra*, *One-mg*, *Snapdeal* (online clothing), *Hike* (messaging app), Faasos (food delivery app), *Zooncart*, Meru *cab*.

(8) **Names of shops, malls, restaurants, etc. in India:** Lucknow Chikan *House*, Aliganj *Plaza*, *cafe Broadway*, *Roof & Soup*: *Café & Restaurant*, Vansh *Square*, Paridhan *Ladies Collection*, *Tumble-dry Laundry* : *Dry Clean*, *Famous Readymade*, H Sugnamal *& Co.*, Shyam *Cloth Stores*, *Shopper Stop, Life Style*, Bangalore Central, Indore *Central*, Panta *Central*, *Pantaloons*, Reliance *Central*, Reliance *Trends*, Reliance *Jewels, Max Fashion*, *Westside*, *Splash fashion*, *Coffee Café*, Hotel Jayanti *Oasis Inn*, Kaveri *Emporium,* UP/Rajasthan *Handlooms,* KD *studio, NOIDA (New* Okhla *Industrial Development Authority*) *Film City,* Krishna *Tea Stall,* Yadav *tea stal and restaurant* (Yadav *Tea stall and restaurant*), *Sweet Shop, Cake Valley,* Bhasin *Medicals, Get-well Pharmaceuticals, Milk Parlour, Ice-cream Parlour, Beauty Parlour, Men's/Unisex Beauty Parlour, Hair-cutting salon, Vision Care, New Light Opticals, Big* Bazaar, Sahara Ganj *Mall, Phoenix United Malls, Phoenix Market City Mall, Fun Republic Mall, DLF Mall of India, Wave Mall.*

(9) **Names of Indian roads, highways, expressways, bridges in EWPNA:** *Ring Road, Outer Ring Road, Inner Ring Road, Link Road, Marine Drive,* Mumbai, *Marine Drive,* Kochi, *Lake View Road,* Bhopal, *National Highway (NH)* 1, 2, 3 ..., *The Golden Quadrilateral Expressway* (connecting Delhi, Mumbai, Kolkata and Chennai), *Elevated Expressway,* Bengaluru-Chennai *Expressway,* Ganga *Expressway,* Mumbai-Pune *Expressway,* Jaipur-Kishangarh *Expressway,* Ahmedabad-Vadodara *Expressway,* Delhi-Gurgaon *Expressway, Western Expressway, Eastern Expressway,* Manali-Leh *Highway,* Dankuni-Palsit *Expressway,*

Allahabad-*Bypass Expressway, Noida-Greater Noida Expressway,* Rameshwaram-Pamban *Bridge*, Bandra-Worli *Sea Link*, Howrah *Bridge*, *Napier Bridge*, Mathur *Aqueduct*, Godavari *Bridge*, Goshree *Bridge*, Zuari *Bridge*, *Broken Bridge*, Chennai, *Adam's Bridge,* Annai Indira Gandhi *Road Bridge*.

(10) **Common words/phrases of EWPNA, widely used in everyday Indian speech** : breakfast, lunch, dinner, strong, weak, weakness, pain, painful, bored, boredom, tired, tiresome, tension, relief, fresh air, smell, yummy, strength, power, energy, news, newspaper, magazine, views, comment, governance, eco-system, law and order, attack, war, judiciary, judgement, acquittal, bail, arrest, terrorist, anti-national, secular, pseudo-secular, human rights activist, liberal, start-up, breakdown, problem, anarchy, holiday, vacation, tour, journey, trip, hill station, tip, pre-paid service, fever, headache, medicine, pharmacy, operation, hospital, nursing home, speciality/super-speciality hospital, trauma centre, diagnostic centre, test (blood, etc) consultation fee, private practice, insurance, life, death, teacher, student, tutor, tuition, principal, director, exam, test, test udaan (flight), clerk, assistant, open university, tele-conferencing, video-chat, cable connection/operator, coaching institute/centre class, English medium school, house, building, housing society, flat, apartment, duplex, gated community, watchman, guard, Security (at the entrance of gated community), bodyguard, house maid/maid, painter, carpenter, cleaner, cook, driver, auto-rickshaw, cab, taxi, result, pass, fail, percentage, struggle, success, emotion, emotional, feeling, beautiful, nice, cute, ok, please, thank you, (you're) welcome, sorry, excuse me, birthday/birthday party, happy birthday, gift, return gift, change, exchange, 'time waste', guest, guest room/house, parking, home/car/agriculture loan, advance (money), credit, credit (also refers to credit balance in mobile phone), ATM (automated teller machine), on-line/net banking, debit/credit card, taxi, cab, office, school/college/ university fee, registration, registration fee/charge, service

charge, repair, last/due date, free, free, free, free offer/service, payment, home delivery, guarantee, warranty, traffic, traffic light, footpath (Indian English word for pavement/sidewalk), bus stand (Indian English word for bus stop), journey, airport, (railway) station, flight, flight/train fare, flight/train timing, domestic/international flight, airport terminal 1, 2…, escort (for VIPs), but, real, really, not really, otherwise, hopefully, not at all, luckily, fortunately, unfortunately, garden, nursery (reference to both nursery class in school and the place where plants and trees are grown for sale), sports, games, coach, instructor, champion, medallist, team mate, team manager, guide, guardian, tourist, friend, enemy, company, factory, sale, purchase, offer, mechanic, technician, (road) divider, circle, cheap, costly, expensive, bargain sale, actor, host, anchor, comedian.

All the instances of English words/phrases, listed above, are extensively used in everyday parlance of IS. Their usage is an absolutely free-will choice of IS participants. This is reflected in sea-change pattern of how IS community at large have virtually discarded even their traditional and centuries-old native terms of addressing their parents, such as **Babu ji/Pita ji/Bapu/Abba, Maan, Mata ji, Amma/Ammi, etc**, in trendy preference for their equivalent terms in English. The same is equally true of other sample instances of English words in Hindi, listed above, in multiple ways.

(11) Code-mixing pattern of EWPNA[7] inprint and visual media of Hindi[8]

Code-mixing pattern of EWPNA in Hindi media is discussed below from twin reference points: visual media, precisely, TV news channels of Hindi, and print media, precisely, Hindi newspaper advertisements, published in Hindi as well as English newspapers.

(a) TV channels of Hindi

(1) *Brand names of Hindi TV channels*

A hallmark feature of an overwhelming majority of Hindi TV

channels is reflected in trendy choice pattern of their brand names, marked by occurrence of EWPNA in the text, either in entirety or EWPNA code-mixed with Hindi.

Listed here are sample instances of the names of Hindi TV channels to illustrate the point.

Note, the occurrence of EWPNA in the list is highlighted in bold fonts whereas Hindi words, code-mixed with EWPNA, are shown in normal font.

ABP News, **NDTV India**, **TV 9** Bharatvarsh, **News 24**, **News 18**, **DD NEWS**, **DD NATIONAL, DD** Bharati, **DD** Kisan, **DD Retro, Republic** Bharat, **TIMES NOW** Nav Bharat, **Zee News**, **Zee Cinema**, **Zee Classic**, **CNBC** Awaaz, **News Nation**, Hindi **News**, Sudarshan **News Channels, & TV**, **Big Music**, **Colors TV**, **Sony Entertainment**, **Colors** rishtey, **Star** Utsav, **Star Movie** Hindi, **STAR HD, STAR PLUS, ST**BHARATI**HD, STAR WORLD**, **B4U Music**, **B4U Movies**, Maha **Movie**.

(2) *Template instances of EWPNA in Hindi TV news channels*

Ahead of further discussion, attention needs to be focused on template instances of EWPNA in Hindi TV news bulletins, listed below, that offer a broad preview of their expansive range of occurrence in Indian speech.

HEADLINES, *BREAKING NEWS*, *News/Interview LIVE, EXCLUSIVE, Zee News DNA (Daily News Analysis), Reality Show; Rescue Operation LIVE, Interview LIVE, test* udaan (flight) (underlined word in HDS), *media, press conference,* Gujarat *Investor summit,* 'Nayi' (New) *scrapping policy, automobile recycling industry*, '*Golden Boy*' (a reference to the Indian athlete who won a gold medal at Tokyo Olympics 2021), *award, prize, reward, hero, super-hero, Sensex, Nifty, tower, multiplex, emotion, emotional, bonanza, bargain, best bargain, summer/winter Sale, parliament winter/budget session, assembly, chief minister, governor, whip, chief whip, marshal, bill* (in parliament/assembly), *NCR* (National Capital Region) Delhi.

It needs special attention that all the numerals and abbreviations occurring in all the Plates (1-8) uniformly follow the script pattern of English in overwhelming preference to that of Hindi/other native Indian languages. The English pattern of abbreviations has been followed in Hindi and other native Indian languages long since, maybe for centuries. What is though special about them is that abbreviations of both English and Hindi words are transcribed now in ERS, as well asHDS, as required, depending on the context of situation, as in 'pee-em' (PM) (HDS) (Plate 1).

Notably, the use of English (ERS) numerals (1, 2, 3...), which was restricted to texts, books, newspapers, documents, etc in English only, earlier in the past, has now become the accepted norm of usage in all books, newspapers, documents, etc, written in Hindi and other native Indian languages as well, though in recent times.

Cited below are more illustrations that highlight the pattern of Hindi, code-mixed with EWPNA :**BRICS**, **JAI** (Plate 1), **NDA : 353**, **UPA : 96**, **MGB : 15**, **OTH: 78**, **G-20** *konferens* (conference) (Plate 3), '**18:36** (Plate 1), **09:02** (Plate 2), **TUE:21:05** (Plate 5), **SAT: 09:00** (Plate 6), **09:04** (Plate 7), **9** baj gaye (It is Nine) (Plate 8), **10** minit (minute) **100** khabaren (news) (Plate 6).

The discussion here centred around *select* TVSI samples of Hindi newscasts, code-mixed with EWPNA. Notably, the occurrence of instances of code-mixing is sprawling, being restricted to the Plates in which they occur here. However, it ought to be added that their pattern of occurrence in IS is becoming largely widespread now, extending far beyond the range of sampled instances from Hindi newscasts to other native Indian language TV news channels as well.

(iv) *Sample texts of Headlines from Hindi TV news channels, code-mixed with EWPNA:*

Cited below are samples of full texts of Headlines of four Hindi TV news channels—**Zee News**,

Republic Bharat, **India TV** and **News 24** —that illustrate *per se*the usage range and distribution pattern of Hindi, code-mixed with EWPNA, in popular Hindi news channels.

Zee News

18th August 2021: "jab *champions* (champion) (HDS) **Met Prime Minister**" (When Champions Met Prime Minister);20th August 2021 : "**NATO** ke videsh mantriyon ki *virtual meeting* (virtual meeting) (HDS) hogi." (A virtual meeting of NATO foreign ministers will be held); 21st August 2021: "**Zee TV** ka sabse bada *komedi sho* (comedy show)" (HDS) (The biggest comedy show on Zee TV.); "2024 ke liye *common minimum programme*" (HDS)" (Common Minimum Programme for 2024 (elections)); **Special Edition LIVE**; 1st September 2021: "Kabul *airport* (HDS)" (Kabul airport); "America-Taliban ki *secret deal ...secret gate* (HDS)" (Secret deal … secret gate between America and Taliban); 2nd September 2021: "Kabul se Ameriki nagarikon ka **EXIT** *plan* (HDS)" (Exit Plan of America citizens from Kabul); "Go hatya par *court* (HDS) ki chote" (Court Ruling on Cow slaughter).

Republic Bharat (HDS)

20th August 2021 : "*PM* (HDS) *walk-way* (HDS) ka udghatan kiya" (PM inaugurated the walk-way); "*Studio* (HDS) se **LIVE**" (Live from studio);"Hajaron nagarikon ka *airlift* karega **US**" (US will arrange airlift of thousands of civilians); "Taliban ne shuru ki *air-patrolling*" (HDS) (Taliban launched air-patrolling). 21st August 2021 : "Aaj ka *video*" (HDS) (Today's Video); "*Surrender* (HDS) karanein walon mein…". (Among those to surrender …); "**US** ka *rescue*" (HDS) Kabul mein kayee jagahon se" (Rescue operation of US from several places in Kabul); "*America* (HDS) ka *most wanted* (HDS) hai Hakkani" (Hakkani is the Most Wanted by America); "Taliban ki tabahi ka *countdown* (HDS)" (Countdown begins for the destruction of Taliban).

INDIA TV

21ST August 2021: "sabhi bharatiyon ko *lunch* (HDS) karaya, *airport* (HDS) rawana kiya gaya" (All the (exiting) Indians were given lunch and sent to the airport); "Sarkar ke sutron ne *kidnapping* (HDS) khabar ko galat bataya" (Government sources confirm that the news about kidnapping is incorrect); 24th August 2021 : "muft *ration* (HDS)" (Free ration);

News 24

Think First, 21st August 2021: "kerala mein corona *out of control* (HDS)" (Corona is out of control in Kerala); 23rd August 2021 : "**BREAKING NEWS, SUPER EXCLUSIVE**" " Jatiya gandana koyee *vote bank* (HDS) nahin" (caste census does not imply *vote bank* (politics)); "Trump se huyee *secret deal* (HDS)" (A*secret deal* was struck by Trump); "Mulla ka '*blue print*' *out* (HDS)" (Mulla's '*blue print*' is *out* (now)); "Roos mein Afganon ki *entry ban* (HDS)" (Russia's *Entry Ban* for the Afghanis).

The occurrence of EWPNA in the cited texts, whether appearing in ERS (shown in bold font) or HDS (marked in italics) indicates a clear pattern of their widespread distribution in IS. However, and most notably, this pattern of Englishisation is distinctly marked by nativisation of the language in IS in the sense that the instances of EWPNA in Hindi appear more often in HDS than in ERS.

(b) Code-mixing pattern of EWPNA in Hindi print media (newspapers)

Much like Hindi TV channels, newspapers, magazines in Hindi, as also in some native Indian languages, tend to show a similar trend of option for brand names in English, though with a difference that branding of their names mostly comprises native terms, code-mixed with EWPNA rather than EWPNA alone.The following list consists of sample instances of such brand names of newspapers and magazines in Hindi as well as some other native Indian languages: Nav Bharat *Times*, Navodaya *Times*, Parichaya *Times*, *Daily* Punjab

Times, New Delhi *Times*, Sandhya *Times*, Ranchi *Express, Mumbai Mirror*, Maharashtra *Times*, Imphal *Free Press*, Mumbai *Mirror*, Gujarat *Today*, Kerala Kaumadi *Flash*, Rozana *Spokesman*, Munsif *Daily*, *The* Inquilab, Navneet (Hindi *Digest*), Hindi *Express*, *Daily* Desher Katha, Dainik *Statesman,* Tripura *Times,* Kolkata *24/7, Independent 24/7,* Kranti Kannada *Daily.*

Attention for now is restricted to instances of only two sub-registral varieties of advertisements in Hindi, widely code-mixed with EWPNA: (i) Government publicity advertisements, published in an English newspaper, and (ii) Commercial advertisements, published in a Hindi newspaper.

Code-mixing of EWPNA in government publicity advertisements in Hindi and commercial advertisements in Hindi is a regular feature of Hindi as well as English newspapers. It thus forms a significant dimension of IS, specially inasmuch as it virtually serves as a role-model template for the evolving code-mixed pattern of everyday Indian speech.

A perceptible difference between code-mixing pattern of the two types of advertisements — government and commercial—is quite revealing. Government publicity advertisements, having a range of readership, normally employ Hindi, code-mixed with EWPNA, as a formidable means to gain access to comprehension level of the widest spectrum of target readership. Commercial advertisements, by contrast, have a limited objective to serve and a rather select range of target readership to access. For this reason, commercial advertisements are always invariably tailor-made, indeed innovatively designed, to grab lion's share attention of target addressee in a highly commercial market. With this end in view, they employ all available/known resources of language (s)to the hilt, for priority attention of prospective customers. These advertisements have thus texts in Hindi, code-mixed with EWPNA, not out of inevitable necessity, but, plainly, as a well-crafted strategy to hog attention of target readership.

Plate 11 is a scanned copy of a premium-value coaching institute commercial advertisement, published in a Hindi daily. It seems a down-to-earth instance of Hindi/IS, code-mixed EWPNA in so far as it has close proximity to everyday Indian speech. The text looks much like a collage of two languages, Hindi and English, too thickly glued with each other to neatly distinguish as to which language it really belongs to. Therefore, it stands out as an iconic instance of code-mixed Hindi/IS.

The advertisement is apparently addressed to intermediate-level middling-order job aspirants, struggling pretty hard not to miss even half-an-opportunity for a somewhat modest job. The text thus naturally employs an alluring variety of Hindi/IS, heavily code-mixed with EWPNA, that just matches their comprehension level.

A close look at the text would show that approximately 80 per cent of its space is covered by EWPNA, whether in ERS or HDS format, while its remaining portion is covered by Hindi. Except that the text is captioned at the top by two headlines in Hindi—— 'seedhe pravesh len' (Get direct entrance) and apnaa saal bachaayen' (save on a year's time)—followed by four headings in Hindi, mixed with EWPNA, later in the text —**(i)** 'kisi bhi warsh men *inter science math* **(PCM)** yaa (or) **ITI Pass**widyarthiyon ko seedhe dwitiya warsh men prawesh uplabdh' (Free and direct entrance for students to the Second Year Class, passing out with Inter Science Math **(PCM)** or **ITI** in any academic session), **(ii)** 'sarkari/ardh sarkari/*praivet* (private) karmachariyon ke liye doorastha uplabdh chhatra/chhtraon ke liye alag-alag *hastal* (hostel) ki suwidha' (Provision of facility for separate boys and girls hostel for out-station government/semi-government/private employees), **(iii)** 'yogyata : **10th Pass**' (Eligibility : 10th Pass), and **(iv)** '**SC/ST** ke liye wishesh chhoot' (Special concession for **SC/ST**),——the remaining portion of the entire text consists of overwhelming instances of EWPNA. Notably, these instances of EWPNA, listed below, appear in the text in either ERS or HDS format. A comprehensive list of the instances of EWPNA occurring in the remaining part of the text, in either ERS or HDS format, is given below to bring home the point :

- "**UGC, DEC, AICTE &UP Govt**. se manyata prapt (recognised)**Regular University** dwara (by)" "***politeknik***" (Polytechnic)
- " **Fee 1000/- Per Sem**"
- "**CIVIL, MECH., ELECTRICAL, CS, EC & AUTOMOBILE**"
- " Kisi bhi warsha men (passed in any academic session) *inter science math* **(PCM)** yaa **ITI Pass"**
- " **100 percent Job Placement Assistance**"
- " sarkari ...... *praivet* (private)......"
- "yogyata (eligibility) : **10th Pass**"
- " **SC/ST** ke liye wishesh chhoot (Special rebate for SC/ST)"

Climaxing this trend for over-all tilt for EWPNA, the text is finally rounded off at the end with a sizeable chunk which is entirely swamped by EWPNA in ERS format. The following citations from the text amply highlight the extent of scale to which Englishisation has impacted everyday Indian speech extensively :

"Contact at once Director ....UPPWD
Annie Besant ....Mgmt
GOMATI NAGAR...........29559251133."

Code-Switching

Code-switching is essentially a registral variety of language of every speech society—monolingual, bilingual or multilingual. Being register-bound, it is quite different from code-mixing which features free/random speech pattern of a bilingual/multilingual speech society. For this reason, code-switching has an added stylistic value in a bilingual/multilingual speech society such as the Indian speech community, if only because it reflects not only the context of text and the context of situation of its occurrence but also interpersonal rapport of formality-informality between speech participants[13].

Code-switching is the next crucial phase of evolution of Englishisation of IS. In variance with code-mixing, code-switching, from Hindi/native Indian languages to English, is a cohesive component of connected speech of pan-Indian parlance. It entails occurrence of EWPNA, though only as its subsidiary constituent, plainly because of its paramount discourse value. Thus instances of EWPNA, code-mixed with Hindi, discussed earlier, would invariably find place in the connected speech of Hindi/IS. What is revealing though about code-switching in Indian speech is its scale of occurrence that varies from higher to lower side in relation to upward/downward placement of IS participants on the cline of socio-economic-professional profile.

In Indian speech, *conversational code-switching* or *style-switching* to English from Hindi/native Indian languages is widespread in Indian parlance. Being a registral variety of language, the pattern of occurrence of conversational code-switching in IS thus naturally varies broadly in relation to social context, context of text and inter-personal relationship between IS participants. Cited below are some template examples of conversational code-switching in Hindi/IS to illustrate the point; herein, the "speaker switches codes (i.e. varieties) within a single sentence..... many times" (Hudson 1980/1987: 57), or in the same stretch of speech, from Hindi to English[14] (highlighted in bold font)back and forth many times over:

(i) *wah achha gaati hai* **but stage-fright** *se* **suffer** *karati hai.* Oose **self-confidence** ki kamee hai. (She sings very well but suffers from stage-fright. She lacks self-confidence.)

(ii) **Public** ko sab maloom hai ki kis-kis **department** *mein sabse zyada* **corruption** hotaa hai, **but, you know**, kaun dekhega. Kissi ko koi **interest** nahi hai. **Political parties** ko kewal apne **vote bank** ki chinta rahati hai. **Most importantly**, sabhi ko kewal **over night rich** banana hai, **by hook or by crook**. (The public knows fully well about the Departments where corruption is most rampant, but, you know, who cares. The political parties are only concerned with safeguarding their vote bank. Most importantly, everybody wants to get rich overnight by hook or by crook.)

In both (i) and (ii), the words in bold font are from English whereas the remaining words are from Hindi. The template illustrations of conversational code-switching in Indian speech, widespread and trendy, feature everyday Indian speech of a majority of mid-level-to-upscale Indians who opt for it quite frequently. They do so as a matter of course, especially by force of habit or for sheer attitudinal reasons, despite having a fair proficiency in Hindi/their native language.Consequently, Hindi and other native Indian languages, suffer irreversible loss of their pristine character, yielding place to progressive Englishisation of Indian speech in course of time.

Indian speech undergoes Englishisation by yet another pervasive pattern of code-switching, called *metaphorical code-switching.*[15] Herein, interlocutors manoeuvre speech norms of code-switching just as naturally as they manoeuvre those of their native language by virtue of their ingrained proficiency in both Hindi/other native Indian languages and English. Since metaphorical code-switching occurs well glued in connected Indian speech, like chaff with the wheat, it goes practically unnoticed by the interlocutors. Its scale of occurrence is also variable, as in conversational code-switching, from higher to lower side in relation to upward/ downward placement of the Indian interlocutors on the cline of socio-economic-professional profile.

Metaphorical code-switching comes with a vital discourse value in Indian speech. It helps interlocutors fine-tune their discourse pattern, more easily while they stay on the same wavelength of interpersonal rapport in the same context of situation. What is more, it often makes their personal rapport more chatty, cohesive and intimate. Metaphorical code-switching occurs in Indian speech mostly, if not always, in informal context of home and casual get-togethers.[16] Being so, IS interlocutors have time and liberty to ramble on diverse areas of conversation, ranging from household affairs, professional life, politics to a lot more.

Metaphorical code-switching seems quite distinctive plainly because of its complex discourse pattern of seamlessly stringing together disparate languages (varieties) in one unit of cohesive discourse.

IS interlocutors resort to metaphorical code-switching to English in formal situation as well, though not frequently, as a handy means to signal their attitudinal/emotional shift vis-à-vis the addressee. For instance, a teacher of Hindi/native Indian language code-switches to English metaphorically to congratulate the students, or signal a stern warning to them against misbehaviour.[17] Similar reasons hold true in case of mid-level-to-upscale IS interlocutors who opt for it in office/work-place to signal a message of vital importance

Code-borrowing

Code-borrowing is distinct from both code-mixing and code-switching if only because it has operational autonomy, which implies that it does not stipulate occurrence of two or more languages to function, though it does not preclude co-occurrence with them. Being free of any 'constraints'—linguistic or socio-cultural (discussed earlier in Chapter 4; cf. Dubey 1978: 40-51)—it may best be considered a *sui generis* type of linguistic occurrence.[18] Nevertheless, it remains a normal and vital component of a language (variety).

Interestingly, the option choice for code-borrowing is voluntary on the part of a speech participant/society. It shows their outright free preference for trendy terms/coinages of dominant language (s) of the day, just to approximate their speech code with that of their evolving language styles, rather than on account of abject paucity of their substitutes in the native language. The option for code-borrowing also reflects, in a way, linguistic laziness of a speech society to innovate new terms/templates to meet surging demands of communication as they emerge from time to time.

Most instances of code-borrowing have a short 'shelf life'. However, some of them last long enough to have cascading effect on speech code pattern of a community. Indian speech, born out of interplay between vast linguistic diversities of the country, offers a most burning example of widespread tilt for code-borrowing from

English. Notably, the spiralling trend of code-borrowing from English has impacted Englishisation of Indian speech in a big way.

Code-borrowing from English in Indian speech has been pervasive in diverse areas of Indian speech since long. However, attention is here restricted to only some of the instances of code-borrowing from English to highlight how crucially they impact various facets of everyday Indian speech.

The instances of code-borrowing, discussed below, are all drawn from comprehensive list of instances of code-mixing, discussed earlier. Hence, they are not all listed here again to avoid their repetition. Instead, attention is focused on only such samples from the earlier list that illustrate how even as they appear, in the first place, as examples of code-borrowing, they also function as instances of code-mixing from English, depending on the context of their occurrence.

Forms of addressing

Forms of addressing[19] such as ***mum/mom/mummy, dad/daddy, uncle, aunt/auntie, sir/madam, doctor*** an***d teach***er in Indian speech are all, in the first place, instances of code-borrowing from English. They function as instances of code-borrowing in Indian speech only till they occur as an isolated utterance, as a form of addressing, as in ***uncle, doctor, sir,*** etc. However, they function as instances of code-mixing if clubbed with a Hindi/other native Indian language word (in italics), as in ***uncle*** *ji,* ***doctor*** *saheb*, ***sir*** *ji*, or when occurring in connected Indian (Hindi) speech, as in '***Mum****ki baat maien hamesa dhyaan sei suntaa hun*'. (I always listen to whatever mum says attentively.)

Forms of greeting and parting

Code-borrowing of various forms of greeting and parting from English is now well ingrained in Indian speech. This is reflected in pan-Indian parlance of a majority of mid-level-to-upscale Indians overwhelmingly, if not absolutely. Notably, this pattern of IS goes together with either complete discard of substitute traditional terms in Hindi/other native Indian languages or their sparing use. Both ways, it has dented the pristine character of native Indian languages irretrievably. Sample instances of English forms of greeting and parting, now a cohesive component of IS, listed below, would illustrate the point :

Hello/Hi (while receiving a telephone call or drawing one's attention), Good morning/Morning, Good evening, Good night, Ok, Thank you, (You're) Welcome (in response to 'Thank you'), Nice to meet you, Bye-bye/bye, See you, Take care.

Exclamation sounds, words and phrases

Trendy code-borrowing of sounds, words and phrases from English in Indian speech, a fairly recent phenomenon, seems rather disconcerting for the cardinal reason that exclamation sounds/ words/phrases are deemed inherent markers of genre code of a speech community. Thus, code-borrowing of exclamation sounds, words and phrases from English, as replacement of existing substitutes in native language (s), seems outright outlandish in Indian speech. Nevertheless, it features high-end style of Indian speech. Amazingly, such instances of exotic code-borrowing from English are gathering fast pace in Indian speech in recent times, especially among upscale-to-mid-level IS participants. Surely, this foreshadows the emerging contour of Indian speech in foreseeable future. Listed below are sample instances of code-borrowing of sounds, words and phrases from English in IS that illustrate the point:

Ow! *Wow*! Ouch! *Shit*! *Cheers! Three cheers! Thumbs up! Congratulations/Congrats! Well done*!

Relationship terms

Code-borrowing of relationship terms from English[20] is yet another salient marker of Indian speech. IS participants, irrespective of their socio-linguistic profile, commonly prefer using English words such as ***father, mother, uncle, aunt, cousin, nephew, niece***, especially in formal context all across the country, discarding native substitutes in Hindi/other Indian languages. This seems not only trendy but sounds outright astounding for the simple reason that, in the process, it ignores, even undermines, the rich repertoire of specific relationship terms in Hindi/other native Indian languages.

As sample illustration, consider the terms **uncle** and **grand father** in English vis-à-vis a range of their precise native substitutes in Hindi/other Indian languages. **Uncle** functions as a cover term in English to refer to brother of both father and mother, husband of both father's sister and mother's sister, whereas, in Hindi, the dominant language of Indian speech, *specific* native terms are available to denote these relationships, *chaachaa*, *maamaa*, *phuphaa* and *mausaa*, respectively. Likewise, **grandfather** is a cover term in English that refers to father of both father and mother, whereas corresponding *precise* relationship terms in Hindi, are *daadaa* and *naanaa*.[21]

Terms of designation

Indubitably, the terms of designation in English have virtually swamped pan-Indian speech, impacting important spheres of Indian life. A reference to their sample instances has already been made in the earlier section on code-mixing. Here, only a select list of their instances is given below to underscore their sweeping range of occurrence in Indian speech.

A select list of instances of code-borrowing of English terms of designation in IS, categorised under broad heads below, would show how it has widely impacted crucial facets Indian speech:

Health : doctor, surgeon, physician, compounder, dresser, nurse, sister, matron, ward boy.

Education : teacher, lecturer, professor, principal, chancellor, vice-chancellor, registrar.

Governance: president, vice-president, prime minister, minister, governor, chief minister.

Judiciary: judge, (chief) justice, advocate, attorney general, solicitor general, counsel.

Administration: magistrate, collector, inspector/superintendent/ commissioner of police.

Security: watchman, security guard, duty officer, captain, lieutenant, major, colonel.

Transport: driver, conductor, pilot, co-pilot, air hostess, purser, ticket collector, sailor[22].

Code-borrowing of English words/phrases in diverse contexts of Indian speech

The pattern of code-borrowing of English words/phrases (EWP) is illustrated with sample instances from diverse contexts of Indian speech, listed below under various heads for focused attention. The listed instances would offer a panoramic view of their heterogeneous pattern of occurrence in IS. More than that, they underscore how, as a catalyst, they crucially contribute to extensive Englishisation of IS.

The trendy choice of code-borrowing of EWP in IS, as mentioned earlier, is absolutely voluntary, not necessarily constrained by lack of their suitable substitutes in Hindi/other native languages. The instances of EWP, listed below, are shown in italics to mark off their pattern and scale of occurrence prominently.

Names of Indian political parties

Bharatiya Janata *Party*, Janata Dal *(United)*, Mizo *National Front,* Indian *National Congress*, *Nationalist Congress Party*, Communist *Party of* India, *All* India MIM, *All* India Trinamool *Congress*.

Names of newspapers, magazines in Hindi and other Indian native languages

Nav Bharat *Times*, Navodaya *Times*, Parichaya *Times*, *Daily* Punjab *Times*, New Delhi *Times*, Sandhya *Times*, Ranchi *Express,* Mumbai *Mirror*, Maharashtra *Times*, Imphal *Free Press*, Gujarat *Today*, Kerala Kaumadi *Flash*, Rozana *Spokesman*, Munsif *Daily*,

The Inquilab, Navneet (Hindi *Digest*), Hindi *Express*.

Names of Indian Apps

KooApp, *Mastodon*, *Paytm*, *Zomato, Swiggy*, *Bookmyshow*, *flipcart*, *Redbus*, *OLX*, *MakeMyTrip*, *Hotstar*, *Map My* India, *ShareChat*, *Bigbasket*, *Dailyhunt* (news aggregator), *One-mg*, *Snapdeal* (online clothing), *Hike* (messaging app), Faasos (food delivery app), *Zooncart*, Meru*cab*.

Names of Indian TV channels in Hindi

ABP News, *NDTV India*, ***TV 9*** Bharatvarsh, *News 24, News 18, DD NEWS, DD NATIONAL, DD* Bharati, *DD* Kisan, *DD Retro*, *Republic* Bharat, *TIMES NOW* Nav Bharat, *Zee News, Zee Cinema*, *Zee Classic, CNBC*Awaaz, *News Nation*, Hindi *News*, Sudarshan *News Channels*, *& TV, Big Music, Colors TV, Sony Entertainment, Colors* rishtey, *Star* Utsav, *Star Movie* Hindi, *STAR HD*, *STAR PLUS, STAR*BHARATI *HD*, *STAR WORLD, B4U Music, B4U Movies*, Maha*Movie.*

Names of shops, malls, restaurants, etc in India

CafeBroadway, *Roof & Soup*: *Café & Restaurant*, *Coffee Café*, *Tumble-dry Laundry* : *Dry Clean*, *Famous Readymade*, *ShopperStop, Life Style*, *Pantaloons*, *Max Fashion*, *Westside*, *Splash fashion*, Hotel Jayanti *Oasis Inn*, Kaveri *Emporium,* UP/ Rajasthan *Handlooms,* KD *studio, NOIDA Film City,* Krishna *Tea Stall*, *Sweet Shop, Cake Valley, , Get-well Pharmaceuticals, Milk Parlour, Ice-cream Parlour, Beauty Parlour, Men's/Unisex Beauty Parlour, Hair-cutting salon, Vision Care, New Light Opticals*, *Phoenix United Malls*, *Phoenix Market City Mall*, *Fun Republic Mall*, *Wave Mall.*

Names of Indian roads, highways, expressways, bridges in EWPNA

Ring Road, Outer Ring Road, Inner Ring Road, Link Road, Marine Drive (Mumbai/Kochi)*Lake View Road,* Bhopal, *National*

Highway (NH) 1, 2, 3 ..., *The Golden Quadrilateral Expressway, Elevated Expressway,* Bengaluru-Chennai *Expressway,* Ganga *Expressway,* Mumbai-Pune *Expressway,* Ahmedabad-*Western Expressway, Eastern Expressway,* Patna *Bypass,* Allahabad-*Bypass Expressway, Noida-Greater Noida Expressway,* Rameshwaram-Pamban *Bridge*, Bandra-Worli *Sea Link*, Howrah *Bridge*, Mathur *Aqueduct*, Godavari *Bridge*, *Broken Bridge* (Chennai), *Adam's Bridge.*

Titles of Indian movies

Hindi : *The Burning Train, Wanted, Guide, Mother India, Leader, CID, My Mary, Love in Tokyo, Love in* Simla**, *Love in*** Goa**,** *Love Story, Street Singer, Taxi Driver, Bluff Master, An Evening in Paris, Five Rifles, Bullet, Warrant, Jewel Thief, Love and God, Fifty-fifty, Houseful 2, Gangs of Wasseypur, Cocktail, Oh My God, Student of the Year, Race 2, Special 26, ABCD—Any Body Can Dance, Murder 3, The Attacks of 26/11, 3 G, Commando—A One Man Army, Go*—Goa—*Gone, D Day, Horror Story, The Lunchbox, Warning, Super Model, Boss, Wake UpIndia.*

Tamil : *Indian, Gentleman, Autograph, Market Street, Jeans, Boys, Anytime Anywhere.*

Malayalam: *Virus, Helen, Bodyguard, Mr Fraud, Law Point, God's Own Country, The Last Supper.*

Telugu :*Leader, Orange, Wanted, Mr Perfect, Oh My Friend, Bodyguard, Businessman.*

Kannada: *Bell bottom, Googly, Love Moktail, K.G.F, I Love You, Mass Leader.*

Code-Intrusion

Code-intrusion stands well apart from code-mixing, code-switching and code-borrowing each, and is yet similar to each of them in a way. Like code-mixing/switching/borrowing, code-intrusion is also a core component of code dynamics of a bilingual/multilingual speech society. Indeed, it is their ultimate outcome as instances of code-intrusion are all initially sourced from code-mixing/switching/borrowing. However, what makes code-intrusion singularly distinctive is the extent of its expanse and select pattern of its occurrence in the relevant bilingual/multilingual speech society.

Code-intrusions relatively take a much longer pace of transition than code-mixing/switching/borrowing to occur and coalesce with the code of a bilingual/multilingual speech society. Plainly, this is because they evolve in stages, from being reversible/partial to becoming irreversible/complete. Likewise, they require more concerted effort and longer time span to reverse and discard, if at all, than code-mixing/switching/borrowing, once they have merged with the code of a bilingual/multilingual speech society.

The canvas of code-intrusion is expansive enough to impact one level or more of linguistic structure, much like that of code-mixing/switching/borrowing. However, its pattern and extent of occurrence varies from one bilingual/multilingual speech society to another. Thus, the pattern of code-intrusions in bilingual/multilingual Indian speech society would be different from that of a non-Indian speech society.

The occurrence pattern of code-intrusions is marked essentially by evolving need-based communicative efficacy/exigencies of a bilingual/multilingual speech society. In this way, it is not precisely conditioned by sequence order in which code-mixing/switching/borrowing normally evolve. Further, even as some instances of code-intrusion, discussed below, also appear as those of code-mixing/switching/borrowing, discussed earlier, only some of them fall within the ambit of code-intrusion in course of time.

The dynamics of code-intrusions of EWPNA in Indian speech is discussed here with sample instances from across Indian speech.[23] Since the pattern of code-intrusions covers a wide spectrum of Indian speech, it seems expedient to discuss it under the following broad heads:

(a) Terms of address

Code-intrusion of English terms of address, greetings, partings and endearment, listed below, is intrinsic to common parlance of Indian speech, irrespective of socio-linguistic-geographical profile of Indian community. However, the occurrence of some terms of endearment such as *hi, dear, darling* and *sweetie* is largely restricted to mid-level-to-upscale Indian speech participants.

Sir, madam, miss, nurse, sister (in school/hospital), *matron* (in hospital), *papa, dad/daddy, mum/mom/mummy*; *good morning, good evening, good night, bye-bye/bye*; *hello* (in telephonic conversation as well as for calling someone's attention), *hi*; *dear, darling, sweetie.*

(b) Choice of initial of a person's forename, or the first letters of all the names of a person or thing,[24] after English orthographic/ ERS (English Roman Script) convention

Indian speech is prominently marked by code-intrusion of English orthographic/ERS convention of abbreviation that employs the initial of a person's forename or the first letters of all the names of a person/thing in English (ERS). This template of abbreviation is the prevailing norm in pan-Indian speech, followed uniformly for ages. Interestingly, recent attempts to reverse this convention in favour of improvised model of abbreviations after Hindi orthography/HDS (Hindi Devanagari Script) convention or that of other Indian native languages have had only display value, restricted to written form.

Sample instances of names of persons, together with initial (s)of their forename (s), are cited below to illustrate how ERS convention of abbreviation is uniformly followed in pan-Indian speech:

S Radhakrishnan : Sarvepalli Radhakrishnana
V V Giri : Varahagiri Venkata Giri
A P J Abdul Kalam : Abdul Pakir Jainulabdeen Abdul Kalam
A B Vajpayee : Atal Behari Vajpayee
L K Advani : Lal Krishna Advani

M S Swaminathan : Monkombu Sambasivam Swaminathan
M S Subbulakshmi : Madurai Shanmukhvadivu Subbulakshmi.

Interestingly, initials of forenames of persons in the list, as also outside it in Indian speech at large, are used as abbreviations after ERS convention, whether they occur in English texts or texts of Hindi or other native Indian languages. What is quite revealing though is how it crucially impacts the code of Indian speech. For instance, the initial 'S' in S Radhakrishnan is spelt as 'es' whenever they occur in the texts of HDS/other native Indian languages in keeping with ERS convention of abbreviation, and ***not*** as 's', the *initial letter and sound* of 'Sarvepalli', after HDS/script pattern of other native languages. Same is the case with the remaining sample names in the list. This underscores how ERS convention of abbreviation has intruded the code of Indian speech quite thoroughly, not only orthographically but also phonetically.

(c) Code-intrusion of ERS in diverse contexts of Indian speech

Code-intrusion of ERS in Indian speech is too massive in scale to be discussed comprehensively in a brief study as the present one. Therefore, its sample instances are only cited below under various heads to illustrate how they have crucially impacted a broad spectrum of Indian speech. Instances of code-intrusion of ERS in the choice pattern of name of organisations, companies, political parties and so on, listed below, along with their abbreviation/acronym, underscore this point.

(i)*Names of organisations and companies and their abbreviation/ acronym*

Union Public Service Commission (**UPSC**), Lal Bahadur Shastri National Academy of Administration **(LBSNAA)**, Tata Institute of Fundamental Research **(TIFR)**, Indian Space Research Organisation **(ISRO)**, Gas Authority of India Ltd. **(GAIL)**, Oil and Natural Gas Corporation Limited **(ONGC)**, Tata Iron and Steel Company Ltd. **(TISCO)**, Tata Engineering and Locomotive Company Ltd. **(TELCO)**, Hindustan Machine Tools Ltd. **(HMT)**,

Bharat Heavy Electricals Ltd. **(BHEL)**, National Thermal Power Corporation Ltd **(NTPC)**, Steel Authority of India Ltd **(SAIL)**, Hindustan Aeronautics Limited **(HAL)**, Hindustan Petroleum Corporation Limited **(HPCL)**. Press Trust of India **(PTI)**, Asian News International **(ANI)**, United News of India **(UNI)**, Unit Trust of India **(UTI)**, State Bank of India **(SBI)**, All India Radio **(AIR)**, Indian Premier League **(IPL)**, The Board of Control for Cricket in India **(BCCI)**, **UP** *Rajya Utpadan Nigam* Ltd (italics in HDS).

Lately, sporadic attempts to coin abbreviations/acronyms in Indian speech after HDS/native Indian languages have been, at best, either casual or partial, and have thus met with little success. For instance, a government organisation in the state of Uttar Pradesh is named in Hindi Devanagari Script (HDS), transliterated, ***oo. pra***. *pradushan niyantran bord* (English version : U.P. Pollution Control Board). The native choice of ***oo. pra*** as abbreviation of Uttar Pradesh after HDS convention has got absolutely no traction in Indian parlance, especially phonetically. The native template abbreviation, ***oo. pra.***, and the like of it, remains, at best, in print only, as it is never so uttered in Indian speech. This foray into nativised version of abbreviation stands out in sharp contrast to the normal practice of using 'U.P.' as abbreviation of Uttar Pradesh after ERS pattern of abbreviation, cited last in the list above, **UP** *Rajya Utpadan Nigam* Ltd (italics In HDS).

(ii) Names of Indian political parties and their abbreviation/ acronym

Code-intrusion of ERS pattern in the choice of name of Indian political parties, as well as its acronym, is quite common in Indian speech. Sample instances of their names, together with their acronym (given in brackets), are cited below by way of illustration.

Asom Gana Parishad **(AGP)**, Aam Aadami Party **(AAP)**, All Party Hill Leaders Conference **(APHLC)**, Bhartiya Janata Party **(BJP**/*bhajapaa*), Indian National Congress **(INC)**, Nationalist Congress Party **(NCP)**, Republican Party of India **(RPI)**, Rashtriya Janata Dal **(RJD**/*raajad*), Indian National Trade Union Congress

(INTUC), Mizo National Front **(MNF**), All India MSajlis-E-Ittehadul Muslimeen **(AIMIM)**, Dravid Munnetra Kazhagam **(DMK**), All India Anna Dravid Munnetra Kazhagam **(AIADMK**), Rahtriya Lok Dal **(RLD**/*raalod*), Communist Party of India **(CPI**), Communist Party of India (Marxist) **(CPIM/CPM**), Socialist Unity Centra **(SUC**), Samajwadi Party **(SP**/*sapaa*), Bahujan Samaj Party **(BSP**/*basapaa*).

The names of Indian political parties and their acronym obviously point to their uniform choice of ERS convention, and there is no sign yet of a let-up in this trend in foreseeable future. Interestingly, a handful of Indian political parties have of late ingeniously employed both ERS and HDS conventions in the choice of their name and acronym, alternating them to match with the context of the text. The acronyms of these Indian political parties are marked out here, as above, in the conventions of both ERS (in bold font) and HDS (in italics):**BJP**/*bhajapa*, **SP**/*sapaa*, **BSP**/*basapaa*, **RJD**/*raajad*, **RLD**/*raalod*.

Apparently, the current practice of using abbreviation/acronym convention of both ERS and HDS by a few Indian political parties seems only a baby step, aimed at eventually phasing out/reversing the prevailing ERS norm of abbreviation/acronym by HDS/native model. However, a majority of Indian political parties have chosen to stay put to ERM convention in selection of their name as well as their acronym. This only points to how massively the ERS code has intruded in selection of name and abbreviation/acronym of Indian political parties, and this pattern is too well entrenched in Indian speech to reverse, let alone discard even partially, at least in the foreseeable future.

(iii) Names of educational bodies/institutions and their acronym

Sample instances of name and acronym of educational bodies/ institutions from across the country, listed below, illustrate how code-intrusion of English has impacted a crucial dimension of Indian speech:

University Grants Commission **(UGC)**, Indian Institute of Public Administration **(IIPA)**, National Council of Educational Research and Training **(NCERT)**, Indian Council of Historical Research **(ICHR)**, Central University of English and Foreign Languages **(CUEFL)**, All India Institute of Medical Sciences **(AIIMS)** Indian Institute of Technology **(IIT)**, Indian Institute of Science **(IISC),** Indian Institute of Management **(IIM)**, Banaras Hindu University **(BHU)**, Aligarh Muslim University **(AMU)**, Delhi University **(DU)**, Jawaharlal Nehru University **(JNU)**, Indira Gandhi National Open University **(IGNOU)**, Academy of Scientific and Innovative Research **(AcSIR)**, National Institute of Securities Markets **(NiSM)**, Securities and Exchange Board of India **(SEBI)**, Indian Institute of Foreign Trade **(IIFT)**, National Institute of Animal Biotechnology **(NIAB)**, Central Board of School Examinations **(CBSE)**.

Most of the Indian educational bodies/institutions, listed above, had initially their name in English only, but have it now in both English and Hindi. Nevertheless, it is the English version of their name which is commonly used in everyday parlance of Indian speech. Strikingly, despite official use of both Hindi and English versions of their name in the written form, it is their abbreviation/ acronym, coined after ERS pattern (marked in bold font in brackets above), rather than HDS, which is uniformly used in pan-Indian speech. This aspect of code-intrusion of English seems patently irreversible, plainly because it has long been looked at as a template model in over-all Indian speech for ages, with no sign of a let-up.

(iv) Names of degrees/diplomas/certificates

Similar to code-intrusion pattern of English in nomenclature of Indian educational institutions and their acronym, code-intrusion of English has also impacted that of Indian degrees/diplomas/ certificates and their acronym, entirely and irreversibly. This is despite their version of name in HDS/other Indian native languages being recently accorded concurrent/priority prominence, along with their ERS version. However, such a move has so far met with only token success inasmuch as their Hindi/other Indian native language version has remained so far confined to written form only. Notably, the use of their ERS acronyms, rather than coinages of their HDS version, whenever opted for, still continues to remain the standard norm in Indian speech.

Both names of degrees/diplomas/certificates and their acronym are patterned after English (ERS) convention in IS as a matter of course, yet it is their acronym, in both written and spoken forms, rather than their full name, that hallmarks code-intrusion of English in Indian speech. Just a few samples from the massive data of names of Indian degrees/diplomas/certificates in English, together with their acronym (given in bold font within brackets), cited below, would suffice to underscore this point:

Bachelor of Arts/Science/Commerce **(BA/BSc/BCom)**;Master of Arts/Science/Commerce **(MA/MSc/MCom)**; Doctor of Philosophy **(PhD)**; Doctor of Literature **(DLitt)**, Bachelor/Master of Technology **(BTech/MTech)**, Post-Graduate Diploma in Management **(PGDM)**, Post-Graduate Certificate in the Teaching of English **(PGCTE)**, Bachelor of Medicine and Bachelor of Surgery (loan word in English from Latin, Medicinae Baccalaureus Baccallaureus Chirurgiae) **(MBBS)**, Master of Medicines **(MD)**, Master of Surgery **(MS)**.

(v) Usage of English (ERS) numerals in Indian speech

Code-intrusion of Hindi Devanagari Script (HDS) numerals, used in Sanskrit/Hindi/their variants in some other Indian native languages/south Asian languages since ancient times, by ERS numerals/Western Arabic numerals is an epochal event in Indian speech in recent times.[25] It has seminal significance as it has drastically altered an elemental character of Hindi, a predominant language of the country with a massive sway over Indian speech.[26] The Table below shows the difference between numeral symbols used in HDS (Modern Devanagari) and those used in ERS/Western Arabic.

It is a paradox that the glyphs of HDS numerals, having origin in Sanskrit/Hindi, both derived from primordial Brahmic family of scripts, vis-à-vis other global languages that evolved later, have now been outright replaced by those of ERS/Western Arabic numerals. Consequently, the pristine character of native numeral glyphs has been decimated for good, absolutely and irreversibly.[27&28] Apparently, there seems hardly any potent or visible reason for such a drastic shift from HDS numerals to ERS numerals in Indian speech today.

Modern Devanagari	Western Arabic	Words for the cardinal number	
		Sanskrit (wordstem)	Hindi
०	0	*śūnya* (शून्य)	शून्य (*śūny*)
१	1	*eka* (एक)	एक (*ek*)
२	2	*dvi* (द्वि)	दो (*do*)
३	3	*tri* (त्रि)	तीन (*tīn*)
४	4	*catur* (चतुर्)	चार (*cār*)
५	5	*pañca* (पञ्च)	पाँच (*pāñc*)
६	6	*ṣaṭ* (षट्)	छः (*chah*)
७	7	*sapta* (सप्त)	सात (*sāt*)
८	8	*aṣṭa* (अष्ट)	आठ (*āṭh*)
९	9	*nava* (नव)	नौ (*nau*)

Source: https:en.wikipedia.org/wiki/Devanagari_numerals

How ERS numerals have swamped the whole gamut of Indian speech now is reflected in comprehensive pattern of occurrence of ERS numerals in Hindi, a predominant and crucial component of Indian speech. This is absolutely evidenced in uniform pattern of usage of ERS numerals even in **Hindi** textbooks, journals, periodicals, print and electronic media, circulars, gazettes, advertisements (both government and private)[29], and so on, let alone in other native Indian languages.

The specious premises, commonly adduced for such a major overhaul such as incompatibility of HDS numerals for computer programming or compulsive necessity to go global with ERS numeral glyphs, just do not hold water. Numeral glyphs of various languages of the world have retained their autonomous character alongside each other while ERS numerals are used by them for higher education and such other crucial areas internationally. One then wonders why the same pattern cannot/could not be applied to Hindi/other native Indian languages as well.

Further, in modern age of computer revolution, innovative ways of computer sciences do/can surely meet evolving needs of diverse languages of the world, if and when required. Languages, therefore, needn't, oughtn't to, alter their elemental character to match with evolving pattern of computer programming. Further, it would indeed be a linguistic catastrophe if languages of the world are/were made to discard their pristine character sheerly because of vagaries of socio-political reasons or short-sighted and idiosyncratic decisions of language policy planners, academics and others. After all, languages of the world, whether spoken by a minuscule few or many, have critical linguistic value inasmuch as each of them functions as invaluable repositories of cultural evolution of human race.

Induction of ERS numerals, together with obliteration of HDS numerals from textbooks, dictionaries, and all other kinds of literature in Hindi, Sanskrit and other native Indian languages, is an irretrievable historical loss. This comes with crucial far-reaching implications for Hindi/other Indian languages as such, as well as for students, academics and scholars of Sanskrit/Hindi/Vedas/Upanishads and other Hindu religious texts and scriptures.[30]

The discussion above revolved around four major dimensions of Englishisation of Indian speech that seem to have evolved in a sequential order, from code-mixing, code-swapping, code-borrowing and then on to code-intrusion. Yet, the four phases/dimensions of code-contact linguistic behaviour in Indian speech are only broad categorisations, functionally variable according to speech context at a given point of time. What is more, there is always an ample room of overlap of instances between these four dimensions, even a slide from one dimension to another in course of time.

Complete/irreversible Englishisation of Indian speech peaks with the stage of code-intrusion of English in Indian speech, a pointed focus to which has just been made earlier. However, quite a few instances of code-mixing/code-swapping/code-borrowing, discussed in earlier sections, seem imminent instances of complete code-intrusion of English in Indian speech in near future. In this category fall proliferating template instances of all types of name-branding in English of shops, organisations etc—big and small, cheap and expensive (listed in earlier sections) that include those of way-side cheap tea/coffee/fruit-juice/dairy shops, budget food joints and expensive restaurants, schools/colleges/universities, malls/departmental stores, Hindi and other native Indian language TV channels, newspapers, organisations, societies, highways, roads, and whatnot.

Let alone name-branding of shops, organisations etc in English, even text contents of their publicity/advertisement discourse are heavily laced with English words and phrases, often written in ERS as well, without an iota of impelling necessity. This is amply reflected in news stories, their banner headlines, write-ups of Hindi newspapers, TV channels and contents of their advertisements, as well as in those of a majority of other native Indian languages. To say the least, this trendy pattern of Englishisation of Indian speech seems essentially born out of one's zest to be exotic or populist, or both, just to grab an edge over their business rivals, or, plainly enough, to toe the prevailing norm of commoner's code of Indian speech.

Undeniably, English remains a most dominant language of the world today if only for its expansive sweep globally in pivotal areas of global transport and communication, international relations and diplomacy, higher education and research, and so on and so forth. Not only for these critical reasons alone but for its crucial value as a co-link language of the country as well, along with Hindi, English remains indispensable for Indian speech today more than ever before. Yet, this hardly ever makes a case for Indian speech, comprising native Indian languages, to be tampered with recklessly through rampant induction of English words/phrases/sentences while their substitutes are readily up for a grab in Hindi/other native Indian languages.

That Indian speech is a myriad times more Englishised today, close to a century *after end* of the British Rule, calls for serious and in-depth attention. Astonishingly, the relentless pace of Englishisation of Indian speech gained faster momentum than ever before quite early on in the fifties or so. More so, this perennial trend has had cascading effect on Indian speech/Hindi and other native Indian languages far and wide.

History has it that a language gains or loses the strength of its survival, even goes extinct, depending on how its speech community, ranging from everyday user of the language to those sitting high up in driving seat, acquit their share of responsibility sagaciously and painstakingly, even at a price. Rapid and reckless pace of Englishisation of Indian speech is surely a retrogressive development if only because of the ominous scale it is fast uprooting the pristine character of Hindi and other native Indian languages. What is more, such a loss is deemed colossal from the perspective of pure linguistics *per se*, which values pivotal role of each and every individual language of the world in the evolving history of human civilisation.

The rising tide of Englishisation of Indian speech may be reversed, even stemmed, if only multi-pronged strong-willed sincere efforts are made well in time by all the concerned stake-holders, from language policy planners of government and private agencies, linguists, academics, language pedagogues, textbook writers, teachers, advertisers, the entire segment of media of Hindi and other native Indian languages, and last but not the least, most crucially, fast-proliferating everyday-participants of Indian speech. The discussion in the foregoing pages was squarely addressed to each of them, though avid readership at large may also find the discussion just as enlightening and relevant, if not more, in their own way.

Notes

1 This chapter is a revised version of my paper presented at the Third International Conference on South Asian Languages and *Linguistics*, held at the Central Institute of Indian Languages, Mysore, India. January 1982.

2 A recent report of the Linguistic Survey of India puts the number of languages and dialects of the country at 179 and 544, respectively. Though the Constitution of India does not accord any Indian language the status of the National Language of the country, Hindi and English have been declared as the official languages, and are widely used in official purposes throughout the country.

A research shows that though Hindi is the dominant language of India, English as a link language is "gaining strength." The study concludes that the probability of two Indians being able to converse in a common language has increased from 0.18 in 1971 to 0.23 in 2011. Courtesy: https://www.google.com

3 Hindi is the most widely spoken language in India, and also one of the country's key official languages. Around 550 million people in India speak Hindi. After Hindi, English is the most widely spoken language in the country, with around 125 million speakers. *Courtesy https//www.google.com*

4 There is a nuanced difference between code-mixing of two or more languages/dialects and loan words in a code-contact situation, the former being a free/voluntary choice of a speech community whereas the latter is its inevitable/involuntary choice for want of a suitable word in one's native language and culture. For instance, the Hindi/IS words 'yoga', 'guru' and 'jungle' are loan words in English whereas 'tea', 'kettle' and 'train' are loan words in Hindi/IS.

5 For a detailed discussion on register, see Ure 1973; Hasan 1973; Gregory and Carroll 1978.

6 To mark their distinction, sample instances of code-mixed English words/phrases, transliterated in the text in Hindi/Devanagari Script **(HDS)**, are italicised, but they are shown in bold font when they occur in the text in English/Roman Script **(ERS)**.However, Hindi words/phrases, wherever they occur together with English words/phrases, are shown in normal script (ERS).

7 As mentioned earlier, **EWPNA** is used here as an abbreviation for English words, phrases, numerals and the scripting convention of writing English abbreviations.

8 The pattern of IS, code-mixed with **EWPNA**, largely holds true for all newspapers and TV channels in Hindi as well as other Indian native languages, though the instances of such code-mixing are currently sampled from only Hindi TV channels and newspapers.

9 Plate 1 is a scanned copy of a full-page Hindi advertisement of the Department of Information and Public Relations, Government of Uttar Pradesh, published in an English daily, The Times of India, Lucknow, dated 19 March 2018.

10 The numerals 1, 2, 3, etc. are also known as Arabic numerals, or Hindu-Arabic numerals, Indian numerals, Hindu numerals, European numerals, and Western numerals. These numerals were first used in India in about 400 BC, were later used in Persia, then were brought to Europe by the Arabs. Hence the name "Arabic numerals". https://omniglot.com/language/numerals.htm

11 "The Devanagari numerals are the symbols used to write numbers in the Devanagari script, the predominant script of India. They are used to write decimal numbers, instead of the Western Arabic numbers."

Devanagari numerals : *Wikipedia, Wen.wikipedia.org/wik:/ Devanagari numerals.*

12 Plate 2 and Plate 3 are a scanned copy each of two commercial advertisements, published in a Hindi daily, Dainik Jagaran, Lucknow, dated 13 June 2013.

13 "The linguistic behaviour referred to as code-switching…can be illustrated by the switch speakers may make (depending on who they are talking to, or where they are) between STANDARD and regional forms of English, between Welsh and English in parts of Wales, or between occupational and domestic varieties." (Crystal 1985/1989 : 53)

14 The sample illustrations in this study are cited from Hindi extensively, a widely spoken link language of the country.

15 "Jan-Petter Blom and John J. Gumperz coined the linguistic term 'metaphorical code-switching' in the late sixties and early seventies. They wanted to "clarify the social and linguistic factors involved in the communication process ... by showing that speaker's

selection among semantically, grammatically, and phonologically permissible alternates occurring in conversation sequences recorded in natural groups is both patterned and predictable on the basis of certain features of the local social system." They wanted to explain why, in a community where all the members of a community have access to two codes, a speaker will sometimes prefer one over another. They therefore did a study in Hemnesberget, a diglossic community in Norway, to test their hypothesis that switching was topic related and predictable."

https://en.wikipedia.org/wiki/Metaphorical_code-switching

16 "Metaphorical code-switching refers to the tendency in a bilingual or multilingual community to switch codes (language or language variety) in conversation in order to discuss a topic that would normally fall into another conversational domain. "An important distinction is made from situational switching, where alternation between varieties redefines a situation, being a change in governing norms, and metaphorical switching, where alternation enriches a situation, allowing for allusion to more than one social relationship within the situation." (1) For example, at a family dinner, where you would expect to hear a more colloquial, less prestigious variety of language (called "L variety" in studies of diglossia), family members might switch to a highly prestigious form (H variety) in order to discuss school or work. At work (where you would expect high prestige language) interlocutors may switch to a low prestige variety when discussing family."

https://en.wikipedia.org/wiki/Metaphorical_code-switching

17 The same is true with a teacher of English as well when he opts for metaphorical code-switching to Hindi/other native Indian language for like reasons.

18 However, code-borrowing is employed globally in specialised areas of science, technology, etc, for quite inevitable reasons.

19 As mentioned earlier, code-borrowing from English is quite a trendy recent practice in Indian speech, not an inevitable compulsion, especially as all the terms of addressing, not just those listed here, have been there in Indian speech since ages.

20 Refer to the earlier section on Code-mixing for a comprehensive list of relationship terms.

21 A comprehensive list of relationship terms in Hindi/native Indian languages is not provided here only to not deflect attention from core focus of this study.

22 Note, these English terms of designation are by far the preferred choice in IS parlance, despite availability/recent coinages of their substitutes in Indian native languages.

23 EWPNA, as mentioned earlier, is used as a cover term for English words/phrases/numerals/abbreviations. Code-intrusion of EWPNA has virtually swamped Indian speech in a massive way. Therefore, only their sample instances are cited here to illustrate their pattern of distribution in Indian speech.

24 Cf. OALD (2020: 816).

25 "A very interesting phenomenon in Indic languages is the usage of numerals. All Indic languages use its own script for representing the text, but the situation is very different when someone needs to represent the numerals. Even though most Indic scripts has its own unique glyphs/symbols ....for representing numerals, many use Arabic numerals (or Indo-Arabic numerals) instead of language's own numeral glyphs."

Source:https://meta.wikimedia.org/wiki/CIS-A2K/Indic_Languages/Numerals_in_Indic_Languages_%26_Indic_language_Wikipedias

26 The Devanagari numerals are the symbols used to write numbers in the Devanagari script, the predominant for northern Indian languages. They are used to write decimal numbers, instead of the Western Arabic numerals. Sanskrit is an ancient Indian language......Devanagari is part of the Brahmic family of scripts of India, Nepal, Tibet, and Southeast Asia. It is a descendant of the 3rd century BCE Brahmi script, which evolved into the Nagari script which in turn gave birth to Devanagari and Nandinagari. Both were used to write Sanskrit, until the latter was merged into the former. Devanagari - Wikipedia

27 (Numeral system) originated in India in the 6th or 7th century and were introduced to Europe through the writings of Middle Eastern mathematicians, especially al-Khwarizmi and al-Kindi, about the 12th century.....................

The most commonly used system of numerals is decimal. Indian mathematicians are credited with developing the integer version, the Hindu–Arabic numeral system. Aryabhata of Kusumapura developed the place-value notation in the 5th century and a century later Brahmagupta introduced the symbol for zero."

www.google.co.in/search?

Source: https://en.wikipedia.org/wiki/Hindu%E2%80

93Arabic_numeral_system

28 "Actually, we don't use Arabic numerals. We use Hindu numerals. Western nations call them Arabic because Europe got the numerals from the Islamic world, which got them from the Hindus."

Source: Numeration Systems - History - Science Encyclopedia https://*science.jrank.org*

29 A detailed discussion of this aspect of Englishisation has already been done earlier.

30 It would be relevant to mention here how, in a similar way, the spelling pattern of Hindi, used for centuries, has undergone drastic changes recently, even more erratically and in a slipshod way. This has caused immense bottleneck real problems of pronunciation for Hindi /speech community, as well as first-time/non-native learners of the language. It is high time this ill-conceived trend is righted promptly before it is too late. Recent quixotic changes in spelling pattern of Hindi have caused far more hurdles to the learners of Hindi than they were perhaps intended to solve. I earnestly believe top-notch academics as well as concerned authorities of Hindi language policy in the government and outside would give urgent attention to this matter of national importance.

References

Bernstein, B (1971) : *Class, codes and control 1 : Theoretical studies towards a sociology of Language (Primary socialisation and education)*. Routledge & Kegan Paul. London. 1971.

Crystal, David (1985/1989) : *A Dictionary of Linguistics and Phonetics*. Basil Blackwell. 1985/1989.

Dubey, Vinod S (1978) : 'A Stylistic Analysis of Mulk Raj Anand's *Seven Summers*: A Dialectal Approach'. *Unpublished MA dissertation*. University of Wales (formerly University College of North Wales), Bangor, UK. 1978.

Ellis, J (1966) : 'On contextual meaning'. In C E Bazell *et al* (ed.) *In Memory of J R Firth*. Longman. London 1966.

Firth, J R (1957) : 'Personality and language'. *The Sociological Review*. 42.

Fishman, J A (1972) : *The Sociology of Language: An Interdisciplinary Social Science Approach to Language in Society*. Newbury House Publ. Mass. 1972.

Gregory, M & Carroll, S (1978) : *Language and Situations : Language Varieties and their Social Contexts*. Routledge & Kegan Paul. London, 1978.

Halliday, M A K (1978) : *Language as social semiotic*. Edward Arnold. 1978.

Hasan, R (1973) : 'Code, register and social dialect'. In *Basil Bernstein ed. Class, Codes and Control,* Vol 2. Ed. Basil Bernstein .Routledge and Kegan Paul. London & Boston. 1973.

Haugen, Einar (1972) : *The Ecology of Language*. Stanford A. Stanford University Press.

Hudson, R A (1980/1987): *Sociolinguistics*. Cambridge Textbooks in Linguistics. CUP 1980/87.

Kachru, Braj, B (1966) : 'Indian English : a study in contextualisation'. In Bazell *et al*., ed. 1966.

______(1969): 'English in South Asia'. In Sebeok ed. 1969.

______(1978 (a): 'Toward Structuring Code-mixing: An Indian Perspective.' In *Studies in the Linguistic Sciences*. Vol. 5, No. 1.

______(1978 (b)): ' Code-mixing as a communicative strategy in India'. Paper presented at the Georgetown University Round Table on Languages and Linguistics. 1978.

LDCE (2014/2020): *Longman Dictionary of Contemporary English*. 2014/2022.

Malinowsky (1923): 'The problem of meaning in primitive languages'. In *The meaning of meaning*. Routledge & Kegan Paul. London.

OALD (2020): *Oxford Advanced Learner's Dictionary*. 10th ed. 2020.

Ure, Jeane (1971): 'Lexical density and register differentiation'. In G.E. Perren and J.L.M. Trim (eds) *Applications of Linguistics*. Cambridge. 1969.

______(1972): 'Code Switching and 'Mixed Speech' in the Register Systems of Developing Languages'. In *Applied Sociolinguistics*. Ed Verdoot, A 1974.

8
Dynamics of Media Discourse in Yemen

Notion of discourse

With increasing interest in linguistic literature and outside in how meanings are structured and negotiated in the society, the notion of discourse has undergone a widened reinterpretation and enlargement of scope.[1] Even as language remains our crucial channel of communication, there is at once a growing common awareness that quite often it is not the only, or even the exclusive, channel of human communication. So much so, while discourse[2] generally implies a " piece of language as a whole as a kind of communication" (Widdowson 1979:98), it is also viewed, at a more abstract level, as "a behavioural unit which has a pre-theoretical status in linguistics" without even any "reference being made to its linguistic structuring" (Crystal 1985:96). The notion of discourse has thus acquired a much broadened implication than just "language as a whole as a kind of communication".[3]

Structures of discourse

Interestingly, our cultural evolution today is being fast patterned by simultaneous use of both verbal (linguistic)[4] and visual channels of communication[5]. Consequently, the notion of discourse extends today beyond spoken and written texts to cover both verbal and visual channels of communication.[5] The fact that communication often occurs at primary (spoken) medium of language at once verbally and visually—through gesture, posture and facial expression — essentially underscores the mixed pattern of discourse structure.[6]

More interestingly, even as the channel of verbal communication has a far more crucial role to play in the discourse structure of a message than the visual channel as a matter of regular course, it is the visual channel that precedes the verbal channel in a most significant way, naturally and primordially: "Seeing comes before words. The child looks and recognises before it can speak." (Berger 1972: 7) This explains why, in the event of a communication bottleneck or breakdown, as in *foreign* language communication, or, in the event of an urgent necessity for a rapid rapport with the interlocutor, as in advertisements or films, as contrasted with the written texts — especially novels — which are filmed, one tends to opt for mixed discourse structure employing both verbal and visual channels of communication.

Dimensions of discourse

Negotiation of meanings in the society is possible through a variety of contributing factors — social, pragmatic, psychological, proxemics, para-tonal, even telepathic, etc. —which constitute the multiple dimensions of discourse. However, attention at present is restricted to only three of the overlapping dimensions of discourse— social, pragmatic and psychological — which seem to have direct relevance to a study of the dynamics of media discourse in Yemen.

The social dimension is obviously the most important dimension of discourse in that human communication, though marked by infinite creativity, is best possible only in a speech community. Discourse is thus closely related to "the social practice" and "the whole process of social interaction" of a speech community and the "social conditions of production and social conditions of interpretation." (Fairclough 1989:24-25)

The pragmatic dimension of discourse envisages the relation between what is said and what is meant, or precisely, the implications which derive from —not based on—linguistic and extra-linguistic context of utterance. In other words, communication occurs through "presuppositions of a pragmatic kind ... which can override the presuppositions which are associated with linguistic forms." (Widdowson 1979:128-9)

The psychological dimension of discourse has been discussed by Sperber and Wilson (1986) in terms of the 'theory of relevance'. Sperber and Wilson conceive of communication as a complementary act involving the communicator and the addressee: "...the communicator produces a stimulus which makes it mutually manifest to the communicator and the audience that the communicator intends, by means of his stimulus, to make manifest, or more manifest, to the audience a certain set of assumptions." (Sperber and Wilson 1986: 63). The use by Sperber and Wilson of the terms 'manifest (ness)' and 'assumption' in preference to more categorical terms `knowledge' and 'propositions' suggests that communication is a matter of degrees of relevance—'manifestness' or 'more manifestness'— and also degrees of commitment to truths —'assumptions', not propositions. In view of this, Sperber and Wilson (*op cit.*) specify the notion of relevance with reference to the following 'extent conditions of relevance':

Extent Condition 1: "an assumption is relevant in a context to the extent that its contextual effects in that context are large."

Extent Condition 2: "an assumption is relevant in a context to the extent that the effort required to process it in that context is small."

A perspective on media discourse in Yemen

Prior to a discussion of the dynamics of media discourse in Yemen, precisely, English advertisements discourse in the Yemeni print media,[7] a reference needs to be made to the overall media communication scenario in Yemen with particular focus on English.

English is used as a foreign language in Yemen. The English media in the country is therefore addressed to a minuscule section of native and non-native target addressees. This explains why there are no English *dailies* published in Yemen, and even the number of English *weeklies* published in the country is just two, namely, the *Yemen Times* (YT) and the *Yemen Observer* (YO). The Yemeni TV and radio of course telecast/broadcast a short news bulletin in English every day, but its target audience remains restricted to a tiny section of people. Obviously, with little scope for advertisements in English over the Yemeni TV/radio, the English advertisements discourse remains highly restricted to the Yemeni print media, and, occasionally, extends to display boards /hoardings in public places as well.

Interestingly, a picture of similarity and contrast emerges from a study of the advertisements published in the *Yemen Times* (YT).[8] Whereas advertisements, with texts in English and those with texts in Arabic — both published in YT — share a pattern of mixed verbal-visual discourse structure, it is the dissimilarity in the choice frequency of this pattern that distinguishes one from the other. While advertisements, with texts in English, almost invariably opt for the visual component as the **text-anchor**, or the dominant component of discourse structure, the advertisements, with texts in Arabic opt for mixed verbal-visual pattern of discourse structure far too infrequently.

Dynamics of media English discourse in Yemen

In the light of preceding discussion, it seems worth-while to explore the dynamics of English print-media advertisements discourse in Yemen with reference to both its structures and dimensions which together help constitute its core pattern.

Structures of discourse

An eye-catching sight for a first-time non-native reader of YT is its advertisements, particularly those published on its front page (see Plates 1-3). Though these advertisements have mostly mixed verbal-visual discourse structure, it is their visual component that prominently functions as the **text-anchor,** or the core component of discourse structure of the text.

The verbal (descriptive) component of the text functions only as a **co-text**[9], or ancillary text, that highlights, in most cases, subsidiary part of the message that mentions only the brand name of the goods/ shop where they are available for sale. This contrasts with natural and primary concern of a customer about details of quality features of the product. Nevertheless, a majority of native customers, users of English as a Foreign Language (EFL), in Yemeni EFL communication, rest content with such a discourse pattern of print-media advertisements in English.

As mentioned above, the visual component functions as the **text-anchor** in the English print-media advertisements in Yemen. This implies that the visual component— display image(s)[10]/ associative image(s) of the product, evoking varied responses, referential or evocative or both —occupies overwhelming space in the text. The crucial discourse value of the visual component in these advertisement texts can be realised if one were to blank it out from them entirely. This will be evident if one compares Plates 1-3 and Plate 7 with the their corresponding Plates 4, 5, 6 and 8, or, for that matter, imagined complete omission of the visual component from Plates 9-24 .

It is worth noting that even in advertisements where the verbal component gets prominent placement in the text, the discourse function of the visual component remains paramount. In Plate 9, the mention of 'UNIVERSAL CONTRACTING & READY MIX CONCRETE CO. LTD - *of ZUBAYEN group*' right at the top of the text, followed by a sub-heading 'HYUNDAI: Heavy Industries Co. Ltd.' makes only a vague idea of a wide variety of equipment/ machines, etc. if considered in isolation by itself, without reference to a wide spectrum of images of the advertised goods in the text.

Plate 1

Plate 2

Plate 3

Plate 4

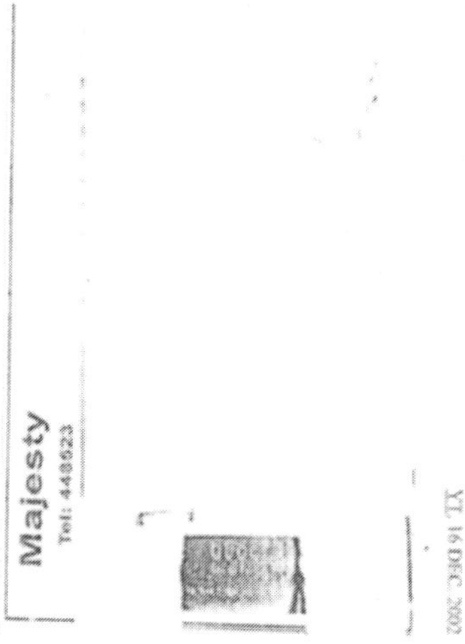

Plate 5

Plate 6

Plate 7

Plate 8

Plate 9

Plate 10

YT, 02 DEC. 2002

Plate 11

YT, 16 DEC. 2002

Plate 12

YT, 16 DEC. 2002

Plate 13

YT, 20 JAN .

Plate 14

Plate 15

Plate 16

Plate 17

Plate 18

Plate 19

Plate 20

Plate 21

Plate 22

Plate 23

Plate 24

Plate 25

Plate 26

Plate 27

How the discourse function of the images in Plate 10 remains vital vis-à-vis the verbal component of the text can be self-checked just by discarding all the images that appear in the text. The same is precisely true of the verbal component, appearing in the following Plates as well, where it functions only as a co-text :'*322 Q*', etc. in Plate 11; '*We bring good thing to life*' in Plate 16; '*NOW: KLCC in Sana'a Opened*' in Plate 17; '*Providing exceptional utility and space*' in Plate 19, and '*Fun on the run: Pathfinder*' in Plate 20. The rationale behind this lies in that the verbal component in all these Plates does not aid transmission of the core message of the text – the products/services advertised —a small bit more in absence of the visual component from the text.

The option for the visual as text-anchor in mixed discourse structure of Yemeni print-media English advertisements may possibly be attributed to a variety of reasons.[11] The choice of an image (bottles: Plate 1), or an associative image (a lady shown beside a bottle: Plates 2 and 3), having an evocative function, in preference to a detailed verbal note on the features of the advertised goods, seems to be a much quicker and handy way of communicating with the target native addressees. Apparently, this seems to be a native pragmatic compulsion, plainly because an overwhelming majority of the target native addressees— precisely, users of English-as-a-foreign language— possess just a bare minimal proficiency in the written form of the language. Indeed, this choice falls in pattern with the natural, pre-verbal and visual channel of communication that primordially precedes its verbal channel (cf. Berger 1972:7).

The choice of the visual as text-anchor is also an effective "tactile means to play upon the spectator's sense of acquiring the *real* thing which the image shows" (Berger 1972:141), or, what is still more remarkable, a discreet way of whetting the reader-spectator's desire to be herself an object of envy: what she would become once she uses the product herself (see Plate 1-3) (cf. Berger 1972 : 13).

Dimensions of discourse

The social dimension

Given the social condition of restrictive occurrence and use of English-as-a-foreign -language, the presence of English media in Yemen is noticeably confined to the print-media channel, precisely, to its two English weeklies, the *Yemen Times* (YT) and the *Yemen Observer* (YO). The English print-media in Yemen thus target a minuscule section of readership, a majority of who make do with English-as-foreign-language only sparingly. In such a social scenario, the advertisement copywriters' sole concern obviously lies in highlighting only the core contents of the advertisement while ignoring details about them. Indeed, this pattern quite adequately meets the Yemeni readership's minimal communication requirements in the foreign language, as is evidenced from regular appearance of identically patterned—prototype— advertisements in the Yemeni print-media English (Plates 1- 24).

Like advertisements in general, the advertised items remain the central part of advertisement texts in the Yemeni print-media

English. However, they are prominently introduced in the text only visually— through their image—and not through verbal description of their features, without causing a problem of social interpretation to the natives. Such a problem of interpretation may however arise for non-natives unfamiliar with the Yemeni socio-cultural reality.

In Plate 1, the image of two bottles with little feature details of the product, precisely, scanty details provided in too fine prints at top right corner of the text to catch adequate attention of the addressee—'*Paul Smith*: Perfume', and at its bottom in bold fonts—'**PAUL SMITH** EXTREME'— is easily interpreted as bottles of perfume in the native perfume-loving society.

Interestingly, in Plates 2-3, even as a non-descript tiny image of a bottle appears at the foot of the image of a woman, it is the prominent anchorage of the woman's image without a veil that unfolds the Yemeni pattern of social interpretation. Notably, the Yemeni society/culture ordains women to wear a veil –*hijab/niqab/burqa*— in public. Yet, the occurrence, rather unusual, of the discreetly-chosen evocative image of a woman without a veil in the text, seems quite significant. What needs special attention is that, in the process, it brings to light the evolving pattern of conservative native socio-cultural interpretation.

How crucially relevant are these images in Plates 4-6, and how difficult it would be to interpret their message value in the native Yemeni socio-cultural context without them, can be well figured out if the same texts, stripped of these images, were offered for interpretation to the same readership.

Plates 7 and 9-24 further reinforce the discourse pattern of Plates 1-3 (discussed earlier) in that they underscore the critical role of visuals *per se* in social interpretation of Yemeni print-media English advertisements, irrespective of anchorage of a verbal footage in the text. This would explain why if the visual anchorage—the images of different types of automobiles, etc.—were removed from Plate 7, the very targeted purpose of the advertisement would stand nullified, because, in that case, the reduced text will be left with the following redundant verbal remainder, "With Best Wishes From..." (Plate 8).

Surely, this advertisement is not really put up to convey greetings from a firm/shop by way of establishing phatic communion with the target addressee. On the contrary, the bottom-line genuine concern of the advertiser is indeed to promote, in right earnest, the sale of the advertised goods. For this reason, the visual anchorage, with minimal verbal footage of description, fits in fairly well with the pragmatics of interpretation of Yemeni English print-media advertisements.

Next to visual anchorage, what seems most striking in the Yemeni English print-media advertisements is its verbal and core part of 'commercial' anchorage, namely, the mention of the name of the firm/shop, along with its address, etc., where the goods are available for sale. Again, the verbal anchorage here contains no reference to the features of the advertised goods. Apparently, the advertiser's sole concern lies in the sale of their goods, and not in the least in spelling out their utility/product features. In spite of this rather scanty verbal information in the text, the prospective native readership/customer seems to have little problem in interpreting the content value of such advertisements. Otherwise, repeat publication of this pattern of sale advertisements in YT would have come to a stop, sooner than later.

The continued and wide acceptance of this type of mixed visual-verbal discourse pattern of sale advertisements in Yemeni print-media, points to a revealing aspect of how English is used as a foreign language in everyday native Yemeni communication. Among the notable factors that seem to account for this communication scenario are briefly listed here. Apparently, the native users of EFL in Yemen either feel too complacent with the visual anchorage of the advertisement text to go through its verbal segment, or do so just out of linguistic laziness, or lack of motivational leanings for the language, or, plainly, lack of basic-level proficiency in the language, or a combination of some/all of these factors.

Notably, Plates 25-27 display a marked irregular discourse structure of Yemeni English print-media advertisements. In Plates 26-27, the verbal anchorage is the sole predominant constituent of the text. Herein, the text comprises only the verbal segment— a reference to Canon, Sony, Aiwa, etc., along with the name of the shop where these products are available for sale–while the visual segment is not included in the text, since both the advertiser and addressee are deemed to be well aware of these world-renowned brand names of electronic goods.

However, in Plate 25, the visual anchorage of a man carrying a tool box seems to be significant in a special way. Even as an elaborate description is given in the text about Suzuki Yemen services, spare parts, maintenance, etc. it is the centrepiece visual anchorage in the text that gets overriding attention of the prospective native customer. Otherwise as well, the addressee's attention would be naturally drawn to the visual first before he chooses to go through the descriptive verbal segment of the text. Nevertheless, in terms of discourse function, the visual in Plate 25 remains ancillary to the text inasmuch as it does not convey much sense by itself without reference to its verbal segment.

The pragmatic dimension

The social interpretation of Yemeni English print-media advertisements is clearly derived, indeed made possible, from pragmatics, precisely, from the pattern of relations between what is said and what is meant, shared by the native participants. Thus, even with little or practically no verbal (descriptive) clues in the text, the visual anchorage in the Yemeni English print-media advertisements often helps establish by itself rapid communication rapport with the native addressee.

Apparently, while composing the discourse structure of advertisement texts for print-media in English, the copywriter richly draws from his real-life experience of how English is used as a *foreign* language in everyday *living* Yemeni communication scenario. Being aware of the challenges and limitations of such a scenario, he perhaps knows it only too well how best to square up to them to the best advantage of his clients, as also, to the maximal comfort-level proficiency of the native users of the language. He therefore makes a skilful choice of minimal use of the verbal and optimal use of the visual segments to structure the discourse pattern of Yemeni print-media advertisements in English.

The overwhelming option trend for the choice of the visual in preference to the verbal as text-anchor in Yemeni print-media advertisement texts in English is basically conditioned by the pragmatics of everyday use of English as a foreign language in Yemen. Thus, while composing the discourse structure of these texts/Plates the copywriter discreetly goes by the premise of 'pragmatic presupposition'.[12] This is to make absolutely certain that the intended message of these texts/Plates is straightaway received by the Yemeni readership of the language without any communication hurdle.

The iconic image of two bottles in Plate 1 and the evocative image of a woman in Plates 2-3, both text-anchors, carry the same implicature in the native Yemeni communication, being an advertisement of a brand of perfume, precisely, a tacit solicitation to buy it. Apparently, for want of a verbal (descriptive) clue, the implicature of the visual is derived, not from the text, but clearly exophorically from the native pattern of social interpretation of images. (This point was also discussed earlier in the section on social dimension of discourse.)

In Plates 7 and 9–27, the implicature of the advertisements is endophoric or text-oriented, its social ramifications notwithstanding (discussed earlier).

Plate 7 draws immediate attention to the overwhelming space and focused prominence that the visual anchorage occupies in the text. Indeed, the extensive space of the text is nearly swamped by a sizeable number of images of various types of automobiles, heavy duty equipment, etc. The crucial discourse value of the visual anchorage can be well guessed if it is blanked out from the text completely, as in Plate 8. Notably, the visual display of images in EFL communication in Yemen seems quite a handy means to project the salient features of the advertised goods.

The verbal (descriptive) segment in Plate 7, placed centrally in the text for focused attention, however, comes with an added crucial commercial implicature. The compliments from the firm-- '*With Best Wishes.........*' are not really intended to establish phatic communion with the addressee. Plainly, the compliments have a polite implicature of discreetly soliciting the native customer's purchase interest in the goods, visually displayed in the text. With this extended commercial implicature, the name and detailed contact address of the business firm, the dealers of these goods, are prominently displayed in the text.

In Plates 9-24, the implicature of soliciting the prospective customer's attention to the advertised goods/services is not as discreetly oblique as in Plate 7. Herein, even as the visual segment occupies a central place of prominence in the text, the bottom-line implicature of the text lies, above all, in primarily soliciting purchase interest of the native customer. This is evidenced by prominent display of the name and detailed address of the dealers in these goods at both the top and bottom of the text.

In Plate 10, the image of two buildings, along with verbal/ descriptive footage of the name and address of the firm, carries an explicit commercial implicature of soliciting business interest of the native customer to the kind of construction services offered by the firm.

Interestingly, Plates 26-27 stand out distinctly apart from Plates 1-25, because of markedly conspicuous absence of any visual images therein. Each of these Plates contains just a mention of the name of the advertised goods, together with that of the shop dealing in them. Despite there being no visual images in them, these Plates adequately cater to the Yemeni EFL communication requirement, and for a pragmatic reason. A visual in these texts would seem only redundant if only because the copywriter goes by his pragmatic presumption that the native readership/customers, already familiar with these global brand names, Canon and Sony, would not really care for the images of these products in the advertisements.

The discourse structure of the advertisement text in Plate 25 is somewhat special for a pragmatic reason. Even as the visual anchorage of an iconic image of a technician carrying a toolbox gets a prominent placement at the centre the text, it offers little clue to the core message of the text. Consequently, the descriptive segment that occurs at both the top and bottom of the text, detailing product features and name of their manufacturers, is an imperative pragmatic necessity. Notably, such a discourse structure runs counter to the sweeping preference pattern of the visual as text-anchor in the Yemeni EFL communication. What is more, the discourse value of the descriptive segment in Plate 25 extends far beyond than being just an information act. Indeed, it has an unmissable bottom-line commercial implicature of soliciting (eliciting?) purchase interest of the native customers:

'SUZUKI YEMEN; **Be safe on the road by using genuine parts; Economy – Durability**;'*All services ... available at: Suzuki Yemen...........*'.

The overall discourse pattern of the Yemeni print-media advertisements in English, discussed above (Plates 1-27), features an admixture of the visual and the verbal (descriptive segment), though the visual segment overwhelmingly functions as text-anchor in keeping with the pragmatics of Yemeni EFL communication. Such a discourse pattern emerges because the copywriter goes by, what Grice (1975) calls, the Maxims of '*Quantity*' and '*Manner*'. It needs to be mentioned that the discourse structure of the texts (Plates 1-27), are representative samples of Yemeni print-media advertisement English. And, fort this reason, they help provide an incisive view of the pragmatics of Yemeni socio-cultural reality in shaping the Yemeni EFL communication.

The psychological dimension

For a comprehensive view, it seems worth-while to explore the dynamics of Yemeni English print-media advertisements from a complementary psychological perspective, precisely, within the broad framework of Sperber and Wilson's 'theory of relevance'

(1986). Obviously, the efficacy of an advertisement crucially lies in its being relevant to the addressee. The notion of 'relevance', or 'more relevance', is indeed behind the notion of communication itself, involving both the addresser and the addressee. Relevance seems to be an interplay of two crucial factors of stimulus and response, and, both, by their very nature, can be conceived only in terms of degrees — degrees of stimulus and degrees of response.

The efficacy of an advertisement clearly lies in how 'relevant', or 'more relevant', it can make itself to the addressee through a stimulus—verbal, visual, or both—made 'manifest' or 'more manifest', and through a response it can evoke from the addressee —the extent of its effects on him in a given context—that would require minimal processing effort on his part.

The regular appearance of similar/prototype advertisement texts in the Yemeni English print-media is an ample testimony to their acceptance by the native readership in Yemeni EFL communication. What is though indeed relevant in Yemeni EFL communication depends on its context of occurrence.

In the light of challenges and constraints of EFL communication in Yemen, the copywriter knows it well enough that the best strategy of stimulating the native addressee's quick response to the advertisement is through use of the visual as text-anchor. After all, naturally and primordially, the visual channel precedes the verbal channel of communication: "seeing comes before words" (Berger 1972/1988:7). Further, since "we only see what we look at" (*op cit.*: 8), the copywriter's next concern is to stimulate the native addressee's interest in the visual by offering him its 'relevant' type, while, at the same time, keeping the verbal (descriptive) segment of the text to its barest level. The verbal/descriptive segment of course gets a placement in the text only when its occurrence is *relevantly* required.

The relevance of the kind of discourse structure, precisely, that of print-media advertisements in English in native EFL communication, is conditioned by discreet interplay between the addresser's stimulus and the addressee's response. In Plates 1-24, the visual as the text-anchor functions as stimulus, through a display of the types of images which would help make the message of the advertisement '*manifest*' or '*more manifest*' to the native addressee. The images are thus selective, requiring minimal processing effort on the part of the native addressee and optimal contextual effects on him. The footage of the verbal segment that goes with the visual segment in the text is often restrictive to just a mention of the core commercial part of the advertisement — the name of the shop/firm, dealers in the advertised goods.

The advertisement texts in Plates 1-3 consist of only what appears most *relevant* commercially from the viewpoint of both the addresser and the addressee. Thus, it contains the visual of the advertised item(s) as well as the name of the shop/firm/dealers in the advertised goods.

The iconic image of a pair of bottles in Plate 1 and the evocative image of a woman in Plates 2-3, both manifesting themselves with the corresponding image of perfume bottles, work as a stimulant of purchase interest of prospective native customer. The verbal segment, giving details of the shop dealing in the advertised goods, is appended to the text just because it is essentially *relevant* for commercial reason. After all, the advertiser's interest in putting out the advertisement is, precisely, commercial, rather than display of images in it.

The same discourse pattern of *relevance* is reinforced in the advertisement texts in Plates 7 and 9-24. What is advertised in these Plates, both visually—different types of images of automobiles, consumer goods, garments, telephones, services, etc—and verbally—the name of the shop/company/ dealers in the advertised goods—seems critically and essentially *relevant* from the standpoint of both the addresser and the addressee in native Yemeni EFL communication.

However, in Plate 25, despite focused placement of the visual at the centre of the text, its *relevanc*e seems rather unclear, even open to question, as it offers little information about message content of the text by itself. However, the verbal/descriptive segment that precedes and follows the visual segment serves this paramount discourse necessity of the text by detailing relevant and precise details of its core message.

It needs a special mention that the discourse value/viability of verbal and visual segments is critically dependent on their *relevance* in the text, precisely, their *degrees of relevance* in the context of the situation, endophoric or exophoric, or both. Thus, the visual segment in the text (Plate 25) has some *relevanc*e nevertheless inasmuch as it stimulates the initial purchase interest of the native customer at a first glance, thus serving a limited discourse function.

By sharp contrast, the advertisements in Plates 26-27 feature complete absence of the visual segment. Such a marked variation from the remaining texts of this study makes them noticeably distinctive in English print-media advertisements in native EFL scenario. Notably, each of these advertisement texts (Plates 26-27) contains only *relevant* and adequate information that exclusively concerns the advertiser and the native customer. Thus, even a brief mention of the globally-renowned brand names, such as Canon, Sony, Aiwa, etc, with which the native customers are well acquainted, together with the name of the shop dealing in these products, seems *relevan*t and sufficiently adequate in Yemeni EFL communication. This would explain absence of any visuals in the text.

The exploration of the dynamics of media discourse in Yemen, precisely, Yemeni English print-media advertisements discourse, has been revealing in quite a number of ways. First and foremost, it reflects the Yemeni English print-media advertisements discourse being in line with the fast-evolving global trend towards mixed pattern of media discourse—simultaneous use of both verbal and visual channels of communication—though this is marked by striking variations from the prevailing global pattern.

The mixed discourse pattern of Yemeni print-media advertisements discourse in English stands out apart from the global pattern if only because of its sweeping tilt towards the visual anchorage in the text. Several functional constraints and imperatives seem critical to this kind of preference tilt under which English as a foreign language (EFL) functions in Yemen. Some of these key factors have been explored in this study under the broad heads: social, pragmatic and psychological dimensions of the dynamics of Yemeni print-media advertisements in English.

The overwhelming pattern of preference for the visual segment vis-à-vis verbal/descriptive segment in Yemeni English print-media advertisement texts seems naturally, indeed intrinsically, derived from the notion of the visual being the primordial and simplest mode of communication. The notion that the visual precedes over the verbal as an easy and more effective communication channel, naturally and primordially, is lucidly explained thus by Berger: "Seeing comes before words. The child looks and recognises before it can speak." (Berger 1972: 7).

Apparently, this reasons out why the native users of EFL, who need to grapple with complex challenges of EFL communication in Yemen, seem naturally inclined to prefer/ look for, above all, the visual anchorage in the text. Apparently, they do so because they deem it an easy option to access the discourse message of the Yemeni print-media advertisements in English. They are thus generally inclined to browse over, even skip, the verbal/descriptive segment of the text as long as it does not lead to a real communication gap. The continued acceptance of this pattern of Yemeni print-media advertisements discourse in English clearly reflects the efficacy of this pattern of Yemeni EFL communication.

Significantly, the mixed verbal-visual discourse dynamics of Yemeni English print-media advertisements best features itself in overlapping terms of its social, pragmatic and psychological dimensions. Indeed, the tripartite socio-pragmatic-psychological framework employed in this study may perhaps seem efficacious in further explorations in communication studies in general as well.

Notes

1 This chapter is a revised version of my paper presented at the *Second International Conference on 'Critical Discourse Analysis: The Message of the Medium'*, Hodeidah University, Hodeidah, Yemen. 2003.

2 The notion of discourse, dealt with in Chapter 6 earlier, is discussed here again of necessity, though briefly and somewhat tailored in keeping with subject orientation requirements of this chapter. This is also done to cater to the requirement of such section of readership who tend to leap-frog from one chapter of the book to another of their own accord to match their reading choice priority rather than go by the sequence in which the chapters occur in the book.

3 Indeed, the mixed — verbal-visual — structure of discourse has not been an uncommon occurrence in the past. For instance, William Blake (1757-1827), the English poet-painter, chose to publish his poems alongside his corresponding paintings to facilitate communication of the intended message of the text.

4 "......human language is primarily spoken, on the grounds that it is originally spoken, both in the individual's acquisition of a language and in the history of language itself. The written language is in both cases based on the spoken, and can be taken as a derived version." (Widdowson 1996/2003 : 7-8).

5 It is "quite artificial to conceive of discourse in exclusively verbal terms" especially when even verbal texts are "visually perceived by interpreters. When we think of written, printed, filmed or televised material, the significance of visual is far more than obvious. Indeed the traditional opposition between spoken and written language has been overtaken by the events, and a much more helpful terminology in modern society would be spoken as opposed to visual language." (Fairclough 1989: 27-28).

6 "Indeed, our cultural evolution today is characterised by 'simultaneous use of verbal and non-verbal communication' as reflected in 'plays, films, television, strip cartoons ... most advertising' (Vestergaard and Schrol,1985:13), photographs, sketches, hoardings and such other visual channels of communication." (cf Dubey 2000: 49-50).

7 The data of this study were sampled from a leading English weekly newspaper of Yemen, the *Yemen Times*, over a period of two

months, between December 2002 and January 2003. Note, during that period, Yemen had only two weekly English newspapers, but no daily English newspaper.

8 Note, this pattern is largely shared by the advertisements on display boards/hoardings in public places in Yemen.

9 The terms 'text' and `co-text' are used here in a restricted sense for reasons explained in the chapter 10 "An image is a sight which has been recreated or reproduced.... Every image embodies a way of seeing. Even a photograph ... although every image embodies a way of seeing, our perception or appreciation of an image depends also upon our way of seeing." (Berger 1972: 9-10)

10 An image is a sight which has been recreated or reproduced. Every image embodies a way of seeing. Even a photograph... although every image embodies a way of seeing, our perception or appreciation of an image depends also upon our way of seeing. (Berger 1972: 9-10).

11 Note, the reference to "Paul Smith: perfume' in extremely fine prints at top corner, is obviously not intended to catch the addressee's attention, for in the entire text it is the visual that functions as text-anchor.

12 Pragmatic presupposition is "defined in terms of assumptions the speaker makes about what the hearer is likely to accept without challenge." (Givon 1979: 50)

References

Berger, J (1972/1988): *Ways of Seeing*. British Broadcasting Corporation and Penguin Books 1988.

Crystal, D (1985): *A Dictionary of Linguistics and Phonetics*. Basil Blackwell, 1989.

Dubey, Vinod S (2000): 'Discourse as weapon: the dynamics of election advertisements'. *Issues in Stylistics*.Ed. Sharma, D.D. & Kumar, A. Gurukul Publications. Lucknow, 2000. Also, in this volume.

Fairclough, N (1989): *Language and Power*. London and New York. Longman, 1989.

Givon, T (1979): *On Understanding Grammar*. New York. Academic Press. 1979.

Grice, H P (1975): 'Logic and conversation.' In P Cole and J Morgan ed. *Syntax and Semantics 3: Speech Acts*. New York. Academic Press. 1975.

Sperber, D and Wilson, D (1986): *Relevance:Communication and Cognition*.Oxford:Basil Blackwell. 1986.

Vestergaard, T and Schrofter, K (1985): *The Language of Advertising*. Oxford: Basil Blackwell, 1985.

Widdowson, H G (1979): *Explorations in Applied Linguistics*. OUP: Oxford, 1979.

__________(1996/2003) : *Linguistics*. OUP : Oxford, 1996/2003.